(1/3/10)

THE NEW JACOBINS

*The French Communist Party
and the Popular Front*

In defense of the Republic: the demonstration of Socialists and Communists in Paris, February 12, 1934. (*L'Illustration.*)

The New Jacobins

THE FRENCH COMMUNIST PARTY

AND THE POPULAR FRONT

Daniel R. Brower

CORNELL UNIVERSITY PRESS

Ithaca, New York

Library of Congress Catalog Card Number: 68–24018

PRINTED IN THE UNITED STATES OF AMERICA
BY KINGSPORT PRESS, INC.

Preface

The communist movement must be homogeneous on the international as well as the national level. This unity may be understood in two ways: as the result of pressure from without, of the mechanical endorsement of or slavish adherence to all directives. . . . But there can also be a unity which is based on the differences and originality of individual experience, on mutual criticism and the enhanced autonomy of the various parties: we feel the need for a unity of this second type.

          —PALMIRO TOGLIATTI [1]

 There are two approaches to the history of the Communist International. They may be termed the institutional and the social interpretations. The institutional approach stresses the uniformities, both institutional and ideological, which existed within the International. The questions it seeks to answer are those relating to any bureaucratic organization—that is, where authority lies and how it is used, and how policies are implemented. The social approach, on the other hand, focuses on the peculiarities of the individual Comintern "sections," each treated as a product, at least partially unique, of the society in which it developed. The usual goal of such studies is to isolate the forces within that society which gave rise to and sup-

---

[1] Quoted in B. Levitski, "Coexistence within the Bloc," in Walter Laqueur and Leopold Labedz (eds.), *Polycentrism* (New York, 1962), p. 29.

ported the Communist movement. The two interpretations are not inherently contradictory. The choice of one or the other, however, frequently represents an implicit judgment regarding the significance of the Comintern. The social interpretation suggests that a form of polycentrism characterized world communism between the world wars, for it breaks up the Comintern into a myriad of socially unique movements. The institutional approach in effect minimizes the importance of this diversity by concentrating on the uniformities of operation and controls within the Comintern organization and the similarities of ideology and tactics among the various sections.

What is the cause of these differing views? In part, the responsibility lies with those authors who let their own prejudice color their treatment of Comintern history. The institutional approach, for example, fits in easily with the belief that communism has been an "international conspiracy." The social interpretation can be used to justify the belief that the principal strength of the Communist movement has always been its appeal to the masses. But the most important reason for the conflict of views lies in the nature of the Comintern, with its peculiar institutional and social characteristics.

There were no purely "national" Communist movements in the Comintern. In the early 1920's, the apparatus of control was in the process of development. Consequently, various movements which styled themselves "Communist" were included within the organization, though their subordination was only nominal. At that time, the activities of the sections were in large part a function of indigenous social and political tensions. By the mid-1920's, however, the Comintern was able to assert effective authority and to enforce discipline according to its standards of "good" and "bad" communism. Its interpretation of "international solidarity" meant first of all acceptance of its instructions; since the voice of the Russian Communists was dominant within the executive organs of the Comintern, the foreign Communist movements came under the control of the Communist party of the Soviet Union. They were caught up in the Soviet leadership struggle of the 1920's, then at the end of the decade submitted to Stalin and his followers. Moscow became the source of all major policy decisions.

In one sense, this situation was not entirely new. The European socialist movement had from the very beginning shared ideas and institutions in its pursuit of the new society. The Comintern was in this perspective an elaborate form of institutional borrowing within one wing of socialism. But its organizational controls were stronger than anything achieved before then. In the Second International, each section was in most instances final judge of its own policies. The Third International left its sections no real independence in policy making. Before World War I, the German Social-Democratic party had, thanks to its size and the authority of its leaders, enjoyed a leading position within the Socialist International. But the Comintern placed one party, the CPSU, in a position to control the activities of the other parties.

Yet these parties were still partly "national." They continued to feel the pressure of events in their country and had to adjust to these pressures. Their members were never completely free of the values of the society in which they had been raised. Indeed, the great imponderable throughout the Comintern's existence was the question to what extent it could impose its values and outlook on the membership of the sections. Even the rejection by these members of prevailing social values continued a situation of social isolation which predated the Comintern. As one French historian has remarked, the Comintern sections existed as "Communist ghettos," with their own image of the world and well-defined political hierarchy.[2] This segregation in preparation for the new socialist society had

[2] Annie Kriegel, "Les Communistes français et le pouvoir," in M. Perrot and A. Kriegel, *Le Socialisme français et le pouvoir* (Paris, 1966), pp. 106–7.

been a part of the experience of earlier socialist movements, though it had probably never been so well attained.

It is this ambiguity in the nature of the Comintern which so confuses the histories of the organization and its sections. Ideally, the social and institutional approaches should be fused to produce a unified picture of the character and activities of the Communist parties. But the obstacles are great. To be meaningful, this approach must unite several themes of historical development. The social development of a given party must be related to its political activity, with each receiving its proper weight. International events, especially those directly affecting the Soviet Union, have to be given adequate attention together with trends within the state and society of that particular party. On a deeper level, developments in different societies must somehow be made relevant one to another. The policies of the Soviet Union in the interwar years in large part reflected the needs of a developing society. This fact sets the context for Soviet history, and also, particularly in the 1930's, for Comintern history. But in the West, society had reached a more complex level of industrialization and urbanization. The importance of the Communist movement there was directly related to this situation. Thus a proper evaluation of the significance of European communism requires a dual perspective comprising both Europe and the Soviet Union.

In the pages that follow, I have tried to find the proper interpretive balance in discussing the history of the French Communist party and the Popular Front. The reader will quickly become aware that the problem of communism as an ideology receives scant mention. The fact is that the ideal of the proletarian revolution is not directly relevant to the events discussed. Ideology alone was not an important factor in the behavior of party leaders, the great expansion of party membership, or the party's increased electoral support. The major event in French Communist life in the 1930's was the party's participation in the Popular Front coalition, and it is the central theme in my study. The setting is French politics; however, the action of the party was only partially related to political developments in that country. Communist policy was set in Moscow, and can therefore be understood only if one take into account the activities of the Soviet Communist leadership. It is fair to say, therefore, that this study falls within the bounds of the institutional interpretation. It straddles the political worlds of France and the Soviet Union. It discusses the rise and fall of the Popular Front from the point of view of the French Communists. It examines the ties between the French Communists and the Comintern. It goes into the murky question of Soviet foreign policy in the 1930's insofar as the French party was involved. It introduces material on the activities of other Comintern sections in an effort to assess correctly the significance of events in France.

Emphasis on institutional uniformities implies a relative neglect of the problem of the relations between the party and French society. It is clear that the introduction of the Popular Front tactics had a profound impact on the character of the party membership. The party in that period put down roots in French society which would endure. Further, the stresses evident in that society in the 1930's gave a particular resonance to Communist activities, which might otherwise have proven much less successful. These questions are discussed in the pages that follow, but they do not receive major attention. I chose to focus on political developments in belief that they were of primary importance. I might still have examined social issues more extensively had it not been for the paucity of sources. With the exception of Gabriel Almond's *The Appeals of Communism*, no one has attempted a sociological and psychological study of the party membership which might be of relevance to the situation in the 1930's. Very little information is available even on the social composition of the party at that time.

In addition, no detailed investigation has been made of the complex ties which developed between the party, the Communist municipalities, the labor unions, and the French workers. With all this in mind, my study might best be viewed as a contribution to the history of the French Communist party during the 1930's.

I owe a debt of gratitude to the many people who have helped me in the preparation of this study. I have included in the Bibliography a list of the individuals, politically active in the 1930's, who consented to discuss their experiences with me. I wish to thank them collectively for their very appreciable aid. In addition, certain scholars were of great assistance. M. François Goguel was generous with his time and advice in guiding me through libraries and interviews, and kindly consented to read and criticize the manuscript. On this side of the Atlantic, Professor Alexander Dallin aided my understanding of the issues and trends in the international Communist movement. The bulk of the research for my study was done in France in 1960–1962, thanks to a grant from the Ford Foundation. Further research was undertaken in the summer of 1964 with the aid of a grant from Oberlin College. I, of course, assume full responsibilty for my interpretations and conclusions.

DANIEL R. BROWER

Oberlin College
December 1967

Contents

Illustrations

xiii

THE NEW JACOBINS

*The French Communist Party
and the Popular Front*

I

"Class against Class"

The working-class movements of the Third Republic were created and supported by a small minority of workers and intellectuals. Though all claimed to represent the proletariat, none succeeded in winning the allegiance of the class as a whole. Class hostility, sustained by strong revolutionary traditions and by deep-rooted class consciousness, clearly separated the workers from the peasant and middle classes. But the hostility did not produce an ongoing class struggle; it led rather to the political and social isolation of the proletariat in French society. Only rarely could radical political or labor groups focus and organize this hostility into a coherent class movement. The agitation of 1919 represented one such movement, the strike wave of 1936 another. But even when one or another political group was able to take the head of a working-class struggle, its large following usually soon dissolved. Whether socialist or syndicalist or communist, it seemed unable to break the isolation of the workers. Thus political activity conducted in the name of the proletariat was for the most part the work of a restricted number of activists led by a small group of leaders. Such was until 1934 the case for the Communist party.

The history of the party in the 1930's is a story of slow decline and dramatic revival. For a variety of reasons, it had been losing strength almost constantly since the year of its formation, 1920, through the early 1930's. The trend had continued through periods in France of internal stability and instability, prosperity and recession, international peace and tension. It was obvious that the problem lay not in the French capitalist economy or class society nor in the relations among imperialist powers, but in the party itself. Supposed vanguard of the proletariat, it had in reality never found the secret to mobilizing the majority of the French proletariat. Its membership was by 1932 so tiny as to resemble that of a radical religious sect, and its electoral and labor-union support came from only a small fraction of the proletariat. Ironically, it had never been closer to the revolutionary ideal of a militant and aggressive organization than during the years of its greatest numerical weakness. Beginning in 1934, the ranks of the party's organizations began to swell for the first time, and the party's slogans won an audience of a size unknown in many years. But the revival came at the expense of the revolution.

The Comintern and Joseph Stalin

In the history of the Communist International, the Sixth World Congress of 1928 marked the beginning of the predominance of Soviet interests over all other issues confronting the international Communist movement. Hitherto, the Soviet leadership had at least taken account of the peculiarities and special problems of the Comintern's various sections in elaborating policy directives. Henceforth, uniformity would set the tone of Comintern activities, a uniformity whose origin lay in the needs created by the great transformation of Soviet life. To be sure, the terminology would remain internationalist and policies would continue to be presented as in the interests of world communism. But the logic behind the argument was founded on the simple postulate that what was in the interests of the Soviet Union was automatically in the interests of the Comintern. The reasoning was applied for the remaining fifteen years of existence of the Comintern in all of its sections, whether in Europe or Asia (China being a partial exception), the Middle East or the Western Hemisphere.

The change did not come all at once. The Sixth Congress itself saw a certain degree of debate and discussion, the last time this would occur publicly in Comintern meetings. The Theses which were drawn up at the close of the Congress stated that the era of "temporary stabilization of capitalism," announced by Lenin in 1921, had come to an end. The world had entered the "third period" of postwar development marked by growing capitalist instability, the most serious effect of which would be the heightened danger of war between the Western capitalist powers and the Soviet Union. By mid-1929, however, the Comintern leaders were arguing that the world was on the eve of a "revolutionary crisis" which would result from the *internal* weakening of the capitalist system and the consequent rise of proletarian discontent. By presenting a uniform model of the internal evolution of capitalism, the Comintern could proceed to prescribe uniform tactics for its sections. The Sixth Congress had defined these tactics as the "united front from below," that is, the unification of the proletariat under the sole leadership of the Communists. The "united front" had first appeared in early 1928 as electoral tactics for the English and French Communist parties. It had been enlarged by the Sixth Congress to include all sections from capitalist countries—and in effect colonial countries—in a struggle to deprive rival organizations, especially the socialists, of influence over the working masses.

But by early 1929, the Communist parties of Europe had moved into a new phase of virtually insurrectionary agitation, including political strikes and violent street demonstrations. To emphasize the class character of the struggle, the tactics came to be described as "class against class." Since the socialists were identified with the bourgeois forces, they too experienced the weight of Communist opposition. In fact, they seemed at times the principal foes of the Communists, who treated them as "social fascists." [1] In Germany, the party minimized the rising Nazi movement after 1930 while pursuing a merciless campaign against the Social-Democratic party; in a somewhat parallel situation in China, the Communist party leadership refused in 1933 to ally with reformist generals leading a military revolt in Fukien province against the Kuomintang. In effect, the Comintern had obliged its sections to fight a battle of "one against all."

There seems little doubt that the introduction of the tactics of "class against class" was connected with Stalin's rise to power. The details of the shift, however, are still poorly known. The first steps in 1928 may well have been due to reverses suffered by the Comintern in 1926–1927 in Britain and China, where alliances with "bourgeois" or socialist forces failed completely. In addition, diplomatic incidents with Western powers in 1927 led to a "war scare" in the Soviet Union which might have been of some influence. As long as the older Bolshevik leaders, men like Nikolai Bukharin, had some voice in Soviet policy, the Comintern was able to preserve an international perspective. But by early 1929, Stalin had removed Bukharin and his followers from the Comintern.

Stalin's impact was unmistakable. He had just embarked on the rapid program of industrialization and collectivization of Soviet society. He personally had a very low opinion of the Comintern, and besides was poorly acquainted with the foreign situation. He pushed for the application of the militant "class against class" tactics certainly not because he thought the world proletarian revolution imminent. Rather, he un-

[1] The best account of the shift of Comintern policy remains Franz Borkenau, *World Communism*, pp. 334–41; the ideological side to the change is explored in K. McKenzie, *The Comintern and World Revolution*, pp. 118–24, 131–35.

doubtedly regarded them as in some way useful to his policies within the Soviet Union. Perhaps he looked upon the Comintern as an instrument for the defense of his country at a time when it was particularly vulnerable to foreign attack. At least within the capitalist regimes in the West, internal dissension created by the Communist movements might weaken the potential for anti-Soviet action. Besides, while fighting for a social and economic revolution in their own country, the Soviet leaders may have felt that the entire world Communist movement had to mobilize as well. The parallel with Chinese revolutionary policies in recent years is so striking as to suggest a common psychological outlook. Whatever the reason for the shift, it was not conceived for the sake of the Comintern itself. Stalin probably cared little whether or not the tactics of "class against class" were an immediate success; the Comintern was in the service of Soviet modernization.

The ability of the Comintern to assure compliance with its new tactical directives was due in large part to the effectiveness of its organizational controls. Alongside the Executive Committee of the Comintern (ECCI) existed a secretarial organization which in fact held the reigns of power. Regional secretariats handled the affairs of the sections of various areas. The French party, for example, was under the "Latin Secretariat from 1928 to at least 1935 was Dimitry Manuilsky, Spain, Portugal, and Latin America. The head of this secretariat from 1928 to at least 1935 was Dimitry Manuilsky, probably the man closest to the Soviet leadership. Though an unquestioned Stalinist, Manuilsky still preserved a certain independence of judgment, as he would prove in 1934. Another key figure in the Comintern leadership was the old Bolshevik Osip Piatnitsky, who was in charge of the International Liaison Section. This body handled the key operations of assigning agents and distributing funds to the various sections. The amount of these subsidies was a carefully kept secret; they may well have represented more than half of the total income of many of the sections. Another important figure in the Comintern was Valdemar Knorin, head of the Central European Secretariat, under whose control fell the very important German section. Both Piatnitsky and Knorin disappeared later in the purges of the late 1930's.[2] In addition, the various sections usually maintained representatives in Moscow, and the Comintern sent emissaries to oversee the activities of its sections. The operations of the Comintern extended even to schools for the training of activists in the sections. This technical training of a special sort was for some of the foreign Communists who came, such as the future French leader Maurice Thorez, the only advanced schooling they would ever receive. This complex network of controls and services could not ensure the flawless operation of the Comintern's sections, but did at least provide the world-wide organization with a unity and discipline comparable only perhaps to the early Jesuits. Like the Society of Jesus, the Comintern was strong in discipline, not in initiative. Its policies were made, or at least approved, by the Soviet leadership, that is, Joseph Stalin. Between 1929 and 1934, Stalin held fast to the "class against class" tactics.

The result was a general decline among Communist parties. Many lost more than half of their members. Leaders came and went during the six years of "class against class" tactics as the Comintern sought to revive the flagging energies of its sections. But the most spectacular reversal of all was the defeat of

[2] Good descriptions of the Comintern organization are found in Gunther Nollau, *International Communism and World Revolution,* pp. 134–35; various essays and notes in Drachkovitch and Lazitch [pseud.], *The Comintern: Historical Highlights.* I obtained valuable information also through interviews with Mme. C. Vassart, wife of the French representative to the Comintern in 1934–1935, and M. H. Barbé, in Moscow in 1928–1929 as French party representative and in 1931–1933 as representative of the French Communist Youth League.

the German Communist party. The largest section in the West, it had been the major exception to the downward trend of the Comintern, gaining after 1930 both in membership and electoral support. In the crisis atmosphere created by the depression and the instability of the Weimar Republic, it seemed to many that the German Communists were at last on the verge of seizing power. Pressured from above by the Comintern leadership (particularly Knorin) and perhaps sustained by the apparent revolutionary enthusiasm of their followers, the party leaders publicly minimized the Nazi threat and rejected appeals from the Social-Democratic party for an antifascist alliance. They continued to apply faithfully the "class against class" tactics, until the Weimar Republic had been overthrown and their own organization crushed by the new Nazi regime. The virtual disappearance of the German Communist party was a stunning blow for the Communist International.

These events did not escape criticism from within the Communist parties in Europe and apparently in the Soviet party as well. Dissension was a private matter in the Comintern in the 1930's, when the rule of public unanimity was supreme. Nonetheless, enough information has filtered through since then to indicate a definite undercurrent of dissatisfaction. According to a former German Communist official who had been transferred to the Comintern apparatus in Moscow in mid-1932, the German Communist leaders were in a "critical mood" and some showed a "marked readiness to set up a united front with the Social Democrats" to fight the Nazis.[3] Following the Nazi seizure of power, leading Communists in Switzerland, Czechoslovakia, and France spoke out against the Comintern tactics.

[3] Ex-Insider, "Moscow-Berlin 1933," *Survey*, No. 44–45 (October, 1962), p. 151.

Discontent was noticeable within the Soviet Union as well. When the Communist official quoted above arrived in Moscow from Berlin in mid-1932, he found "in the Comintern apparatus and its policy-making bodies the [same] critical mood . . . encountered among the German party leaders." But criticism in Moscow was "expressed much more widely and in a sharper form." [4] From the evidence available at present, it appears that Dimitry Manuilsky himself advocated a revision of Comintern tactics to meet the rising fascist threat. Defending the *status quo,* on the other hand, were Piatnitsky and Knorin. [5] This controversy over tactics was never brought out into the open. At the Thirteenth ECCI Plenum in December, 1933, the official Comintern line was respected by all the speakers. Yet between the speeches of Piatnitsky and Manuilsky there existed a subtle but significant difference in tone. Piatnitsky defended all the old tactics, and included a sharp word of defense for the policies of the German Communist party before and after Hitler's rise to power.

Manuilsky, on the contrary, admitted that "the setting up of a fascist dictatorship in Germany has inflicted a most severe defeat on the whole international working class." It was therefore "impossible" for Communists to "disregard this event, to neglect to make use of the lessons which all the other sections

---

[4] *Ibid.,* p. 155.

[5] According to M. Henri Barbé, Manuilsky told him personally in June, 1933, that a change in tactics was necessary, but gave no instructions (personal interview with M. Barbé). M. Albert Vassart found this split among the Comintern leaders upon his arrival in Moscow in April, 1934 ([Vassart], "Compte-rendu d'une conférence," *La Révolution prolétarienne,* No. 414 [February, 1957], p. 23). Borkenau asserts, without giving any source, that Manuilsky had "cautiously advocated a more elastic Comintern policy" at least since 1931 (Borkenau, *European Communism,* p. 132). According to the "Ex-Insider," the "dogmatic" Knorin had "thwarted" a united front in Germany between the Communists and the Social Democrats in late 1932 ("Comintern Reminiscences," *Survey,* No. 32 [April–June, 1960], p. 113).

of the Comintern have to learn from this murderous blow." [6]
A plausible argument has been made that Manuilsky hoped
Maurice Thorez, head of the French section, would follow his
lead and criticize the application of the "class against class"
tactics in France.[7] But Thorez was too cautious—or too
naïve—to take such a dangerous initiative. Manuilsky himself
drew no "lessons" from the German events for the benefit of
his fellow members of the Executive Committee Plenum.
Until he had some support from the Soviet leadership, he was
powerless to change policy.

Perhaps even the leaders of the Soviet Communist party
participated in the controversy. Evidence to this effect is
found in the "Letter of an Old Bolshevik," written in late
1936 by Boris Nicolaevsky on the basis primarily of talks with
Bukharin several months earlier. The letter asserted that a
"great deal of discussion" occurred in the winter of
1933–1934 within the Soviet leadership over issues of both
foreign and internal policy. It identified Sergei Kirov, the
rising young Leningrad leader, as the man who led the drive
for a re-evaluation of Soviet policy.[8] If true, Kirov kept his
views a closely guarded secret.

[6] Piatnitsky, *International Press Correspondence* (abbreviated *Inprecorr*), March 5, 1934, pp. 371–73; Manuilsky, *ibid.*, May 7, 1934, p.
710. This is the English edition of the weekly Communist journal of
opinion published in French as *Correspondance internationale* (abbreviated *Correspondance*).

[7] Cécile and Albert Vassart, "The Moscow Origin of the French
Popular Front," in Drachkovitch, pp. 240–41; when Vassart arrived
in Moscow in April, 1934, Manuilsky encouraged him to express
before the Comintern his opposition to the "class against class"
tactics (Lazitch, "Informations fournies par Albert Vassart sur la
politique du PCF entre 1934 et 1938," p. 9, manuscript in possession
of the Hoover Institution; part of the material from this manuscript
has been included in Vassart, "The Moscow Origin," pp. 243–44).

[8] "The Letter of an Old Bolshevik," in B. Nicolaevsky, *Power and
the Soviet Elite*, pp. 30–34; for a discussion of the writing of the
letter, see *ibid.*, pp. 3–9.

It is now known that Stalin, upon whom fell the major responsibility for the "class against class" tactics and thus for the German defeat, was not secure in his position as General Secretary of the Soviet party in that period. According to L. Shaumian, delegate to the Seventeenth Party Congress of January, 1934, certain of the delegates (among whom he implicitly includes Kirov) thought that "the time had come to shift Stalin from the post of General Secretary to other work." Shaumian does not, however, indicate that Stalin's mismanagement of foreign policy was at issue. He attributes the desire to remove Stalin to "alarm" caused by "the abnormal situation that arose in the Party in connection with the cult of the individual." [9] No information has been published in the Soviet Union explaining how the potential conflict was resolved at the Congress. Leonard Schapiro, in his book *The Communist Party of the Soviet Union,* has found evidence of a "compromise between Stalin and the more 'moderate' members of the Politburo." He maintains that the Congress elected a Central Committee, a majority of whose members might oppose Stalin's extremist policies. Similarly, the new Politburo elected by the Central Committee was not completely "reliable" from the Georgian dictator's point of view. Finally, Kirov was now a member of the Secretariat, while Stalin was no longer referred to as "General Secretary," but simply "Secretary." [10] It does not seem that Stalin's position as head of the party was in any immediate danger; his policies and person were praised by every speaker to the Congress. Nor is there any indication that Soviet foreign policy and Comintern tactics were in any way

[9] *Pravda*, February 7, 1964.
[10] Schapiro, *The Communist Party of the Soviet Union*, pp. 395–98; for further speculation on factional disputes within the Soviet party, see Robert Slusser, "The Role of the Foreign Ministry," in Ivo Lederer (ed.), *Russian Foreign Policy*, pp. 217–22; George Kennan, *Russia and the West under Lenin and Stalin*, pp. 278–84; Robert Daniels, *The Conscience of the Revolution*, pp. 380–82.

modified as a result of the Congress. All that can be said at present is that conditions after the Congress were such that Stalin might feel obliged, whether willingly or not, to moderate his former policies in both foreign and internal affairs.

Key to Soviet foreign policy in Europe were relations with Germany. Ever since the Rapallo Pact of 1922, the German alliance had stood as a guarantee against a united Western assault on Russia. Fear of capitalist aggression continued to dominate the Soviet attitude toward the West—witness the "war scare" of 1927—and became, if anything, even stronger after 1928 during the critical years of rapid industrialization and collectivization. Thus preservation of the German pact remained a major goal of Soviet foreign policy in the early 1930's. Stalin apparently foresaw little change in German-Soviet relations in the event of Nazi control of the German government. Despite overt signs in 1933 of Nazi hostility, he strove to maintain the alliance. At the same time, though, he did leave the way open for a diplomatic realignment by sanctioning improved relations with Poland and France.

His most spectacular gesture toward the Nazis came in the course of his speech to the Seventeenth Party Congress. He denied assertions by "certain German politicians" that the Soviet Union had sought more cordial relations with Poland and France in the preceding months as a result of the "establishment of a fascist regime in Germany." "Fascism," Stalin argued, "is not the issue here." The Soviet leaders were concerned solely with the protection of the interests of their country. They would "not hesitate" to strengthen their ties with any country "not desirous of disturbing the peace," if this step was in the Soviet interests. The Soviet Union would support all "those who want peace and are striving for trade relations with us." [11] In effect, Stalin was outlining for the sake

[11] *Pravda*, January 28, 1934.

of the German leaders the basic Soviet conditions for the preservation of good relations between their two countries. The
German ambassador in Moscow reported to the Foreign
Office in Berlin that Stalin's speech revealed an attitude of "ex-
pectation . . . that Germany is, by means of a statement from
an authoritative source, going to state its position respecting
Russian fears." [12] A group of Soviet leaders, including Kle-
menty Voroshilov, People's Commissar for Defense, and Nikolai Krestinsky, Deputy Commissar of Foreign Affairs,
apparently hoped these "fears" would be put to rest, and that
the German alliance would be preserved.[13] But Hitler made no
move.

Stalin's declarations could also be read in another light. For
while he denied any permanent attachment to Poland and
France, he defended the improved relations with these two
countries as a justified reaction to the "growth of revenge and
imperialist moods in Germany." In other words, he was stating the alternative Soviet policy, one perhaps not much to his
liking but necessary if Hitler persisted in his anti-Soviet trend.
The *rapprochement* with France had been under way for
several years, as part of a "general pattern of improving political relations and increasing trade with as many of the great
industrial powers as possible." [14] It was the work primarily of
Maxim Litvinov, People's Commissar of Foreign Affairs and
one of the few men within the Soviet leadership who appeared
genuinely concerned over growth of an aggressive nationalistic spirit in Germany. The signature in November, 1932, of
the Franco-Soviet nonaggression treaty was the first sign of
substantial progress. In itself, however, the treaty was no more
than a platonic expression of mutual good will, and marked no
new policy on either side.

[12] *Documents on German Foreign Policy* (hereafter referred to as
German Documents), C, II, 436.
[13] William Scott, *Alliance against Hitler*, p. 98.   [14] *Ibid.*, p. 73.

The situation was altered by the beginning of negotiations for a mutual security pact between the two countries. In the summer of 1933, Litvinov began pressing the French government for stronger ties. By early November, diplomatic negotiations for a Franco-Soviet mutual assistance pact had begun between the Soviet ambassador in Paris and the French Foreign Minister, Joseph Paul-Boncour. The evidence would indicate thus that in the winter of 1933–1934 Stalin had not yet abandoned hope for the continuation of the German alliance, but was also considering an alternative alliance. Karl Radek, one of the former "oppositionists" in the Soviet party restored to some power in early 1934, declared to a German reporter in January of that year that "Stalin does not know where he stands with Germany. He is uncertain." [15] It might be fair to conclude that uncertainty characterized both Soviet policy toward Nazi Germany and the Comintern evaluation of the new fascist threat. But while the Soviet Foreign Commissariat enjoyed sufficient liberty of action to begin preparing for the eventuality of a rupture with Germany, the Comintern was frozen in its "class against class" tactics.

The French Communist party had not taken easily to the new tactics. Even the application of a more aggressive electoral policy had stirred up resistance in late 1927 and early 1928. Traditionally, French socialists and liberals had united in parliamentary and even local elections when a second ballot was necessary (the electoral rules before 1919 and after 1927 required a second ballot when no candidate had received an absolute majority on the first) in order to defeat the conservatives. This practice was known as "republican discipline," since at its origin it was intended to defend the parties loyal to

[15] Interview reported by the German ambassador on January 10, 1934, in *German Documents*, C, II, 333; the best account of the origins of the Franco-Soviet alliance is Scott, pp. 92–99, 116–21, 135–38.

the Republic. It still enjoyed general support on the Left in the 1920's, though the Third Republic was long since secure. Apparently, even a sizable number of Communists felt the same way. To fight this "opportunism" and generally to pull the party together, the Comintern decided in 1927 to break "republican discipline" in France.[16] Under strong pressure from Moscow, the party's Central Committee issued in November, 1927, an "Open Letter" condemning electoral coalitions. The initiative was justified by the argument that the party had to lead the workers in a "united front from below" against the bourgeoisie, among whose supporters the Central Committee included the Socialist party. The Communist campaign for the national elections of 1928 was therefore to be waged under the slogan "class against class" (the first time this slogan appeared).[17]

Opposition to the new tactics among the French party leadership continued. At a stormy meeting of the Central Committee in January, 1928, one speaker warned that the workers would "accuse us of playing the game of the reactionaries and would break away." The party would consequently be "isolated from the masses." [18] In the Politburo, the new tactics were actively supported by only a small minority, among whom was the young Maurice Thorez.[19] One of the most dynamic leaders of the party, Jacques Doriot, never

[16] See the letters of Jules Humbert-Droz, Swiss Communist who in 1927 was head of the Comintern's Latin Secretariat, in *"L'Oeil de Moscou" à Paris: Jules Humbert-Droz, ancien Secrétaire de l'Internationale communiste* (Paris, 1964), pp. 248–54.

[17] "Lettre ouverte," *L'Humanité*, November 19, 1927; the slogan "class against class" was thought up by Humbert-Droz himself (J. Humbert-Droz to D. Brower [November 7, 1964], letter in my possession).

[18] Quoted in *Classe contre Classe: La Question française au IX Exécutif et au VI Congrès de l'Internationale communiste*, pp. 6–8.

[19] See Thorez's letter to Humbert-Droz, in *"L'Oeil de Moscou" à Paris*, pp. 236–41 (the letter should be dated May 16, 1928, not 1926).

accepted the extremist tactics and the wholesale condemnation
of the socialist movement. After having reviewed this sorry
situation in a speech before the Comintern Latin Secretariat in
June, 1928, Pierre Sémard, General Secretary of the French
party, sadly concluded that the Communists had not "completely broken" with France's "strong democratic traditions."
The "lack of understanding" of the tactics of "class against
class" was due particularly to the adherence of "many comrades" to the tradition of "the necessity of 'republican discipline' . . . on the second ballot to defeat the so-called
reactionaries by allying with the 'democratic' parties." In sum,
the new policy had produced within the party "difficulties"
and "lapses" (*défaillances*) and even "utter foolishness" (*co-
chonneries*)! [20]

The result was precisely what the critical Central Committee speaker had predicted: isolation from the masses. Party
statistics tell a large part of the story. Membership declined
from 50,000 in 1928 to 29,000 in 1933, the lowest in the
party's history.[21] The major Communist newspaper,
L'Humanité, was at an all-time low in 1932 and 1933, printing between 100,000 and 110,000 copies on an average per day
and actually selling 70,000 to 80,000.[22] Just as fewer people
were reading Communist publications, fewer voters were supporting Communist candidates in the national elections for the
Chamber of Deputies. The total party vote on the first ballot
fell from 1,063,000 in 1928 to 796,000 in 1932. Further, on the
second ballot the Communist candidates in 1932 lost 55 per

[20] *Classe contre Classe*, pp. 111–12.

[21] Annie Kriegel, "Le Parti communiste français sous la Troisième
République: Evolution de ses effectifs," *Revue française de Science
politique*, February, 1966, pp. 21–25.

[22] Information provided in a personal interview by P.-L. Darnar,
on the editorial board of *L'Humanité* from 1932 and actual editor-
in-chief from 1934 to 1939, when he broke with the party.

cent of their first-ballot vote.[23] This electoral infidelity was the direct result of the "class against class" tactics. The Communists were breaking the tradition of "republican discipline" by refusing to withdraw their less-favored candidates to aid their leading left-wing opponent. The startling loss of second-ballot support indicates that Communist voters went right on honoring the tradition.

Party representation in the Chamber of Deputies was minute: fourteen deputies elected in 1928, ten in 1932. In addition, the presence of the Communist candidates on the second ballot split the vote of the Left, and thus benefited the candidates of the Center and Right. According to one estimate, the result was the loss by the Socialist party of from 20 to 25 seats in 1932, by the Radical party of about 20 seats, and by the Communist party of from 12 to 15 seats.[24] Communist intransigence thus modified significantly the power balance in the legislature which was to rule France from 1932 to 1936.

The decline of party support was paralleled by the weakening of the Communist-controlled organizations, of which the most important was the Communist labor-union confederation, the General Confederation of United Labor (*Confédération générale du Travail unitaire*, or CGTU). One of the most important aspects of the "class against class" tactics was worker agitation, accompanied by campaigns against the "reformist" labor organizations. Consequently, the CGTU was kept in a state of permanent unrest through repeated strikes and violent demonstrations. Its leaders attempted in every manner possible to weaken and disrupt the much larger General Confederation of Labor (CGT). These tactics met with little success. Membership in the CGTU declined from

---

[23] André Ferrat, "Le Parti et les Elections legislatives," *Cahiers du Bolshevisme* (hereafter referred to as *Cahiers*), June 1, 1932, p. 722.

[24] Article by Jean Longuet, Socialist deputy, in *L'Oeuvre*, September 6, 1934.

323,000 in 1930 to 264,000 in 1934.[25] Other party organizations were little more than skeletons. Both the Communist
Youth League and the Republican Association of Veterans
had only a few thousand members. The General Confederation of Farm Workers, founded in 1929 in an attempt to
capture the support of the "rural proletariat," was only 9,000
strong.

A new initiative to increase Communist influence over the
masses throughout Western Europe had been the creation in
1932 of an international movement against "imperialistic
war." Patronized by the French novelists Romain Rolland and
Henri Barbusse, its nominal president, the organization was
controlled by the German Communist Willi Muenzenberg.
After the Nazi victory in Germany, it became the "World
Committee against War and Fascism," frequently referred to
as the "Amsterdam-Pleyel Movement" since its first two congresses had been held in Amsterdam and at the Salle Pleyel in
Paris. It was originally intended specifically to capitalize on
the antiwar sentiment in Europe while fighting outright pacifism (its slogan was *Pacifisme combattant!*). Many national
committees with local chapters were established, with the
French committee (also under Barbusse's official leadership)
one of the most important. The leaders claimed by 1934 five
hundred local chapters in France. The organization could not
be considered an effective mass movement, however. It could
never overcome, neither when it preached "combative pacifism" nor later when it urged collective security, the almost
visceral distaste of left-wing Western Europeans for any kind
of fighting. Further, its membership, in France as elsewhere,
left much to be desired. Outside of its Communist members, it
lacked real internal strength.[26] The only significant actions

[25] Antoine Prost, *La C.G.T. à l'époque du Front populaire*, p. 35.
[26] See R. Hunt, "Willi Muenzenberg," in David Footman (ed.),
International Communism (Carbondale, Ill., 1960), pp. 76–78; also,

undertaken by the French committee were conducted in conjunction with the Communist party.

The inability of the party to hold the support of the masses led the Comintern to experiment with new forms of leadership. In the face of the initial resistance to the "class against class" tactics, the Comintern decided in late 1928 to call on the aid of the Communist Youth League. The idea, one applied also in England, was that "young blood" would be more amenable to extremist policies. Therefore, members of the French League were introduced throughout the party hierarchy. At the same time, a system of collective leadership was created, including Henri Barbé and Pierre Célor from the League, Benoît Frachon and Gaston Monmousseau from the CGTU, and Maurice Thorez from the party Secretariat. This scheme was partially abandoned in 1930, when Thorez was made "politically responsible" to the party. Actual control was still parceled out, though it is impossible to say how. Finally, in mid-1931, the Comintern completely abandoned the attempt to use the Communist Youth League, removed the "Barbé-Célor Group" from positions of leadership, and placed Thorez at the head of the party.[27] The only thing actually accomplished by the shuffling about of leaders was to prove that real control over the French party lay in Moscow.

Thorez was 32 when officially declared Secretary of the Central Committee at a party congress in March, 1932. Born into a poor miner's family in the north of France, he had joined the Socialist party in 1919 and had backed adherence to

Arthur Koestler, *The Invisible Writing* (New York, 1954), pp. 207, 313. Koestler was for a while Muenzenberg's assistant.

[27] Information on this murky period in party history can be found in Vassart, pp. 22–23; H. Barbé, *Bulletin de l'Association d'Etudes et d'Informations politiques internationales*, No. 76 (November 1–15, 1952), pp. 25–27; H. Barbé and P. Célor, "Le Groupe Barbé-Célor," *Est et Quest* (continuation of *Bulletin*), No. 176 (June 16–30, 1957), pp. 1–4, and No. 177 (July 1–15, 1957), pp. 7–9.

the Communist International the next year. By 1923, he had become a "professional revolutionary," devoting all his time to party activities and supported by the party in return. His entire career was to be made as a Communist. His higher education, travels, and eventually leadership of the French party were all benefits derived from his party work and the support he received from the Comintern. Part of the explanation for his lifelong fidelity to the Russian Communists may lie in the very real gratitude he felt for all they had done for him. In 1924, he became a member of the Central Committee, in 1925 a member of the Politburo, in 1926 a member of the Secretariat, and in 1928 Secretary for Party Organization.

He owed his rapid climb primarily to a remarkable ability to do his work without becoming overly involved in the factional disputes which almost tore the party apart in the 1920's. He was a capable organizer and good administrator, not an independent leader or creative intellectual. His tenacity paid off when he was made "politically responsible" for leadership action in 1930, then finally titular leader of the party following the dissolution of the "Barbé-Célor Group" in 1931. Yet he was too young and inexperienced to be given the full confidence of the Comintern, and of Manuilsky in particular. Aiding him was the leading Comintern emissary in France, the Czech Eugen Fried. Sent to France in 1931, Fried played an anonymous but important part in the elaboration of Communist policy until his departure in 1939. Albert Vassart, member of the party Secretariat from 1932 and representative to the Comintern in 1934–1935, knew Fried well and esteemed him as a very capable political leader. He later wrote that the Czech "played a decisive role" in the training of Thorez, who "did not possess much initiative or political courage." The young Secretary did have the quality of being an "excellent 'loudspeaker'" in elaborating on the suggestions of others." Thus Fried could "use Thorez as an intermediary to guide the French Communist Party" while at the same time "working to correct the latter's defects and inadequacies to make him a real leader."[28] Until 1934, however, the new party Secretary was still very much "on trial."

Thorez was assisted in his work by three other Frenchmen of importance. In the Secretariat were Jacques Duclos and Marcel Gitton. Duclos was born in southern France in 1896, and had worked as a baker before devoting himself completely to the party. He took charge particularly of the parliamentary affairs of the party; in addition, he was for a while at least a part of the Comintern espionage network involved in spying for the Soviet Union.[29] Gitton was the youngest, born in 1903, and a construction worker by trade. He had played a leading role in the CGTU before becoming a member of the Secretariat in 1932. Leadership of the CGTU passed then into the hands of Benoît Frachon. He was also of proletarian background, born in central France in 1892 and becoming a metallurgical worker before going into labor-union and Communist party work. Frachon had risen in the party at the same time as Thorez, and had been a member of the collective leadership in the period 1928–1931.

Outside this "inner group" was André Marty, who had been catapulted to fame by his participation in the Black Sea mutiny of the French Navy in 1919. Marty was aggressive, suspicious, and extremely difficult to work with. For reasons that are unclear, he also was made a member of the Secretariat in 1932, and held the key role of delegate to the ECCI from 1932 until January, 1934, when he was sent back to France to

[28] Albert Vassart, "Le Rôle du délégué du Comintern en France," manuscript in possession of Hoover Institution; excerpts from the manuscript were published in Lazitch, "Two Instruments of Control by the Comintern," Drachkovitch, pp. 52–54; see also A. Ferrat, "Contribution à l'histoire du Parti communiste français," *Preuves*, February, 1965, pp. 58–59.

[29] See Lazitch, "Two Instruments," p. 58.

become (temporarily) editor-in-chief of *L'Humanité*. Another man with a famous past was Marcel Cachin. He had been a very important "national defense" Socialist before being won over by the Bolsheviks in 1920. At that moment, he had played a major role in swinging the majority of the French Socialists to support entry into the Communist International. Fame did not, however, bring him power: his opinions were of little importance in determining party policy, and his participation on the editorial board of *L'Humanité* was purely nominal.

The most outstanding of the young generation of Communists was Jacques Doriot, born in 1898. He was a talented orator and gifted leader. He had created in one of the working-class suburbs of Paris, Saint Denis, a stronghold for the party—and for himself. If one may judge by his later career as a fascist, Doriot was strongly attracted by power. He had found it first in the Communist party and was one of the leaders in the 1920's of the Communist Youth League. He frequently disobeyed party orders, however, particularly after 1928 when he refused to follow the "class against class" tactics. His talents were so great, though, that his indiscipline went unpunished, and he was even included on the Politburo in 1932. He was the logical candidate to succeed Thorez as party leader should the latter fail. In general, the French Communist leadership of the early 1930's was composed of men of the war generation, including some who fought in the trenches, some who labored in the factories, and some, too young to fight, who still experienced the hardships and shared in the passions of the war.

The situation in which Thorez found himself as newly appointed Secretary in 1932 was anything but secure. His party was declining, and there was little he could do about it. He—or someone around him—attempted in 1933 to revive *L'Humanité* under the leadership of a new editor, only to have the conservative Marty descend upon the editorial staff of the paper in early 1934.[30] He agreed in late 1932 to initiate discussions with the Socialist leaders on the question of proletarian unity, in the hopes probably of maneuvering the Socialist party into an unfavorable position in the eyes of the workers. But it was the Socialists who outmaneuvered him.[31] He, and other Communist leaders, admitted publicly that the rank and file were unhappy with the state of the Comintern and of their party in particular. The only hope for real improvement lay in the modification of the "class against class" tactics. But as long as the Comintern refused to take this step, Thorez would not—and could not—take it himself. As a result, his party remained for the time being a political sect of little importance either in the international Communist movement or in French political life.

The Crisis of the French Republic

France in the early 1930's was no longer a land of unity and stability. The delicate social balance which characterized it earlier was being disrupted and undermined by the depression; its complex parliamentary regime was less and less able to satisfy the demands of its citizenry. The success of the Third Republic in surviving internal and external crises had made France the center of republicanism in Europe; it had established a political tradition of freedom with order which had won the allegiance of almost all Frenchmen. Yet its social foundations were still weak. Prior to the 1930's, France was, in the words of Stanley Hoffmann, a "stalemate society" marked by a complex blend of industrialism and agrarianism, of social rigidity and mobility, of authoritarianism and indi-

[30] Personal interview with M. Darnar.

[31] A history of the affair is given in *La Vie du Parti, Supplément au Populaire*, February 20, 1933.

vidualism. The secret to the long life of the Third Republic was its ability to protect this intricate social system. It lost this ability when, in the 1930's, the depression and the rise of a powerful German totalitarian state created new needs which the republican institutions were unable to meet. The result was political and social crisis.[32]

The first major blow to the French regime came from the depression. Slower to react than the more industrialized countries, France experienced from 1930 a gradual economic decline which became abrupt only in late 1933. Industrial production was then 14 per cent below its 1928 level, and fell by April, 1935, to 24 per cent below. Total unemployment, for which no completely reliable figures exist, rose to a peak estimated at 800,000 to 850,000 in early 1935, and was perhaps one-half as great a year earlier.[33] In addition, partial employment—that is, a work week of less than the legal forty-eight hours—affected a great number of workers, particularly in large-scale industry where the recession was most sharply felt. Farmers suffered from the drastic fall in prices paid for farm commodities. The French standard of living fell, particularly among the farming and middle classes. Definite signs of social unrest began to appear by the end of 1933, and the chief focus of discontent was the government.

The difficulties of the French government were basically financial. A falling national income brought a decline in tax revenues. Reduced receipts in their turn further unbalanced a government budget already far out of balance. The French cabinet leaders, staunchly orthodox in their refusal to use

[32] Stanley Hoffmann, "Paradoxes of the French Political Community," in S. Hoffmann *et al.*, *In Search of France* (Cambridge, 1963), pp. 3–34.
[33] Henry Ehrmann, *French Labor from Popular Front to Liberation*, p. 16; also, *Mouvement économique en France de 1929 à 1939* (Paris, 1941), p. 118.

public finance to promote economic growth, felt obliged to cut expenditures, primarily those devoted to payment of civil servants and social dependents such as veterans. Unpopular under any circumstances, this Spartan program was the major cause of the rapid series of cabinet crises which followed the elections of May, 1932.

These elections had been a victory for the liberal and social-ist forces in the legislature. The Radical party (*Parti républi-cain radical et radical-socialiste*) claimed the largest number of deputies in the Chamber of Deputies. Yet the state of the party was not good. Indeed, it was hardly a party at all as the term is understood in Anglo-Saxon countries. It had few mem-bers and a virtually nonexistent organization. It was domi-nated at the base by local notables and at the top by its deputies. A recent historian of the party has very aptly de-scribed it as "a collection of politicians masquerading as a party." [34] In the early years of the Third Republic, it had been the chief defender of the republican institutions; its leaders had been among the greatest men of the time. By the 1930's, its vigor had left it. The quality of its leadership had declined markedly, while its political attitude had become much more moderate, even conservative.

Only in the field of foreign policy did the Radical party show some degree of political audacity. It had supported its president, Edouard Herriot, in his policy of *rapprochement* with the Soviet Union. As Premier in 1924, Herriot had granted *de jure* recognition to the U.S.S.R.; as Premier again in 1932, he had supported the Franco-Soviet Treaty of Non-Aggression. On a trip through Russia in September, 1933, he was received with an enthusiasm reserved for few politicians from Western Europe. A further token of Soviet esteem was a New Year's greeting sent Herriot in early Janu-

[34] Peter Larmour, *The French Radical Party in the 1930's*, p. 99.

ary, 1934, by Maxim Litvinov. The Commissar of Foreign
Affairs described the Radical leader as "a reliable and devoted
champion" of "that peace so necessary to our peoples," and
expressed the wish that "long years of close and fruitful collaboration await us both." [35] Soviet confidence in Herriot
would later become a key factor in French Communist policy
toward the Radicals.

But there was on the whole little in the Radical party to
interest dynamic young leaders. A few did enter, but others
left. One of those to leave was a deputy named Gaston Bergery. Accusing his former party of "lack of courage," he set
up in 1933 an organization called the *Front commun* (a title
commonly confused later with the "United Front" of the
Communists and Socialists). Its goal was the achievement of
complete unity of action among all the left-wing parties in
order to push reform of the French regime and to fight "fascism." Bergery's call for unity received little response.

The other member of the parliamentary coalition created
after the elections of 1932 was the Socialist party (*Section
française de l'Internationale ouvrière*, abbreviated SFIO).
Thanks to energetic leadership, it had recovered remarkably
well from the 1920 crisis, when the members faithful to its
prewar doctrine and organization had been a very small minority. By 1933, it was the largest mass party in the country.
It too suffered from internal dissension. A revolutionary left
wing was counterbalanced by a very reformist right wing.
The party leadership tried to steer a middle course by approving parliamentary reformist action while refusing to accept
participation of its deputies in the cabinet. The compromise
policy was difficult to apply, however, for it left open the
question of how much responsibility the deputies should ac-

[35] Quoted by Herriot in his memoirs, *Jadis*, II: *D'une Guerre à
l'autre, 1914–1936*, 373.

cept in support of cabinets of which they generally approved. The latent conflict broke into the open in the fall of 1933, when a group of right-wing deputies voted for a bill rejected by the party leaders. Their argument was that opposition to the measure would lead to the defeat of the Radical cabinet then in power, a far more serious matter than the bill itself. The rebels, baptized "neo-socialists," took out of the party 30 deputies and some 20,000 members. Thus the SFIO had purged itself of its right wing. There still remained in the party an unruly radical faction, whose strength lay in the Paris region. Still, the SFIO was more united in early 1934 than it had been before. It retained 110,000 members and 99 deputies, a numerical strength far exceeding that of the Communist party.

The Socialist and Radical parties together were able to control a majority of votes within the Chamber of Deputies. Yet they were not able to agree on financial policy. The Radical party was the bastion of financial orthodoxy. The SFIO, on the other hand, favored government policies to fight the recession, such as public-works programs, and disapproved of financial austerity, harmful to the economy—and to their own voters. Thus the coalition was deeply divided on the fundamental issue confronting the legislature after 1932. The Radical leaders obtained control of the cabinet and set out on their program of financial austerity. Yet they could not hold a majority in the Chamber without the support of the Socialists, who opposed this program. The Radical cabinets were doomed from the start. In the period between the national elections of May, 1932, and February, 1934, France was governed by six different cabinets, a luxury even in normal times, a scandal in the agitated years of the early 1930's.

This situation produced a steady decline in the prestige of democratic government in France. By January, 1934, a violent campaign had begun against the "corrupt" and "outmoded" parliamentary regime. It was conducted in the pages of certain reactionary newspapers and in meetings and demonstrations organized by private paramilitary leagues. Though not united on ultimate objectives, these leagues had the great psychological advantage of being in complete opposition to the regime of the Third Republic. Theirs was a union of negation, satisfactory enough for the discontented whose numbers were legion.

The most dynamic of these organizations was the royalist League of French Action, or *Action française*. Its newspaper, *L'Action française*, spearheaded the public campaign against parliament. In addition, it was supported by a small "fighting wing," the *Camelots du Roi*, ready at the slightest pretext to take to the streets to demonstrate and to fight the police.

Among the other leagues, the most mysterious was certainly the *Croix de Feu*, whose emblem was a skull set over a fiery cross. It was primarily a veterans' organization, with strong overtones of authoritarianism. It impressed Frenchmen most by its perfect discipline in demonstrations. Though the real fame of the *Croix de Feu* came later, it was already an influential organization in early 1934. In all, five major groups were active. Only one or two were professedly fascist—though all were spoken of as such by their opponents—but all were certainly a threat to the French republican regime. Their total membership was perhaps one million; [36] their effectiveness in mobilizing large and aggressive crowds was soon to be proved beyond any doubt.

The opportunity for action came in January, 1934, when a financial scandal involving a petty swindler named Alexander Stavisky broke into the news. The shady financial dealings of Stavisky would have passed unnoticed, had not some members of the Chamber of Deputies compromised themselves by lend-

[36] Georges Lefranc, *Histoire du Front populaire* (Paris, 1965), p. 62.

ing their support to his slightly less than legal operations. It was even said—by the opposition—that certain Radical ministers were involved. The Stavisky affair had little to distinguish it from the usual run of parliamentary scandals, but it came at the worst possible moment.

The opposition mobilized both in parliament and in the country. In the Chamber of Deputies, the conservatives were only too happy to find an excuse to attack the rule of the Radical party, for they hoped to shift the parliamentary majority from Left-Center to Right-Center. Outside, the widespread discontent among many segments of the population was directed against the ineffectual and apparently compromised Radical cabinet. On January 7, the first call was sent out by *L'Action française* for demonstrations against the "rotten" government. The agitation rose to a crescendo in early February after a new premier, the Radical Edouard Daladier, took punitive measures against the Paris police chief, who was accused of being lenient toward the demonstrators. The Chamber of Deputies was to convene on February 6 to approve Daladier's cabinet. On the morning of the sixth, *L'Action française* proclaimed in bold headlines: "Everyone Out This Evening in Front of the Chamber to Oppose the Robbers and the Despicable Regime!" Plans for giant demonstrations were made by the leaders of *Action française, Croix de Feu,* and the other leagues.

The Communist party felt in its turn the effects of the rising rightist extremism in the country. In response to the agitation of the paramilitary leagues, Jacques Doriot proposed at the meeting of the Central Committee on January 25 that the leadership modify the "class against class" tactics. For him as for others in the party, a very real distinction had to be made between fascism and the bourgeois democratic regime, supported by the Socialists. The "fascist forces," he warned, were well on their way to winning the "allegiance of the masses" in France. To fight them, unity of action among the working-class parties was necessary. It was especially important that an alliance be sought with the "revivified" Socialist party. Doriot proposed openly that his party form a "united front from above" with the Socialist leaders, a policy formally condemned by the Comintern. The Secretary of the party did not agree. The "party line," he reportedly declared, would be "compromised" were Doriot's proposals adopted.[37] If the Comintern had said that there could be no united front with the Socialist leadership, then it could not be. Nonetheless, Doriot received the support of several other members of the Central Committee.

Despite the continuing street demonstrations in Paris, the Communist leadership preferred to minimize the danger of league agitation. On February 2, Doriot proposed that the party organize a counterdemonstration against the "fascist provocations," and that the Socialist Federations of the Paris region be invited to participate. His proposal was turned down. On the very next day, André Marty published an editorial in *L'Humanité* calling for "no weakening" (*pas d'énervement*) and attacking "anarcho-syndicalistic" proposals for "monster demonstrations" on the boulevards of Paris. The most the Communist leadership consented to do was to organize in the first days of February small, local demonstrations to protest against the Stavisky scandal, to defend unemployed workers, and so on. In effect, they were denying that a fascist menace existed in France. They, like their German comrades earlier, were simply applying the "class against class" tactics. The enemy was the bourgeois class, of which

[37] [Jacques Doriot], *Lettre ouverte à l'Internationale communiste*, pp. 10, 24. This "letter," written and made public in April, 1934, is an invaluable source of information on the strife within the party in the early months of 1934. Also very useful is Pierre Frank, *La Semaine du 6 au 12 Février.*

fascism was a by-product. The leagues by definition could not represent a separate and important threat. Hence, their agitation did not require any special defense measures. Ignoring the dissension within the party, the Communist leadership adhered steadfastly to this policy.

The growing crisis of the Republic was a major test of the party. It had absolved itself of responsibility for the fate of French liberties. On ideological grounds, the argument was sound, but it ran counter to a very strong tradition of republican defense. This attitude of loyalty had overcome many previous ideological splits, such as that dividing Socialists and Radicals prior to the Dreyfus affair. The Communist position rejected any compromise with the past. Party tactics since 1928 had consistently violated the electoral understanding of support of "republican" candidates against conservatives. But the stakes were higher in February, 1934. The Republic itself appeared threatened. The moment had come for French Communists to take the true measure of their attitude toward the Republic.

II

The New "United Front from Above"

The "February days" of 1934 revealed a new and unexpected face to French communism. After the antirepublican leagues launched their attack on the Chamber of Deputies on February 6, party members violated or simply ignored the tactics of class struggle. Despite the orders from above, they united with liberals and socialists in defense of the Republic. Even the leaders gave in temporarily, agreeing to participate in the demonstration on February 12. In the weeks that followed, pressure from within the ranks grew in favor of united action with the Socialist party. But it had no apparent effect. For while a sizable fraction of the membership was ready to break Comintern discipline, the party leadership was not. It clung firmly to the "class against class" tactics. Its faithfulness testified to the effectiveness of Comintern control over the party organization, though clearly not over all the members. The French party did finally modify its tactics to meet the new political situation, but not because the membership wished it, rather because Moscow ordered the change.

The "February Days"

By February 6, the agitation in Paris was at its peak. A monthlong newspaper campaign and small but violent demonstrations had prepared the way. The demonstration on February 6 promised to be of major proportions. The leagues had decided to concentrate their forces in the small area around the Palais Bourbon, meeting place of the Chamber of Deputies. They had appealed to all Parisians to participate, and could expect a large turnout.

The Communist party had to respond somehow to the challenge from the Right. Its campaign against the Republic had been fully as violent verbally as that of the leagues, though it had not been able to mobilize crowds so large. The party called therefore for a demonstration of its own on February 6. But, unlike the leagues, the party deployed its forces throughout the city. The plan was to hold many demonstrations, in factories, in the railway stations, along the major Parisian boulevards. The Communist veterans' organization was to demonstrate at the Rond-Point des Champs-Elysées, quite near the Place de la Concorde and Palais Bourbon. These instructions were made public in *L'Humanité* on the morning of the sixth in banner headlines on the front page, together with an appeal to "all workers" to demonstrate "at one and the same time against the fascist gangs and against the government which protects and encourages them, against social democracy which, by its division of the working class, tries to weaken it and thus to permit a rapid worsening of the brutal class dictatorship." The Communist party was continuing along its solitary political path.

In mid-afternoon, a crowd began to gather in the Place de la Concorde, directly across the river from the Palais Bourbon. By the middle of the evening, 100,000 or more demonstrators had assembled in the area around the Palais.[1] Though

---

[1] I have found only one eyewitness estimate of the numbers of February 6 demonstrators, given by Doriot in his newspaper, *L'Emancipation de Saint Denis*, February 10, 1934. Doriot estimated that there were present 20,000 "fascists," 30,000 "sympathizers," and 50,000 "curiosity seekers dragged into the struggle."

they never penetrated into the building, which was protected by an imposing mass of policemen, the fighting was vicious. For a few hours Paris experienced virtual civil war. One policeman was killed and 1,664 were injured, while 14 demonstrators (and onlookers) were killed and an untold number injured.[2]

In the midst of the rioting, the Communists went ahead with their own demonstrations. There were from 2,000 to 3,000 Communist veterans parading around the area of the Place de la Concorde; later in the evening, two Communist deputies, Arthur Ramette and Renaud Jean, led another group of from 200 to 300 demonstrators across the Place.[3] The Communist cries of "Long live the soviets!" and their song, "L'Internationale," were lost in the uproar. Soon, the Communist demonstrations lost even their identity as a separate movement. Though some fighting did occur between Communists and leaguers, a common hatred of the police frequently united both in attacks on the forces of order.[4] In the end, the general impression was that the fascists and the Communists had united against the Republic.

Only the conservatives in the Chamber profited from the violence. On February 7, Daladier resigned, fearing more rioting if he remained Premier. Two days later a new cabinet was formed under the leadership of the venerable and conservative Gaston Doumergue, with the support of all the deputies in the Chamber save the Communists and Socialists. The Radicals had at last given up their attempt to govern France.

---

[2] The best account of the February 6 events and of the demonstrations that followed is by Laurent Bonnevay, *Les Journées sanglantes de Février 1934;* see also Beloff, "The Sixth of February," in Joll, *The Decline of the Third Republic*, pp. 36–66.

[3] Testimony given by Jacques Duclos, head of the veterans' organization, to a parliamentary investigating committee looking into the events of February 6. *Le Temps,* March 31, 1934.

[4] "Le six Février," *Cahiers des Droits de l'Homme,* No. 25–26 (October 10–20, 1934), pp. 638–39.

Within the Communist party, the tactics were still unchanged. *L'Humanité*, probably under Marty's control, cried out on February 7 against "the killers Daladier and Frot" (Frot was Daladier's Minister of the Interior). It accused the government of shedding the blood of the "French people." On February 6, the Socialist Seine Federation leadership had sent a letter to the Communists proposing unity of action against the leagues. After the riot that evening, it sent a delegation to *L'Humanité* headquarters, the only Communist offices open at that time of night, but Marty refused to receive the delegates.[5] It is possible that Marty was in fact responsible for the intransigent Communist tactics at that time; after his expulsion from the party in 1955, he was blamed for the "sectarian errors" committed in February, 1934.[6] While the Communist leadership stood still, others began to move. The Socialist party called for an antifascist demonstration on February 12, the same day the CGT had decided to organize a general strike. Even local Communist organizations began taking independent action. Socialist demonstrations organized in various cities on February 6, 7, and 8 were joined by Communists. Pressure was growing within the party for some sort of action.

On February 8, the Communist leaders altered their tactics. Perhaps they felt they risked losing control of their followers; perhaps they feared being left behind by the Socialists; perhaps they hoped to reassert their revolutionary virtue, gravely compromised by the events of February 6. Whatever the reason, "no weakening" suddenly became a slogan of the past. *L'Humanité* launched an appeal on the morning of the eighth for a mass demonstration to be held the next day to demand the arrest of the fascist leaders and of the "killers Daladier and

[5] Information given by P.-L. Darnar in a personal interview.
[6] *L'Humanité*, May 25, 1955.

Frot." A call was also made for a twenty-four-hour general strike in the Paris region to be organized by the local CGTU and CGT unions.

But the party leaders still had little stomach for heading a full-scale antifascist movement. The call for the Paris strike was abandoned on the ninth, when *L'Humanité* published the decision of the CGTU to join in the general strike organized by the CGT. So hesitant were the leaders concerning the demonstration to be held on the evening of the ninth that all the members of the Politburo were ordered to "stay low." There was some justification for this decision, for the Paris Police Prefect had forbidden the demonstration. The Communist leaders, Thorez in particular, had already had one unhappy experience with police repression in 1929 and probably feared a repetition.[7] Thorez continued to minimize the danger from the leagues, remarking in a private speech on February 8 that "certain comrades display an incomprehensible agitation in the face of the fascist maneuvers."[8] His reluctance to organize the Communist resistance did not augur well for the February 9 demonstration.

The plans went awry from the start. To prevent any trouble in the Place de la République, originally to be the meeting place for the demonstrators, the police had filled the large square and surrounding streets with a force of almost 6,000 men. In these conditions, the absence of almost all the Communist leaders was sorely felt. Doriot declared later that the demonstration was "very badly organized and very badly directed."[9] Of the three columns of demonstrators coming in from the working-class regions of Paris and outlying suburbs, none penetrated to the Place de la République itself. Instead,

[7] Doriot, *L'Emancipation*, February 9, 1935; Vassart, "Conférence," p. 23.

[8] [Doriot], *Lettre ouverte*, p. 10.

[9] *L'Emancipation*, April 28, 1934.

Communists and sympathizers haphazardly built barricades and fought the police all over the east side of Paris. Doriot was there with his followers from Saint Denis and the other northern suburbs, plus a contingent of Socialists from Saint Denis. In all likelihood, no more than 12,000 to 15,000 demonstrators were present that evening.[10] Before the fighting was over, four of the demonstrators were killed and 64 known wounded (i.e., hospitalized), and 141 policemen were wounded.[11] The Communists had shown an undeniable force, but it was not at all clear to what end this force had been mobilized.

Was the Communist party fighting the entire bourgeois regime in France or simply the fascists? The Socialist party was fighting only the extremists, and had organized the February 12 demonstration for this purpose. The CGTU had implicitly associated itself with this movement by supporting the general strike of the CGT. If the Communists refused to participate, they would appear still the enemies of all the republicans and would be cutting themselves out of what already looked to be a powerful mass movement. If they joined, they would in fact be admitting that their sectarian tactics of "united front from below" had been wrong. For two days the party leaders hesitated, until finally Fried, the Comintern representative in France, took upon himself the responsibility of approving participation.[12] There was to be unity of action with the Socialist party after all.

There would have been joint action on a local level with the Socialists in any case. Demonstrations in the provinces continued to unite members of the two parties. Further, local committees were formed with the collaboration of Communist representatives to prepare for the events of February 12. In taking this action, the local Communist cells were acting com-

[10] Information given by two participants, MM. Henri Barbé and Giles Martinet, in personal interviews.
[11] Bonnevay, p. 211.   [12] Vassart, "Conférence," p. 23.

pletely on their own initiative. The extent of this insubordination is unknown. But it was apparently widespread. It was the
outward sign of strong pressure from within the party for
immediate joint action with the other proletarian groups.
With or without the approval of the national organization,
there would certainly have occurred a provincial "united
front from above" on February 12.

The antifascist movement that day was a tremendous success. The CGT had never before shown such political
strength in the country. Its general strike virtually paralyzed
the economic life of Paris, and made a strong impact on the
provinces. The demonstrations were impressive, too, particularly in those cities where there existed a strong labor-union
movement.[13] February 12 was truly the day of the CGT. In
Paris, an estimated 150,000 people demonstrated their opposition to the leagues. Though the Communist leaders tried to
maintain their own separate column behind that of the Socialists, the two soon mingled in one great line of marchers. Fears
of strife between Socialists and Communists turned out to be
groundless. Léon Jouhaux, general secretary of the CGT, was
correct when he concluded that the French proletariat "did
not intend to let any harm be done to the democratic regime
or to the established liberties." [14] Though the French workers
were socially isolated and economically oppressed, they remained loyal to the basic principles of the regime. Their
loyalty had a long history behind it, going back to the Jacobin
rule of 1793–1794 and the *levée en masse* against the internal
and external enemies of the First Republic. This "Jacobin
myth" was one of the few elements serving to unite the
working and middle classes in the Third Republic. It had first
shown its force during the Dreyfus affair; almost two genera-

[13] A. Prost, "Les Manifestations du 12 février 1934 en province,"
Mouvement social, No. 54 (Jan.–March, 1966), p. 16.
[14] Quoted in Bonnevay, p. 217.

tions later, February 12 proved that the myth was still strong. The events of that day, and of the days before, showed too that a substantial number of Communists responded to the Jacobin appeal. After six years of "class against class" tactics, the party had still not broken all its ties with French society.

The Return to Intransigence

After February 6, the right-wing leagues continued to organize meetings, parades, and demonstrations. These activities were very often accompanied by violence and bloodshed, and kept French politics in a state of permanent effervescence. Among those organizations which had taken part in the February 6 rioting, the *Croix de Feu* profited most in rising membership. Its discipline and the energetic leadership of its president, Colonel de la Rocque, soon gave it first place in importance among the leagues, and made it the center of attack for those who feared the growth of fascism in France.

In opposition to these reactionary organizations stood the forces of the French Left, still disunited but now conscious of the threat to the democratic regime of the Third Republic. In a spontaneous movement to solidify their power to resist violence from the Right, Radicals, Socialists, Communists, labor-union members, and members of other organizations came together in many communities to form "vigilance committees." Meetings and demonstrations by the leagues met often with counterdemonstrations from the Left, and violent clashes between demonstrators and counterdemonstrators were frequent.

Above this civil strife, yet a product of it as well, the Doumergue cabinet tried to present itself as a government of "National Union." The Radical party constituted the left wing of the new coalition, with ministerial portfolios in the hands of Edouard Herriot and four other Radicals. A political "truce" was called among the parties supporting the government. Good feeling and unity were to replace the previous polemics and bitter struggle.

A sizable group on the Left and Extreme Left of the Chamber of Deputies refused to be parties to the "truce." The Radicals themselves were not united in their support of Doumergue. Edouard Daladier was one of those hostile to the new political formation, and was backed by other Radical deputies. The Socialist party was definitely in the opposition. Its leaders suspected Doumergue and one of his influential collaborators, André Tardieu, of being accomplices of the leagues and of seeking to introduce a more authoritarian form of government. Thus the Communists, even more violently opposed to the Doumergue cabinet, found themselves voting alongside the Socialists in parliament, after having demonstrated alongside them on February 12.

The Communist party leadership reacted at first to the events of early February by continuing to minimize the threat posed by the rightist agitation. The attacks of *L'Humanité* were still directed at the government. Scorn was heaped on the growing movement to defend "a democracy which is gradually being transformed into fascism." Every effort was made to obliterate the precedent of cooperation with the Socialist party. The Central Committee, meeting in early March, declared that the only way to "defeat fascism" was "to win over the Socialist workers to the class struggle, to tear them away from the paralyzing influence of their party." [15] Party leaders showed marked displeasure at the participation of Paris Socialists in Communist demonstrations which took place on February 17 and March 4. If there was to be any joint action at all, it had to occur with the Amsterdam-Pleyel Movement. In early March, the Movement called for a national antifascist

[15] *L'Humanité*, March 3, 1934.

congress in mid-May. In addition, it directed its local "committees of struggle against fascism and war" to propose unity of action to local Socialist organizations. But this was no more than a gesture.

The Socialist leadership was much more flexible in its response to popular pressures. On March 11, the SFIO National Council gave official approval to Socialist participation in independent local "vigilance committees." A number of these committees were direct descendants of temporary committees set up for the organization of the February 12 strike and demonstrations. Others had been set up in the month that followed. In all cases, the vigilance committees had as their goal the defense of the Republic and of democratic liberties against the threat from the leagues. Any organization could join on a basis of complete equality. As the most numerous and most active participants, the Socialists were the unofficial leaders of the movement. Those from the Paris region were particularly active, even organizing with other left-wing groups a "Liaison Center of the Anti-Fascist Forces of the Paris Region." Within a few months of the March meeting of the National Council, the Socialists claimed, there were "hundreds, then thousands" of these vigilance committees in France.[16] The SFIO had placed itself at the head of the antifascist movement.

From the Communist point of view, the situation was growing steadily worse. The Socialist Seine Federation initiated negotiations with the Communist organization of the Paris region in an attempt to achieve unity of action. Meetings were held on March 6 and 9 but failed because of the Communists' refusal to abandon the class against class tactics.[17] Yet at

[16] Statement made by Emile Farinet, one of the Socialist leaders from the Paris region, in *Le Populaire*, May 30, 1934.

[17] A detailed history of Communist-Socialist relations during the first six months of 1934 can be found in a long article, "La Marche à l'Unité d'Action," *ibid.*, February 10, 1935.

the same time the Amsterdam-Pleyel Movement recognized the force of the vigilance committees by inviting them to participate in its antifascist congress. On March 9, it published a laconic statement in *L'Humainté* "noting that committees of vigilance have been formed lately under the leadership of the Socialist party" and "asking that these committees take part in the May 20 assembly." In effect, the party leaders had to accept a very weak form of cooperation with the Socialists.

Within the party, the current of opinion favorable to united action had grown stronger since February 12. In mid-March, Marcel Gitton noted in a speech to the Central Committee that some Communist cells were issuing statements in which they declared themselves ready to defend "republican liberties" and to support a "common front of the Left to insure the respect of the parliamentary regime." [18] Certain local Communist organizations entered vigilance committees, organized meetings with Socialists, and even signed agreements to cease criticism of the Socialist party for the duration of the common action.[19] In particular, Jacques Doriot had continued to defend in party meetings the necessity of proposing a pact for united action to the Socialist party. He had kept alive the Saint Denis Vigilance Committee, formed on February 11. His independent policies received wide support and he was in fact looked upon as spokesman for the tactics of "united front from above." He received backing from a few members of the Central Committee, especially Renaud Jean and André Ferrat, a young party leader in charge of the Politburo's section on colonial affairs. According to Doriot,

[18] Marcel Gitton, *Le Parti communiste dans la Lutte anti-fasciste,* p. 21.
[19] The only available source of information on the vigilance committee movement is *Le Populaire.* For the period February–May, 1934, I was able to find 40 cases of Communist participation in these committees.

one regional party official from Paris warned that "in the present state of passive opportunism in our party, Doriot and his position would without doubt have had a majority if discussion had been opened." [20] The Saint Denis Party District was already well under control. On March 10–12, the District held a prolonged meeting to discuss the issue. By a vote of 120 to 55, it decided to support a policy of united action with the Socialist party. It also voted to send a report to the Comintern Executive Committee in Moscow, exposing the reasons for its refusal to follow the tactics defended by the Central Committee. The resistance to the "class against class" tactics was creating a very undesirable, even dangerous situation for the party leadership.

A campaign against united action with the Socialists had already begun. After the January Central Committee meeting, the leaders had started a drive within the party for resolutions condemning "opportunistic deviations," that is, tactics having for a result cooperation with the Socialists. Following the "February days," *L'Humanité* had set out on a public campaign against the "errors" of certain Communists from the region of Saint Denis, all supporters of Doriot. At the same time, the word was circulated in private that the real culprit was the Saint Denis leader. To keep Doriot from making converts in the provinces, he was prevented from speaking in the name of the Central Committee at any party meeting and was never made speaker at any demonstrations.[21] But by mid-March, it was apparent that the campaign was not having the desired effect.

The party leadership decided then to take a small step

[20] *L'Emancipation*, April 24, 1934.

[21] Information on the activities of the Saint Denis Communists, and on the campaign by the party leaders against them, can be found in various issues of *L'Emancipation* in April and May, 1934, and in [Doriot], *Lettre ouverte*.

toward satisfying demands for antifascist action. Another meeting of the Central Committee was held on March 14. Marcel Gitton delivered the major speech, whose theme was that the party had to modify its attitude toward fascism. He criticized the slogan "no weakening" (launched by Marty in early February) and admitted that "the masses were conscious of the fascist danger and wanted to fight." He declared that the "central task" of the party was "to defeat fascism." His treatment of "fascism" as distinct from the class interests of the bourgeoisie was a significant modification of the Communist view of earlier years; however, the means he recommended to combat the French paramilitary leagues marked no innovation at all. Though he made a slight gesture toward cooperation with the Socialist leaders, Gitton nullified the effect of his offer by repeating the old charge that the SFIO was "the party of social fascism." Reiterating in effect the old tactical instructions, he stressed the "mass political strike" as the weapon which would assure the defeat of "fascism." [22] Gitton's speech indicated that the party leaders had simply adjusted their analysis of the French situation to justify the continuation of the "class against class" tactics.

The Central Committee meeting of March 14 was in fact the beginning of a more energetic campaign against the Socialists and against those "rightist opportunists" within the party who advocated united antifascist action. Thorez gave voice to the new militancy in an editorial in the April 1 issue of the *Cahiers du Bolchevisme*. He called for a "constant and pitiless attack on the Socialist party." It would be a "crime against the working class and against the Communist party," he declared, to view the Socialists as anything other than "agents of the bourgeoisie in the ranks of the working class." As for the Communist "opportunists," their demands for real

[22] Gitton, pp. 18–28.

unity of action would lead inevitably to the "liquidation of our party." [23] Thorez was clearly intent on defeating Doriot, who was a personal threat to his leadership in addition to being an undisciplined Communist. In early April, he tried to stop the Saint Denis leader at the conference of the Northern Paris Region of the party. He presented a motion condemning any "collaboration" with the Socialist party and any discussion of "anti-Comintern and anti-party ideas." The motion carried by 30 votes, 84 to 54. The support given Doriot was significant, for he had as yet made no attempt to publicize his views.

Within a few days, however, the dispute was in the open. On April 11, Doriot made public the *Letter to the Communist International* decided upon by the Saint Denis District. The *Letter* presented a clear argument against the tactics defended by the Central Committee and for united action with the SFIO. It appealed to the Comintern Executive Committee to intervene in French Communist affairs to rectify the "errors" of the party leadership. [24] The struggle had reached the critical stage.

In the weeks following the mid-March Central Committee meeting, the Communist leaders waged an aggressive and abusive campaign against all advocates, within the party and without, of united action. Doriot was the chief target. *L'Humanité* published almost daily resolutions by party cells condemning his "anti-party attitude," often ending with an appeal to the erring Communist to admit his mistake and end his struggle. In the privacy of party meetings, speakers from the Central Committee sounded a more militant note. According to the Saint Denis paper, one Communist worker asked Benoît Frachon why Doriot had not yet been excluded from the party; the answer was that "we want to win over the

[23] "Accélérons la Cadence," *Cahiers*, April 1, 1934, pp. 387–98.
[24] [Doriot], *Lettre ouverte*.

workers first; then we shall exclude him." The plan of action was "maneuver, isolate, liquidate." [25] In sum, the French party leaders were applying the Soviet techniques of totalitarian control to purge Doriot. Bitter attacks were also launched against non-Communists urging antifascist unity. The Paris Socialist leaders Marceau Pivert and Jean Zyromski, who were the most ardent defenders of united action with the Communists, were accused of "demagoguery" and "insincerity." The only unity the Communists were to have was that provided by their own party.

Faithfully applying the "class against class" tactics, the party leaders set out to disrupt the meetings and demonstrations organized by other left-wing organizations. At times, they called for demonstrations at the same time and place as the Socialists in an effort to "capture" the Socialists who would be present. At other times, they attempted to create incidents or even to sabotage meetings. When the CGT tried to organize a large public meeting in Paris in support of its own program to end the economic crisis, they called for a counterdemonstration to oppose the "fascist plan" of the Confederation. Fearing violence, the owners of the stadium in which the meeting was to be held backed out of the affair, and the meeting had to be canceled. For the Communist leadership, there could be no compromise with social democracy and its allies; there could be no "marriage between fire and water." [26]

Unfortunately for the party, fewer and fewer Frenchmen supported its revolutionary intransigence. Signs of disaffection were everywhere. The Communist tactics of the "united front from below" met with little success. Where they were opposed by real united action among the other left-wing parties, they apparently failed completely. According to the Socialist

[25] Quoted in *L'Emancipation*, April 24, 1934.
[26] *L'Humanité*, April 13, 1934.

newspaper *Le Populaire* (admittedly a biased source), the
Rouen Anti-Fascist Committee, non-Communist, held a meeting in mid-April attended by a crowd of 1,800 people. When
the Communists held an antifascist meeting two weeks later,
there was an audience of 300.[27] In by-elections on April 22 in
the Paris suburb of Mantes, the renegade Radical Gaston
Bergery ran as an independent with a program of antifascist
united action on the Left. The Communist vote dropped by
almost 50 per cent on the first ballot by comparison with the
1932 vote. Despite the fact that the Communist candidate had
received fewer votes by far than the other left-wing candidates, he stayed in the running on the second ballot against the
two remaining candidates, Bergery for the Left and a right-
wing candidate. As a result, the Communist lost over 60 per
cent of his first-ballot vote.[28] Popular sentiment continued to
run strongly in favor of united action against fascism, and
many disciplined Communists realized this. Thorez attacked
in the pages of *L'Humanité* these "scare-mongers and ob-
structionists [*paniquards et freineurs*]" within the party. He
complained that a "pessimistic" Communist had even written
to the Central Committee to complain of the "incompetence"
of the leadership. This critic had accused the party of permitting the Socialists to " 'organize thousands of committees at
the base in which our members take their place' " and to
appear " 'in the eyes of the workers as the champions of the
united front. We are losing our position as leaders . . . while
isolating ourselves from the masses.' "[29] Never since the introduction of the "class against class" tactics had the state of the
French Communist party been so desperate.

[27] *Le Populaire*, May 5, 1934.
[28] *Le Temps*, April 24 and May 1, 1934.
[29] Quoted by Thorez, "Paniquards et Freineurs," *L'Humanité*,
April 21, 1934.

Comintern Intervention

In mid-April, the Comintern finally intervened. On April 21, a telegram was sent from Moscow to the French Politburo, calling on Thorez and Doriot to come in person to Moscow and to stop the "divisive struggle." This was an unusual move. Rarely did the Comintern try to solve internal quarrels in its sections by calling on both sides to explain their differences to the Executive Committee. The French party leaders appeared to accept the order from Moscow, sending off Thorez on April 26 and declaring in *L'Humanité* that the dispute was really only a question of "internal differences of opinion." The public campaign against Doriot and the "opportunists" was stopped.

Doriot was not so cooperative. Though he was told in a telegram from the Comintern received in late April that "there is no question of your exclusion," he refused to go to Moscow. In all, he received three telegrams, the last on May 10.[30] None had any success. Doriot gave several excuses for his refusal; at heart, he had probably already decided to break with the Comintern. He had been in disagreement with the "class against class" tactics since 1928; in the dispute within the party in the early months of 1934, he had continually asked the Comintern representative for support against the position of Thorez, but had received none. Fried apparently was unwilling to commit himself in the dispute. Though he sent copies of Doriot's speeches on to Moscow, he gave "evasive answers" when asked his opinion of these speeches, and in general supported the position of the Central Committee.[31] There was nothing to indicate that the Comintern's position had suddenly changed in late April. Judging matters from

[30] *L'Emancipation*, May 25, 1934.   [31] *Ibid.*

Saint Denis, it might well have appeared to Doriot that the Communist leadership merely wanted to remove him from the country in order to isolate him.

The party leaders in France did not respect in private the truce they had publicly declared in their quarrel with Doriot. A meeting in Saint Denis on April 26 was sabotaged, and it ended in full-scale fighting between "Doriotites" and "Thorezists." Attacks on Doriot continued to be made by Communists in private meetings. According to Doriot, "the entire apparatus of the party remained mobilized for the struggle against us." [32]

In mid-May, the Saint Denis leader at last came under the ban of the Comintern. In a curiously worded statement, the Executive Committee "refused" him "the protection of the Comintern" and let the French Central Committee take "all the measures against Doriot, ideological and organizational, which it considers necessary in order to assure the unity of the party and the victorious struggle against fascism." [33] Strangely enough, the Comintern did not itself make the decision, as was its practice, to exclude Doriot.

A few days later, the Comintern action took on an entirely new meaning. The May 23 issue of *Pravda*, official newspaper for the Soviet Communist party, published two long articles, one anonymous, entitled "For the United Front, against Discord," the other signed by Maurice Thorez, "Secretary of the French Communist Party," entitled "The French Communist Party in the Struggle for the United Front." The tone was set by a paragraph in the anonymous article stating that "hundreds of thousands of social-democratic workers in all the capitalistic countries want the struggle against fascism. One would commit a crime against the working class not only by opposing this desire for the united front but even by underes-

[32] "Lettre de Jacques Doriot à l'Internationale communiste," *ibid.*
[33] *L'Humanité*, May 19, 1934.

timating it." The Communist parties had therefore the obligation to offer a "united front of struggle" to the leaders of the
socialist parties. This was especially true in France, where
"social democracy has not yet been in power, where, the
elements of the Extreme Right having left the Socialist party,
the Socialist workers think that their party will not follow the
path of German social democracy." [34] The Comintern, "in
agreement with the Central Committee of the French Communist party," was "of the opinion" that an appeal to the
leadership of the Socialist party for a "united front of struggle" was "not only . . . justified but . . . necessary under
certain conditions." Thorez was even more specific in his
article when he wrote that "the situation in France is shaping
up in such a manner now that the Communist party will once
again have to make a frank proposal to the leadership of the
Socialist party and of the reformist labor confederation
[CGT] for a joint struggle against the fascist threat." [35]
Though Thorez devoted a considerable part of his article to a
condemnation of the "insubordination" of Doriot, he was also
writing an implicit self-criticism for tactical incompetence. It
was clear that, under a mask of fictitious continuity, the Comintern was beginning to implement a radical change in tactics
for the French Communist party.

What brought on this change? Why had fascism suddenly
assumed such threatening proportions in the eyes of Comintern leaders? To this day the answer remains obscure. Our
sources of information are still far from complete. Reliable
eyewitness accounts are few in number; the most revealing is

[34] This was almost word for word the argument used by Doriot to
support his proposal for unity of action with the Socialist party, in
Lettre ouverte, p. 23.
[35] The *Pravda* article, "For the United Front," finally appeared in
L'Humanité on May 31; the article by Thorez never appeared in the
French newspaper!

that of Albert Vassart, who from mid-April, 1934, to June, 1935, was French representative to the Comintern Executive Committee, and who resigned from the party in 1939. He wrote later that the Comintern leadership in the spring of 1934 was in "complete confusion." "Violent discussions" were occurring between Manuilsky, defender of "more supple and audacious tactics for the French party, and Piatnitsky, openly fighting any "innovations." [36] Vassart later revealed in conversations with the historian Branko Lazitch that Manuilsky had declared in early May, 1934, that the French party had to be given a new policy for a "mass movement against fascism" by mid-June. Sometime in early June, he told Vassart that Stalin had approved the tactical revison. Perhaps the Soviet leader had actually made the decision earlier; the *Pravda* articles of May 23 clearly indicated the change to come. In any case, Manuilsky apparently felt that Stalin's approval was only conditional, and that he was running some risk in taking the initiative of modifying the Comintern "line." [37]

The fact remains that Stalin had at last sanctioned for some reason a partial abandonment of the "class against class" tactics. The reason or reasons behind his action remain a mystery. The most obvious clue is provided by Soviet foreign policy in the spring of 1934. The situation confronting the Soviet leaders in Europe had been considerably clarified by events which occurred in April and May. On April 14, the German ambassador had officially informed Maxim Litvinov of the refusal of his government to accept the Baltic protocol proposed by the Russians. This protocol, which would have guaranteed the independence of the Baltic states, appears to have been the last Soviet attempt to preserve the German alliance. The German

[36] Vassart, "Conférence," p. 23.
[37] Lazitch, "Informations," pp. 10–12.

ambassador had been told earlier by Krestinsky and Voroshilov, two of the most active partisans of this alliance, that the protocol was of "great importance," and that a "negative or evasive reply from us [i.e., the German government] would . . . have an unfavorable effect on our relations." [38] In fact, the German refusal apparently convinced the Soviet leaders of the futility of seeking to preserve the German ties. In July, the Italian ambassador informed the German chargé d'affaires that "there was no longer a pro-German trend" within the "leading Soviet circles." [39]

By that time, Franco-Soviet relations had picked up considerably. The new French Foreign Minister Louis Barthou was slow to resume the negotiations begun between his predecessor Paul-Boncour and Litvinov. Barthou came to office in early February, but it was not until late April that he showed any real determination to seek a Franco-Soviet alliance. From that moment on, however, negotiations went smoothly and quickly. Litvinov showed great eagerness to resume negotiations. Personal meetings between Barthou and Litvinov began on May 19 in Geneva; by June 4, they had reached a firm agreement on a regional security pact for Eastern Europe, the "Eastern Locarno," and a Franco-Soviet pact.[40] The Russians were clearly eager for the alliance. By the end of May, *Pravda* was spreading the good news of the improved relations between France and the Soviet Union.

The coincidence in time between the reorientation of Soviet foreign policy and the revision of Comintern tactics is striking. It suggests that a common decision lay behind both actions. Perhaps the Soviet leaders had finally been convinced by Nazi hostility that fascism was a unique and dangerous enemy. The simplified Soviet view of the world had pre-

---

[38] *German Documents*, C, II, 686. [39] *Ibid.*, III, 150–51.
[40] The most complete history of these negotiations is in Scott, pp. 167–71.

viously interpreted the Nazi movement as no more than an emanation of the bourgeoisie, seen as the major foe. Since Nazism was defined as one form of fascism, a re-evaluation of the former necessarily entailed a review of the general importance of the latter. Recognition of the Nazi threat thus discredited the old view that fascism as such was a minor factor in the capitalist world, and that the "class against class" tactics were valid for the entire Comintern. If there was actually a current of opinion within the Comintern and the Soviet party favoring stronger measures to fight fascism, it would certainly have been strengthened by the break between Germany and the U.S.S.R. To carry this speculative reasoning even further, there might be some connection between the "moderate" new Central Committee and Politburo elected by the Seventeenth Congress of the Soviet Communist party and the revision of Soviet foreign policy and Comintern tactics. On the other hand, there is no proof that Stalin did not himself decide on the change. He was after all the man to approve Manuilsky's new policy in late May or early June. For the time being, his motives must remain unknown.

It is important to note, however, that in 1934 Comintern affairs and Soviet diplomatic relations with foreign powers were still separate. Evidence of this can be seen in the fact that the French Communists remained resolutely antiwar and anti-national defense after their change in tactics despite the Franco-Soviet diplomatic *rapprochement*. They pursued this policy until the moment the Franco-Soviet pact was signed in May, 1935. Further, the campaign against fascism was not modified by the character of Soviet diplomatic relations with any particular country. By August, 1934, the same new tactics were being applied by the Communist organizations in France, Czechoslovakia, Switzerland, England, Austria, Belgium, and Spain, and even by the exiled Italian Communists. To be sure, they would not have been adopted had they not been in the interests of the Soviet Union. But Soviet use of the Comintern was still restricted generally to the mobilization of mass movements which might weaken forces hostile to the U.S.S.R., such as the Western bourgeois parties or fascism. Only after May, 1935, did Stalin attempt to use certain Comintern sections as a constructive instrument of Soviet foreign policy. The antifascist campaign in 1934, once approved by Stalin, was a Comintern affair, one in which the French Communist party was designated to play a leading role.

Somehow, the French party had to be made to do a tactical about-face. The simplest method, one quite in line with Comintern technique, would have been to change the party leadership. Thorez had shown himself an uninspired Secretary; a replacement might therefore have been called upon, had one existed. Unfortunately, the most likely candidate, Jacques Doriot, had made himself unavailable by his refusal to go to Moscow. Had he done so, undisciplined though he had been, the Comintern might have handed him control of the party. Thorez, who arrived in Moscow at the end of April, was treated like dust. His queries as to why he had been called went unanswered, the only response being that he must wait until the other French leader had arrived. Ignored by all, he whiled away the idle hours by practicing his German with the German-born wife of Albert Vassart, French representative to the Executive Committee.[41] Sometime before May 20, he returned to Paris, at last conscious of the important tactical changes to be made but probably without any precise instructions.[42] Ever since his rise to power, he had minimized fascism

[41] Personal interview with Mme. Vassart.
[42] In addition to the sources already cited, information on Comintern relations with the French party in the spring of 1934 can be found in Ypsilon (pseud.), *Stalintern*, pp. 212–23, and especially in the note on page 213 by the remarkably well-informed translator (this book first appeared in English as *Pattern for World Revolu-*

and had heaped abuse on the Socialist party, "lackey of the bourgeoisie." Now, he was confronted with the task of suddenly reversing tactics and seeking cooperation with the Socialists in an antifascist campaign. At this critical juncture, he probably could not even count on the aid of Fried, who was discredited in Manuilsky's eyes as a result of his handling of French affairs in the preceding months.[43] It is thus not surprising that Thorez dragged his feet in applying the new tactics, until finally Moscow had to tell him specifically what to do.

The first proposal to the Socialist party was made shortly after Thorez's return from Moscow. The French Communist leader had apparently decided to present the National Committee against Fascism and War as the rightful partner for the SFIO. The Committee already had plans well under way for a national antifascist congress on May 20 and 21. The meeting offered a likely occasion for proposing such a plan. Actually, the Amsterdam-Pleyel Movement was too insignificant a force in French politics to be seriously considered by the Socialists. Only the Communist party itself was suitable for united action. But Thorez refused to see things that way. Speaking directly to the issue before the congress on May 21, he declared: "Don't expect us to change, don't expect us . . . to be able to permit the development in our ranks . . . of a policy which, under the deceitful mask of 'united front,' begins by creating disorganization and scission within the ranks of the Communist party." Unity was necessary but could come only "with Amsterdam [-Pleyel] and around

---

tion); also, *Bulletin d'Etudes et d'Informations politiques internationales*, No. 77 (November 16–30, 1952), p. 20; also, André Marty, *L'Affaire Marty*, p. 97; also C. and A. Vassart, "The Moscow Origin," Drachkovitch, pp. 244–46.

[43] Vassart, "Le Rôle de Délégué," p. 2. Vassart defended Fried in discussions with Manuilsky in Moscow.

Amsterdam." [44] At the close of the congress, a vague resolution was voted which called for the national coordination of antifascist organizations. At the same time, a telegram was quietly sent off to the Socialist party, meeting at that moment in a national convention, asking the party to join the National Committee against Fascism and War and its local committees in common action against fascism. This initiative, a minor revolution in itself, was turned down by the Socialists, who considered Amsterdam-Pleyel too "limited" in scope to associate with their party on a national scale. Instead, the Paris Socialists, working within the local Anti-Fascist Liaison Center, invited the National Committee to join forces with the Center. [45]

The Socialist leaders were at heart still suspicious of the new Communist initiatives. For one thing, they feared the ruthless dynamism of the Communists. Marceau Pivert and Jean Zyromski, Paris region Socialist leaders, were eager for immediate cooperation, but others were more reserved. For their part, the Communists did little to overcome this suspicion. During the demonstration in late May honoring the 1871 Commune, they showed their old hatred of the "social traitors." Refusing to organize a joint demonstration, they did everything possible to disrupt the Socialist demonstration, and showed once again what one Socialist called their "blind, senseless sectarianism." [46] At the same time, the Communist leaders continued their violent campaign against Doriot, the one outspoken Communist defender of unity of action with

[44] "Compte-rendu," *Front mondial*, No. 17 (June 1–15, 1934), p. iv.
[45] *Les Communistes et Nous*, p. 61. This brochure, put out by the Socialist leadership during the 1936 electoral campaign, contains much interesting information on relations between the Socialist and Communist parties in the period 1932–1936.
[46] Jean Longuet, in *Le Populaire*, May 28, 1934.

the Socialists. On June 1, the Rouen Anti-Fascist Committee, grouping Socialists, Trotskyites, and members of the League of the Rights of Man, organized a meeting at which Doriot was invited to speak on unity of action. The speech was never made, though, for a group of Communists created an uproar the moment he appeared at the podium and the meeting ended in a general free-for-all. Such events brought cooperation with the Socialists no closer to achievement.

Yet the Communist leaders continued, in a curious, crablike manner, to move toward unity of action. On May 29, *L'Humanité* announced the convocation of a national party conference for June 23–25, the theme of which was to be "The Organization of the United Front of Anti-Fascist Struggle." Thorez, in an accompanying editorial, explained the calling of the conference as a question of *noblesse oblige*. Since the party had such an immense following among the working class, it had the "responsibility" to organize the "united front." This in its turn, Thorez explained, would prove the "unshakable unity of the Communist party in the face of the confusion and decomposition of the parties of the bourgeoisie, including the Socialist party." In fact, of course, the party had no wide following among the workers and its unity was shaky at that moment.

Like it or not, the French Communist leadership had to take action. On May 28, the Presidium of the Comintern Executive Committee met in Moscow. It announced that the much delayed Seventh World Congress would be held later in the year, with the major speech to be made by the Bulgarian George Dimitrov on the antifascist struggle of the proletariat. The announcement was the first public sign from the Comintern itself that something new was ahead. Perhaps the Presidium took the occasion to push the dilatory French comrades in the direction of united action. Only two days later, the French Central Committee came together for what was a historic meeting. It made the first direct offer to the Socialist party to organize common action against fascism.[47]

The Socialist leaders were not willing, however, to begin cooperating immediately with their erstwhile rivals. After an exchange of letters, a meeting was arranged between representatives of the two parties for June 11. There, despite pressure from the Socialists, the Communists refused to make any promise to cease their "criticism" of the SFIO and its leaders. For the Socialists, this was the key question. They had no intention of working with the men who had made a habit of scurrilous public attacks on their party. They repeated their demand for an agreement to end mutual criticism in a letter sent June 12. The Communist leaders answered by letter two days later, calling for a decision on united action "within 48 hours," protesting at the same time that "insult and defamation are methods foreign to our party." In the next breath, they warned that "we intend to retain our entire right to doctrinal criticism, to analyze the facts and events and to draw the tactical conclusions in the exclusive interest of the working masses." [48]

The significance of this warning was made clear in the June 15 issue of the French Communist review, *Cahiers du Bolchevisme*. Once again, the Socialists were attacked as "the principal social defenders of the bourgeoisie." Thorez himself, in the lead editorial, declared that the leaders of the rival party were "social reformists" whose only intention was to "fool the working class and to maintain it partially under their influence." [49] Other articles carried the same aggressive mes-

[47] Published in *L'Humanité*, May 31, 1934; according to Albert Vassart, the decisions for the changes in tactics came from Moscow in the form of "imperative directives sent by coded telegram" (Vassart, "Conférence," p. 24).

[48] *Le Populaire*, June 16, 1934.

[49] *Cahiers*, June 15, 1934, pp. 708–11.

sage. If the Communist leaders had sought to sabotage unity of action with the Socialists, they could not have found a better means.

The real reason for this sudden explosion of polemical violence remains a mystery. Such attacks had been absent from *L'Humanité* since early June. The most probable explanation is that the French Communist leaders had had enough by mid-June of seeking the hand of the "flighty" Socialists. They had never felt any enthusiasm for the marriage—Thorez had expressed open hostility in his speech before the antifascist congress on May 21. After two weeks of desultory negotiations, it was apparent that the Socialist leaders would not accept a pact without provision being made for an end to criticism of their party. Thorez was not willing to make the sacrifice, and revealed his opposition to further negotiations—at the same time that he made continuance of the negotiations virtually impossible—in his vitriolic editorial. His move was not unprecedented. Between 1921 and 1928, the Comintern had applied "united front" tactics which provided for just such a mixture of cautious negotiations with the social democrats and bitter polemics. What Thorez did not—or would not—understand was that Manuilsky believed the fascist threat in 1934 so important that the old maneuvering was no longer called for. Then, too, Thorez was not alone in his hostility toward the new tactics. The Comintern leadership was still divided. Discussions continued throughout the summer of 1934. Though supporters of the change were, in the words of a recent Soviet study, an "overwhelming majority," they still encountered "a certain resistance." The opposing groups were much the same as earlier, with Dimitrov, Manuilsky, and the Italian Togliatti backing, and Piatnitsky, Knorin, and the Hungarian Bela Kun, among others, resisting the new tactics. Though the ECCI had set up committees to prepare for the Seventh World Congress, they could not yet agree on the instructions to be presented at the Congress.[50] The divided counsel within the Comintern may well have aided in slowing down the shift in France.

As a result of the outburst in the *Cahiers*, contacts with the French Socialist party were set back to their pre-June level. On June 20, the Socialist leadership met and decided to suspend the negotiations with the Communists. In a letter to the Communist Central Committee, it declared that "under the cover of common action, you continue in your goal to undermine and dishonor our party." [51]

Prospects for a united front between the Socialist and Communist parties were thus very dim when the Communist delegates gathered in the Paris suburb of Ivry on June 23 for their special national conference. The speeches which marked the early days of the conference did not improve the situation. They were full of the "old-style" rhetoric, defending the tactics of "class against class," belaboring the Socialists for their "anti-unitary" policy and "constant abandonments," grudgingly defending "democratic liberties" against the fascists while attacking the "reactionary degeneration of bourgeois democracy." The old apocalyptic vision of history was revived by Marcel Cachin when he stated that "between fascism and the dictatorship of the proletariat, the development of the crisis does not permit much longer the existence of intermediary forms." [52] The necessity of creating an "anti-fascist united front of the working class" was emphasized, but there seemed to be little room in it for sincere cooperation with the Socialist party. Thorez insisted on the "necessary

[50] Leibzon and Shirinia, *Povorot v Politike Kominterna* [The Change in the Policy of the Comintern], pp. 77–82; "VII Kongress Kommunisticheskogo Internatsionala," *Voprosy istorii KPSS*, August, 1965, pp. 49–50. The material used in these studies was apparently drawn from unpublished minutes of the ECCI meetings.

[51] *Le Populaire*, June 21, 1934.   [52] *L'Humanité*, June 24, 1934.

criticism of the Socialist party and of its leaders when the latter perform anti-proletarian acts or oppose the united front of the working class." [53] Alone, Thorez would never have achieved united action with the Socialists.

At that moment, the Comintern intervened. In the midst of the national conference, probably on June 24, the party leadership received a secret telegram from Manuilsky's regional secretariat for Latin countries. The Comintern categorically ordered the party to reach an agreement quickly with the SFIO. It even included in the telegram the draft of a unity pact, to be used apparently if the French Communist leaders could not achieve a more advantageous pact of their own. [54] The party conference, scheduled to end June 25, was suddenly prolonged another day. On June 26, Thorez spoke once again. His speech had a new tone of urgency. The success of the "united front," he declared, was "a matter of life or death for the proletariat." The immediate task confronting the party was "to prevent a fascist dictatorship from establishing itself in France, and as a result to prevent to the very best of our ability the outbreak of war." Therefore, unity of action was necessary *"at any price."* If such unity was obtained, "neither from the mouth of any of our propagandists, nor from the pen of any of our writers, in *L'Humanité* or even in the *Cahiers du Bolchevisme*, as in our entire press, will there be the slightest attack against the organizations or against the leaders of the Socialist party." [55] Even more pointed were the remarks made

[53] *Ibid.*, June 25, 1934.

[54] According to André Ferrat, the instructions were received 48 hours before the slogan "at any price" was launched (which he mistakenly puts in the month of May), that is, June 24 ("Le Parti communiste," *Esprit*, No. 80 [May, 1939], p. 167). This is confirmed by information given in a personal interview by Mme. Vassart, who was in Moscow with her husband Albert Vassart at that time.

[55] "Le Front unique pour battre le fascisme," *L'Humanité*, June 29, 1934.

on the same day by one of the Communist deputies in the Chamber of Deputies, Arthur Ramette. Turning to the Socialists in the course of his speech, he declared that his party was ready to "put aside the difficulties" raised by the contents of articles in the June 15 *Cahiers*.[56] The way was at last open for united action.

Ironically, it was at this very moment that the last act of the "Doriot case" was played out. On the day after the close of the conference, June 27, the Central Committee finally expelled Doriot from the party. One must admire the skill with which the rebel was eliminated without serious damage. Doriot had previously had a large following among the Communist rank and file, but by late June, he had been so thoroughly isolated that his ejection left the party almost intact. Thus Maurice Thorez was the man to be credited for the ultimate success of the antifascist campaign.

But he was not the author of the pact itself. He made one last attempt to entice the SFIO into accepting united action on his own terms, which included the freedom to continue verbal attacks on the Socialist party and leaders. On June 26, the national party conference concluded its action by passing unanimously a motion calling for a united action pact without restriction on criticism. The only response from the SFIO was a long letter demanding a clear answer from the Communists to the question: Were they ready or not to cease their attacks upon the Socialist party and its leaders?

The Moscow instructions had the answer. They contained the preliminary draft of a pact, prepared by Albert Vassart, French representative to the Comintern Executive Committee and partisan of the new tactics. Vassart's inspiration and model was a proposed "Pact of Socialo-Communist Non-

[56] *Journal officiel, Débats parlementaires, Chambre des Députés,* No. 58 (June 27, 1934), p. 788. Hereafter referred to as *JO, Débats, Chambre.*

Aggression" (a parody of the Franco-Soviet Non-Aggression Treaty of 1932), published by the Socialists on June 23 for the benefit of the Communist national conference.[57] Received by the Comintern Secretariat in Moscow on the same day, the Socialist document was seized upon by Vassart as a bond by which, willy-nilly, Communists and Socialists could be united in common action. The contents of the suggested pact, providing for the end of mutual criticism and for mutual aid in case of attack by the leagues, were maintained as such. Vassart himself merely added an opening section on the aims of the action, which he fixed as the "mobilization of the working population against fascist organizations," and a section calling for a strike campaign against the government's decree-laws for financial austerity. He also included a clause providing for the "denunciation" by either party of those who did not adhere to the conditions of the agreement. Manuilsky, presented with the proposal the next morning, gave his immediate approval, and the document, called now the "Pact for Unity of Action," was sent on to the French party.[58] On July 2, it was presented to the SFIO and appeared as well on the front page of *L'Humanité*. The move was an audacious one. Jean Lebas, author of the Socialist "Non-Aggression Pact" and strong opponent of the Communists, had probably thought his document a means to embarrass the Communist leaders. No one expected that the Communists would willingly silence their attacks on the Socialists. But the unexpected had happened. Vassart's audacity would pay off richly, for it would help earn for the Communist party the credit for the achievement of united action.

[57] Originating in the Socialist Federation of the Nord, the pact was published in *Le Populaire*, June 23, 1934.

[58] Vassart, "Conférence," p. 24. Also, interview with Mme. C. Vassart; also, C. Vassart, "The Moscow Origin," Drachkovitch, pp. 248–51.

An important factor working for Socialist-Communist cooperation was the strong current of popular opinion running in favor of some sort of unity of the Left against fascism. Both Communist and Socialist parties had felt the push earlier, but as long as the Communist leadership fought unity, the Socialists had contented themselves with organizing the local vigilance committees, with or without the participation of the Communists. Now that the Communist party had thrown itself, in effect, into the current, the pressure upon the Socialists was redoubled. This was apparent when Parisian Communists and Socialists, the latter going against the wishes of their national party leaders, organized a common meeting against fascism on July 2. The crowds which presented themselves at the entry to the meeting hall that evening were so great that two additional halls had to be opened. The tone of the speeches was generally in harmony with the popular enthusiasm. One Socialist speaker exclaimed that "I've waited 15 years for this evening, and I hope now it will not be without its sequel." Jacques Duclos declared that "we are ready to put aside anything which might appear to impede unity of action. We want the united front with all our might." The only sour note was struck by Marcel Cachin, who harped on the slogans "bourgeois democracy, the mother of fascism," and "class against class," and concluded with an appeal to the Socialists "to take the road to Moscow." [59] Despite this echo out of the past, however, comradeship was the order of the day.

The pressure for unity affected the various non-Communist worker organizations in different ways. The CGT had after February returned to its traditional nonpolitical pattern of action. It took the position that if the Communists sincerely wanted to reinforce the working-class movement, they had to accept the reintegration of their labor confederation

[59] *L'Humanité*, July 3, 1934.

(CGTU) into the CGT. The CGTU was pressing the CGT for a united action pact of labor confederations, but would not consider its own dissolution. On this point, apparently, there was strong pressure from Moscow for resistance. Consequently, negotiations stalled. But the Socialist leaders were more vulnerable. Blum was uneasy about the motives of the Communists, but was conscious of the popular desire for unity. He described this feeling as an "electrical current" spreading through the Paris region and out into the provinces.[60] Under strong pressure from the ranks to achieve united action, the SFIO leaders could not turn down the new Communist offer without gravely endangering the unity of their party.

On July 15, the SFIO National Council met to consider the Communist proposals. Many at the meeting expressed doubts that, after fifteen years of bitter struggle, the Communist party could suddenly turn ally. There were those who looked on the new Communist initiatives as hypocritical "maneuvers." Still, general opinion was in favor of common action, but under certain conditions not included in the proposed pact. The National Council urged that there be "reciprocal good faith," with no criticisms either in the course of or outside the common action, and no doctrinal controversies to disturb joint meetings. It insisted that "the struggle against fascism . . . will necessarily imply the defense of democratic liberties." Finally, it asked that the "control of common action" belong to each party, in other words, that the Communist party be deprived of any voice in Socialist affairs. In place of mutual denunciation of violations of united action, it proposed that a "Committee of Co-ordination" be created, with representatives from both parties, to settle any disagreements

[60] *Le Populaire*, July 7, 1934; see also J. Colton, *Léon Blum*, pp. 101–2.

arising out of the implementation of the pact.[61] Only under these conditions would the SFIO accept a united front.

By July 27, the Pact for Unity of Action was ready to be signed. The Communist party had agreed to all the major Socialist demands. In its final form, the pact provided for a campaign of joint meetings and demonstrations in order to "mobilize the working population against the fascist organizations." It also called for support of "democratic liberties" and for opposition to "war preparations," the decree-laws, and "fascist terror in Germany and Austria." [62] The agreement did not provide for parliamentary action; the only mention of politics was a passing demand for new elections to the Chamber of Deputies. But it was a major event in French political life. The two most powerful mass parties, erstwhile bitter enemies, had united in defense of the Republic. Together, they represented a popular force stronger than that of all the leagues. The problem of the defense of republican institutions was on its way to solution. To be sure, the pact could do nothing about the still graver issues of the deepening recession and the growing threat of foreign war. But these problems did not appear to dampen the enthusiasm which greeted the signature of the pact. As in 1899, the Republic had found its champions.

The French Communist leaders had reason to be satisfied with the outcome. Nowhere else that year did a Communist party apply so successfully the new tactics of the united front. In Czechoslovakia, England, and Switzerland, the socialists had turned down Communist offers. Only the Austrian and Italian socialists accepted united action, but neither agreement had any impact on developments in those countries. The French pact stood out as the tactical model for other Communist parties. Nothing like it had existed before. Though Com-

---

[61] *Le Populaire*, July 16, 1934.   [62] *Ibid.*, July 28, 1934.

munists referred to it as the "united front," it represented
something different in Comintern tactics from the "united
front" of the 1920's. For the first time, a Communist party had
to restrict its propaganda and activities for the sake of a
short-run alliance with socialists.[63] This fact did not prevent
the Communists from playing on the ambiguity of the term
"united front" to claim that they had desired united action
from the early 1920's. The SFIO leadership, with disarming
frankness, admitted that it had been influenced by popular
wishes and that it was still not united in support of the pact. It
did not even try to make political capital of the fact that it had
supported the vigilance committee movement. It was thus not
difficult for the Communists to convince many Frenchmen
that credit for unity of action belonged to their party.

The signature of the Pact for Unity of Action marked the
close of an extraordinarily agitated period in the history of the
party. The "class against class" tactics, though not officially
renounced, were in fact dead. The grave internal crisis which
the party had experienced in the first months of 1934 was
ended. Unity had been restored. The movement among the
members for united action had been satisfied without compromising the principle of centralized party control. At the same
time, the principal advocate of the new tactics and greatest
threat to the leadership, Jacques Doriot, had been expelled.
Despite his original fears, Thorez had every reason to be
pleased with the result. He had proved once more his fidelity
to the Comintern by accomplishing a radical reversal of party
tactics with little harm to himself or to the party.

It is unlikely that any of the Communist leaders anticipated
the effect this initiative would have on the French party.

[63] The unique character of these tactics was implicitly recognized
in an article in the Comintern theoretical journal in December. See
"Ot rasshatyvaiushcheisia stabilizatsii . . . ," *Kommunisticheskii Internatsional*, December 1, 1934, p. 6.

Their goal was in the immediate situation to block the rise of French fascism. But in seeking to achieve this end, they had aligned French communism with the French Jacobin tradition. Party members had already shown their support of Jacobinism; now the party itself had officially sanctioned the defense of the Republic. Ideologically, the party was in an ambiguous position between the proletarian revolution and the liberal republic. There was not far to go before party members would see themselves, and be seen by others, as latter-day Jacobins.

III

From the United Front to the Popular Front

The signature of the United Action Pact was a turning point in the history of the French Communist party. It set the party on a path of action which eventually altered the nature of French communism. The stresses of the postwar period had set the party going, but could not sustain it; its conversion into a movement dependent in organization and action on the Comintern assured discipline, but not popular success. The United Front put the party in touch with old political traditions still acceptable to many Frenchmen. In the name of the Republic *and* of social justice, it demanded a better living for the poor of the cities and the countryside. It castigated the rich and appealed to all the underprivileged classes to support its action. It once again respected "republican discipline" in the elections. As a result, many more Frenchmen than before found in communism a viable political expression of their problems and aspirations.

In mid-1934, the "united front" tactics were limited to cooperation with the Socialist party. Within a few months, however, they were widened to include other groups in French society. The party leaders introduced a new slogan, the "popular front," to designate the broader mass movement. They enjoyed greater freedom of movement than they had ever known. They presented a program for immediate reform capable of attracting the electoral support of the masses. The antifascist struggle was the immediate task, but to it they attempted to add economic issues of interest to a broad segment of the French population. But while they could propose modifications of the United Front, they could not force the Socialists to accept them. Unwilling to be carried along on anyone else's coattails, the latter refused the Communist advances. The deadlock almost broke the United Front, until a new Comintern initiative made the dispute irrelevant. In May, 1935, the Communist leaders had once more to give proof of tactical agility as they sought to convert the mass movement into a political coalition uniting all left-wing parties. Their quick response and adroit maneuvers, though unsuccessful, showed that they had improved considerably in the year since the introduction of the United Front. They, too, were learning the skills of democratic politics.

At the same time, the conservative government was finding it more and more difficult to cope with the problems caused by the depression. By the end of 1934, French economic activity had fallen off 30 per cent by comparison with its 1928 level. A slow recovery did begin in the spring of 1935, but it was too modest to be noticed by contemporaries. For the government, public finance was still the thorniest problem. The budget deficits were greater than ever before; to fund the tremendous public debt, cabinet ministers found no better solution than to compress public expenditure and request special financial powers from parliament. The policy was a political liability, and was an important factor in the fall of two "National Union" governments between June, 1934, and June, 1935.

To the Masses

The signature of the Pact for Unity of Action on July 27 marked the beginning of the official United Front, but not of effective common action. The federal structure of the Socialist party made application of the pact dependent upon the wishes of the federal and local leaders. In certain regions, such as Paris and Lyon, united action was undertaken immediately after, or even before, the signature of the pact. In other regions, particularly the industrial north and the provinces of Alsace and Lorraine, the pact was applied later, and in a much weaker manner. By the end of 1934, it was effective throughout France. Still, there was some justification for the reproach by the Communists that unity of action was most energetically applied where they were strong and the Socialists weak, and was "underestimated and scorned" where the balance of power was reversed.[1] The basic cause of this situation was not Socialist disloyalty to the pact—though it did exist—but rather a sincere difference of opinion concerning the aims of united action.

There was no question as to the necessity to fight the growth of fascism in France and to take measures to stop the agitation by the reactionary leagues. Meeting after meeting echoed this antifascist theme, and demonstrations were organized to oppose the leagues. These meetings and demonstrations drew large and enthusiastic crowds, much larger than those of the leagues. Proof of the effectiveness of united action could be seen, in fact, in the decline of league demonstrations, which were less and less frequent in the months following the signature of the Socialist-Communist pact. Something had changed in France. In Léon Blum's words, unity of action had provoked an "electric current among the masses" and had once again given the workers their "*élan*, confidence, and enthusiasm." For him, there could be no doubt that the pact had "barred the path of fascism in France." [2] It had fulfilled its immediate goal.

[1] André Blumel, "La Lune rousse," *Le Populaire*, February 23, 1935.
[2] "L'Unité d'Action," *ibid.*, February 26, 1935.

Beyond this point, the agreement ended. For the Communists, united action offered an excellent means to activate the masses, to heighten their "political consciousness" and readiness to follow political leadership. True, the Communists were interested above all in combatting the "fascist forces" in France. However, this campaign was not to be limited to antifascist slogans alone, but was to include other themes capable of gaining the adhesion of the French people. The Communist leaders wished to reinforce the antifascist movement by supporting and encouraging "the struggle for the immediate economic and political demands of the working class, of the peasant workers, as well as of the working strata of the urban petty bourgeoisie." [3] Later, when the leagues no longer posed a threat to the French regime, even the antifascist slogan became but one appeal among others to animate a mass movement. The Socialists, on the other hand, saw in the pact a weapon to be used to fight the activities of the leagues; outside of this action, each party was to pursue independently its own campaigns. It was for this reason that certain Socialist organizations, particularly those in the more conservative provinces, went ahead cautiously with united action.

Repeatedly, the Communist delegates to the National Coordination Committee sought to expand the mass movement. In September, they urged that measures be taken to combat the austerity policies of the Doumergue government. In December, they tried to obtain Socialist support for a strike campaign by the workers. In both cases, they were unsuccessful. Maurice Thorez summed up his party's discontent with unity of action as practiced by the Socialists at a Central Committee meeting on November 1. He complained that united action "is limited to meetings and a few demonstra-

[3] *Internationale communiste* (abbreviated *Internationale*), September 5, 1934, p. 1102.

tions" and that the "content of the action is meager." [4] The
Communists wanted more action over more issues.

At the same time, they were taking steps to increase their
following among the masses. Elections for local departmental
and district (*arrondissement*) councils were scheduled for
October 7 and 14, and constituted the first serious test of the
united front tactics. In previous years, Communist participation had been minimal. This time, however, the party committed itself, in an electoral "Manifesto" published on August 19
in *L'Humanité*, to presenting candidates in as many contests
as possible. Further, the Manifesto put aside in large measure
the old revolutionary jargon and proposed limited reforms,
for the middle classes as well as for the proletariat. This
concern for the bourgeoisie was something quite new. Its
justification was found in Germany, where the lower middle
classes, abandoning their traditional parties, had formed one of
the pillars of support for the Nazi party. The Communist
leaders showed every sign of wishing to prevent a similar
occurrence in France. So concerned were they to attract support from the poorer strata of the bourgeoisie that they even
borrowed certain planks of their new platform from the programs of middle-class associations. The combination of intensive electoral activity and a moderate platform brought the
party comparative success at the polls. Its vote on the first
ballot on October 7 showed an increase of 15 per cent over its
1932 vote.[5] To be sure, a few old-line Communists were not
satisfied with the reformist tone taken by party propaganda.
Some "anarcho-syndicalists and Blanquists," as one leader dis-
paragingly described them, regretted the absence from the
Manifesto of such traditional slogans as "the dictatorship of

[4] "Sur la Voie du Parti unique," *L'Humanité*, November 7, 1934.
[5] T. Ferlé, *Le Communisme en France*, p. 147, n. 2.

the proletariat" and "revolutionary defeatism." [6] But these ideological misgivings made no impression on party policy.

The innovations were not yet at an end. For the purposes of united action, the Communist party scrapped its obstructionist electoral tactics of maintaining its own candidates on both ballots. A declaration from the Co-ordination Committee on October 9 proclaimed that wherever a second ballot was to be held, there would be no competition between Socialists and Communists. The candidate from either party receiving the greater number of votes was to run alone, while the candidate from the other party was to withdraw and to steer his votes to his more successful rival.[7] The United Front had become an electoral coalition.

The major victim of this new situation was the Radical party. Traditionally allied with the Socialists for electoral purposes, its leaders had hoped to preserve this tie in the 1934 elections, despite the reversal of alliances in parliament. In the Communist electoral manifesto of August 19, Radical candidates were promised support, but only on condition that they reject "avowed or masked representatives of fascism," and disavow the government of National Union, its decree-laws, and its Radical ministers. The Socialists joined the Communists in making a withdrawal on the second ballot for a favored Radical candidate contingent upon the rejection by this candidate of the Doumergue government. Not surprisingly, cases of Communist and Socialist support for a Radical candidate were extremely rare. When the final returns of the second ballot of October 14 had been counted, the Communist party found itself with 17 more seats on the departmental councils (now 34 in all), the SFIO with three more (from 115

[6] Gaston Monmousseau, "Pour l'Alliance avec les Couches moyennes," *Cahiers*, September 1, 1934, p. 102.

[7] *Le Populaire*, October 11, 1934.

to 118), the left-center parties, including Radicals, Independent Radicals, and some splinter groups, with 49 fewer (from 765 to 716), and the conservatives with 29 more (from 621 to 650).[8] Though the Communist leaders had reason to be satisfied with their own gains, their final judgment was much more reserved. The Left had gained, but so had the Right, with the Center paying the price. A few months later, a party spokesman stressed this disturbing "polarization to the extremes." He concluded that "we risked experiencing in France what had happened in Germany, where for years our party had gained in each election, but where . . . Hitler's party gained more rapidly."[9]

It was urgent, therefore, that the Communists expand their campaign to win over the middle classes, and that they define more clearly their policy toward the Radical party, the leading political representative of the petty bourgeoisie. The first move came immediately after the first ballot. At a meeting of the Co-ordination Committee on October 9, Thorez proposed the elaboration of a "positive program" of reforms, which would interest the middle classes in the United Front. "Don't you think," Thorez asked in presenting his proposal, "that we must rally certain elements [of the French population] which do not follow us as yet?"[10] In a speech on October 10, the idea became a slogan, the "common front of liberty and peace" which would unite the middle and the working classes. Thorez suggested that it would be possible to prepare a "list of legitimate demands for the workers of all categories," the aim of which would be to give more "positive content to the common struggle of the working masses" against fascism. Two days later came the finishing touch. The speech by

[8] *Le Temps*, October 17, 1934.
[9] Florimond Bonte, "Les Etapes du Front populaire," *Cahiers*, July 1, 1935, p. 720.
[10] Quoted by Jean Lebas, *Le Populaire*, February 2, 1936.

Thorez was reprinted in *L'Humanité* on October 12 under the title, "At All Costs, Defeat Fascism; For a Wide Anti-Fascist Popular Front." According to M. André Ferrat, member of the Politburo at that time, it was Fried, the Comintern representative in Paris, who had hit upon the new slogan of "popular front" and had had it substituted for Thorez's very unoriginal "common front." [11] The party was beginning to give proof of real political initiative.

The popular front was not at that time looked upon as a political alliance which might include the Radical party. Rather, it was intended as a mass movement which would appeal to the liberal politicians and masses. Certain prominent Radicals, a minority to be sure, were in open disagreement with the policy of their party leaders to support and participate in the National Union. Edouard Daladier called for the "union of all democrats" from the working and middle classes; Pierre Cot attacked the "paralyzing" alliance with the center and conservative parties and demanded a more dynamic program.[12] In his speech on October 10, Thorez cited the proposals of both men as proof that parts of the "middle classes" were already receptive to the idea of a "common front." The new campaign was in general aimed at that floating mass of petty bourgeois which might be influenced by the fascist movements. Included also were those groups still faithful to the Radical party who "are not yet convinced that the position of Herriot and his friends results in preparing the bed of fascism." A "positive program" presented by the United Front would give them a "pole of attraction" to their left.[13]

[11] Information given by M. André Ferrat, personal interview; see Ferrat, "Contribution," p. 61.

[12] Daladier's appeal was published in *L'Humanité* on October 5, 1934, with comments; Pierre Cot's article appeared in *L'Oeuvre*, October 7, 1934.

[13] Joanny Berlioz, "Les Elections cantonales," *Correspondance*, October 20, 1934, p. 1509.

The popular front was a weapon to be used against the Radical party as long as it supported the National Union.

This goal was made even clearer later in the month. The Radical party held its annual convention from October 24 to 26 in the city of Nantes. On October 24, Maurice Thorez made a speech in that city in which he called for "a popular front of liberty, of work, and of peace" against the "front of reaction and of fascism." Recalling that certain members of the Radical party were opposed to the National Union, he offered to collaborate with anyone ready to defend "the interests of the working masses of the cities and of the countryside." The only positive suggestion made for the organization of this collaboration, however, was the formation of "committees elected by all the workers" in the towns and villages.[14] Thorez later stressed that this "wide popular front" should group all those "workers, peasants, and little people of the middle classes who are still outside the influence of the [Socialist-Communist] Pact." The popular front committees "even" had room for the "local sections of the Radical party and of the League of the Rights of Man which oppose the so-called policy of National Union and the evil deeds of the fascist gangs."[15] Addressed to a party whose center of power had always been parliament and whose local organizations were rarely more than committees of notables, this invitation was poorly inspired.

The Radical convention at Nantes gave the Communist leadership virtually no satisfaction. The current of opinion hostile to the policies of the Doumergue government was much too weak. The final motion supported the participation of the Radical leaders in the cabinet, declared the party's continued fidelity to the political "truce," and even accepted the prospect of constitutional reform. Daladier's speech did offer

[14] *L'Humanité*, October 25, 1934.   [15] *Ibid.*, January 3, 1935.

the Communists some consolation, especially his declaration that the working class was "on our side" for the defense of the Republic. *L'Humanité* commented that he spoke like a "future head of government destined to destroy the 'enemies of the Republic.' " But the most important lesson drawn by the Communists from the convention was that the active members of the Radical party still had to be brought over to "our side"! [16]

The fact was that the Communist leaders did not yet think in terms of parliamentary action in the framework of the popular front or even of the United Front. The reversal of tactics was still limited to the field of mass action; "bourgeois parliamentarianism" remained, as Jacques Duclos declared at a Central Committee meeting on November 1, a "caricature of democracy" to which the Communists opposed the "real democracy" of the dictatorship of the proletariat.[17] Though ideologically correct, this attitude was much too dogmatic given the new situation created by the formation of the United Front. The "positive program" suggested in October could even have been used as a parliamentary "pole of attraction" to form a new Center-Left coalition had the Communists directed their efforts to that end. Yet the idea was never so much as hinted at; much later, in March, 1935, Thorez stated flatly that "obviously no parliamentary program is called for." Further, the Communists would have "no confidence" in a left-wing government. They might at most support measures enacted by such a government which were "in the interests of the working class." [18]

It may well be that the parliamentary strategy of the Communists was simply nonexistent in November, 1934. Though

---

[16] *Cahiers,* November 1, 1934, p. 1292.

[17] *Corps à Corps avec le Fascisme,* p. 9.

[18] "Le Parti communiste français et la Lutte pour le Front unique," *Internationale,* March 5, 1935, pp. 332, 335.

violently hostile to the political formula of National Union and even more so to Doumergue's proposals to reform the Constitution, they could offer nothing to replace the existing political coalition. This was made clear when a cabinet crisis broke out in early November as a result of the refusal of the Radical ministers to accept a demand by the Premier for special financial powers. The rebellion of the Radicals ought to have suggested to the Communists the possibility of a reversal of political alliances. The Socialists made an attempt at one, offering to the Radical group in the Chamber to form a "strong republican government" with a limited program of defense of public liberties and measures to fight the economic crisis.[19] The Communists said nothing. Later, Thorez declared that the Socialists' move had been an act of "disloyalty" to the Unity Pact which his party should have publicly criticized.[20] The Socialist offer was ignored by the Radicals. A second government of National Union, headed by Pierre-Etienne Flandin, was formed within a few days. It is extremely unlikely that Communist support for the Socialist move could have swayed the Radicals in their determination to remain in the Center-Right coalition; the Communists' lack of support merely underlined the parliamentary weakness of their tactics.

At that moment, the real complaint of the Communist leaders was the lack of success of their plans for a massive popular front. The "positive program" suggested on October 9 seems to have been neglected until late November. The National Council, supreme executive body of the Socialist party, was to meet on November 25. On the day before, the Politburo sent a letter to the Council suggesting a "program of the popular front" which included measures calling for the dissolution of the leagues, new elections, the forty-hour week, generalized

[19] Léon Blum, *Le Populaire*, November 11, 1934.
[20] *Internationale*, March 5, 1935, p. 324.

aid to unemployed workers, aid to poor farmers, a moratorium on commercial debts, a public works program, and a reduction of taxes on the poor. This untidy bundle of reforms was not to the liking of the Socialists, who declared "impossible" the signature of "a 'common program' which does not contain *a single measure of a socialistic nature*." [21] They proposed that the program be reinforced by the addition of measures for the "socialization of the large means of production and of exchange," plus a price support program for the farmers. The Communists refused to consider these measures, which they felt might frighten away the peasants and small merchants. The negotiations were broken off "amicably" on January 9, 1935, with no agreement in sight. The Socialists sought a "common program" uniting the two Marxist parties on ideological grounds. The Communists desired a tactical program which was meant, in Léon Blum's opinion, to "set forth the themes for action around which could be created a large mass movement going beyond the limits of our two parties and of the masses which follow them." [22] Between the intellectual rigidity of the Socialists and the tactical expediency of the Communists, there could as yet be no compromise.

As a result, the popular front marked time, and the United Front limited itself to fighting the leagues. The Communist leaders regretted the failure of the common program, whose absence, they said, made the United Front "too abstract and too restricted to the domain of general agitation." [23] They continued to seek some organization around which to construct their popular front. They tried in January, 1935, to build up the Amsterdam-Pleyel Movement as a potential leader, but with no effect. They continued to urge the forma-

[21] Quoted in *Le Populaire*, November 28, 1934.
[22] "Le Programme commun," *ibid.*, January 20, 1935.
[23] Berlioz, *Correspondance*, January 26, 1935, p. 101.

tion of "democratically elected committees of the popular front," but none apparently was ever formed. They were left with only a few meetings organized under various auspices which grouped a wide popular following. For example, they claimed for the popular front a meeting held in Paris on January 18, 1935, in support of the antifascists of the Saar. In reality, the reunion was organized by the Committee for Unity of Action, founded by the Paris Socialists with the participation of the local Communist and Radical organizations. The "wide popular front" did not exist, and never would.

The Comintern had thus some reason not to be completely satisfied with the first six months of united front tactics in France. The seemingly grave fascist menace had been parried by the Pact for Unity of Action, but on the conditions set by the Socialists. Further, nothing had been accomplished beyond the terms of the pact. There was no common program, no mass movement uniting middle and working classes, no campaign in support of strikes. The SFIO had not proven a pliable partner. The Comintern, in an editorial in the September 5 French issue of *Communist International*, had encouraged the French party to overlook minor difficulties in applying the united front tactics. Taking these instructions literally, the French leaders had accepted later Socialist rebuffs loyally and without controversy. Then, at the end of the year, the attitude of the Comintern changed.

The first sign of discontent with the united front tactics came in an anonymous editorial in *Communist International* on December 1. The theme of the article was the approach of the "second cycle of revolutions and wars," a revival of the "class against class" analysis. The new militancy implicit in this choice of subject became quite explicit in the treatment of the united front tactics. The alliance with social-democratic parties was approved only as a means of fighting fascism,

1. The leagues against the Republic: the Place de la Concorde, February 6, 1934. (*Illustrated London News.*)

2. The new allies: Pierre Laval in the Kremlin, May, 1935 (*from left to right*, Litvinov, Molotov, Potemkin, Stalin, Laval). (*L'Illustration.*)

3. The well-fed among the lean: Edouard Herriot meeting Russian workers during his visit to the Soviet Union, September, 1933. (*L'Illustration.*)

defending the democratic rights of the workers, and delaying war. This "defensive" operation was definitely subordinate to the "principal aim" of the united front, which was to "facilitate the passage of the social-democratic masses to communism." Therefore, the Communists were never to cease criticizing "the program, strategy, and tactics of those with whom we have signed the agreement [for a united front]." In effect, the editorialist was recommending that the Communist parties return to the united front tactics of the 1920's. His only concession to the "new" united front practiced by the French Communist party was to warn that attacks on social democracy should be made "without any uproar" which might break the agreement! Such contradictory advice was virtually useless.

The author of the editorial was just as ambiguous in his criticism of "our French comrades." He noted that they had succumbed to the "rightist danger" in the application of the Pact for United Action. He accused them of "giving in to the pressure of the Socialists" and of having "at times interpreted incorrectly the conditions of the pact." He further declared that the French party had neglected to "underline with sufficient clarity for the masses the differences of principle which exist between the Socialists and us" and of having failed to "prepare and conduct strike action, after the Socialists refused to include strikes in the clauses of the agreement." [24] The French Communist leaders were being ordered—for the advice given in the editorial was clearly a command—to become more militant in their relations with the SFIO. Yet at the same time they were made to understand that the pact, with its provisions for no criticism, was still to be preserved.

[24] "Ot rasshatyvaiushcheisia stabilizatsii ko vtoromy turu revoliutsii i voin [From the Unsteady Stabilization to the Second Cycle of Revolutions and Wars]," *Kommunisticheskii Internatsional*, December 1, 1934, pp. 6, 19–20.

It could be that the obscurity of the editorial reflected a real disagreement within the Comintern concerning the united front tactics. Significantly, the editorial itself was presented as a "basis for discussion" of Communist tactics in general prior to the meeting of the Seventh World Congress. For some unexplained reason, the Congress had been put off by the Comintern Presidium of September 5, 1934, until the first half of 1935. In the early months of 1935, the Comintern review published a series of articles under the heading of "Tribune of the Seventh Congress." Here, Communist leaders from many countries discussed tactics ranging from the united front to armed insurrection. One of those who favored the united front was George Dimitrov. Writing in the Comintern weekly journal *International Press Correspondence* in late November, 1934, he had declared that the application of these tactics was "the most urgent task of the working-class movement in all countries." Obviously referring to the French experience, he had warned that there should be no "stereotyped and uncritical transfer of political and organizational experience." Still, he had not restricted the united front to a purely "defensive" role. On the contrary, he had affirmed that "the formation and strengthening of the united proletarian front is now the *main link* in the preparation of the world proletarian revolution." [25] Further information on Dimitrov's position is provided by the testimony of a former Chilean Communist leader, Eudicio Ravines, who was in Moscow in late 1934. He witnessed a personal clash between Dimitrov and Manuilsky over Comintern tactics. Dimitrov defended the use of the new united front tactics "everywhere"; Manuilsky wished to see these tactics applied only in "liberal countries like France and Spain" and urged "armed insurrection in

[25] "The Struggle for the United Front," *Inprecorr*, November 24, 1934, pp. 1581–83.

some places." [26] For the time being, no final decision was made.

Perhaps this indecision among the Comintern leadership was the cause for the delay shown by the French party in responding to the "recommendations" contained in the *Communist International* editorial. On January 10 and February 1, Thorez did publish two articles in the Comintern review in which he assessed the accomplishments and insufficiencies of his party's "struggle for the united front." On the whole, he painted a rosy picture. He did, however, accept the need "to expand the guiding role of the party" in the united action with the Socialists. He promised that the party would lead the workers on an offensive against capitalism, would "create a vast network of local committees in the cities and the countryside," and would strive to obtain a popular front program as another means of achieving the "mobilization" and the "extra-parliamentary action of the masses." [27] Finally, on February 15, the Central Committee approved the tactics outlined by its secretary.

Application of the modified party line was difficult to achieve. In fact, part of the tactical recommendations were never applied. There was no strike movement. The economic depression made the French proletariat more than cautious, as even the Communists realized. The workers hesitated to take action because of "their poverty, of the risk of losing their jobs," and asked to have the "guarantee that they are undertaking action in the best possible organizational conditions." [28] In the face of such obstacles, Communist labor leaders could do nothing. There was really no mass agitation at all. The

[26] Eudicio Ravines, *The Yenan Way*, p. 145.
[27] *Kommunisticheskii Internatsional*, January 10, 1935, pp. 14–21, and February 1, 1935, pp. 24–31. Thorez's articles did not appear in the French edition until March 5!
[28] Joanny Berlioz, *Correspondance*, February 9, 1935, p. 201.

popular front was never "mobilized"; when it finally appeared in June, 1935, it did so in an entirely different form and for entirely different reasons than those invoked during the campaign in February. The "vast network of elected committees" remained invisible. The French Communists, in sum, had no more influence over the masses after December, 1934, than before.

The only tangible results of the heightened militancy were strained relations with the Socialists. The Communists set out systematically to take the credit for joint demonstrations, to criticize certain members or leaders of the SFIO, and to vaunt the qualities of the "real" proletarian party. All of this made the Socialist leaders even less willing to go out of their way to appease their supposed partners in the United Front. Their discontent with Communist tactics was made public at a meeting of the National Council on March 3. Speaker after speaker rose to complain of the "unfriendly procedures" of the Communists. Their irritation was not great enough to cause them to denounce the Pact for United Action. It was sufficient, though, to lead them to make demands of their own, chief among which was the beginning of negotiations for the unification of the two parties of the proletariat, the eternal dream of the SFIO. In the two months that followed the meeting of the National Council, the Communists made token gestures toward accepting the Socialist proposals for unification, while continuing to act independently. The joint meetings and demonstrations were few and far between, and were held on Communist terms.

By this time, Moscow had almost decided to abandon entirely the French experiment. According to Albert Vassart, both the Comintern and French Communist leaders were convinced that united action with the Socialists "would not last and was not profitable." Preparations were made for a break;

Vassart even wrote a pamphlet for use by the French party in which blame for the failure of the pact was placed squarely on the Socialist party.[29] In one sense, the Communist appraisal of the situation was accurate. The United Front had accomplished its immediate goal of creating a strong antifascist movement; by the spring of 1935, its moment of greatest importance had passed. But it had only begun to show its real and potential profitability. The municipal elections in May, 1935, and the parliamentary maneuvering at the end of the month were proof of that. The United Front was not yet dead.

Elections, Pacts, and Politics

Despite strained relations, the Communist and Socialist parties went into the municipal elections of May 5 and 12 more allies than enemies. Each party conducted its own electoral campaign. Communist propaganda stressed more than ever the party's concern for the "people." The front page of *L'Humanité* on the day of the first ballot became one big electoral poster, calling on one and all to "vote Communist for honest management of municipal affairs in favor of the working masses, for lower taxes for the poor and higher taxes for the rich!" Still, the Communist leadership was willing to continue cooperating with the Socialists on the second ballot, and even softened its attitude toward the liberal candidates. On May 7, two days after the first ballot, the Socialist-Communist Co-ordination Committee declared that withdrawals on the second ballot to the benefit of the most favored candidate would again be the rule between Socialists and Communists. The Committee added that these withdrawals would even be

[29] Lazitch, "Informations," p. 17.

extended to "candidates who are partisans of liberty and who are leading against the reaction."[30] Contrary to the position taken in the elections of October, 1934, this declaration left the door open for support of Radical and other liberal candidates. It is impossible at present to determine whether the Communists were following a Socialist initiative in May, 1935, or vice versa. They continued their attacks on the leaders of the Radical party, such as Herriot, who had "capitulated" to the reactionaries—that is, who had supported the National Union government. But their primary concern was to defeat the reactionary leaders themselves. In the fifth ward (*arrondissement*) in Paris, their candidate led all other left-wing candidates, but was far outdistanced in his turn by a prime enemy, Lebecq, the president of one of the organizations active in the February 6 riots. The Socialist, Radical, and dissident Radical candidates withdrew from the second ballot in favor of a newcomer, Paul Rivet, President of the Committee of Anti-Fascist Intellectuals, who ran under the title of "candidate of union for the defense of democratic liberties." The Communist candidate backed out as well. Between a liberal and a "fascist," the French Communists, as against their German comrades earlier, could make the sensible choice.

The most notable result of the municipal elections was the Communist gain. In control of 150 municipalities, large and small, since the last elections of 1929, the party increased its holding in May, 1935, to 297. The increase was most spectacular in the Paris region and the industrial north. In the working-class suburbs surrounding Paris in the Seine department, the number of Communist city governments rose from 9 to 27; the total population of these 27 cities was over 700,000. The contrast with the cantonal elections of October, 1934, was striking. The 1934 elections were dominated by French

[30] Quoted in *Le Populaire*, May 8, 1935.

rural voters, of whom still very few supported the Communist party. Most municipalities in predominantly rural departments were non-Communist, too; only in the central and southwestern departments did the party begin in May, 1935, to show some strength.[31]

On the whole, the party's centers of electoral strength were the industrial areas. By the spring of 1935, these regions were feeling the full weight of the depression. Unemployment was at its peak. The new Communist tactics appealed to a proletarian population having good reason to feel discontented with things as they were; the result was Communist success. The effect on the party was great. In these industrial areas, the Communist-controlled municipal government provided a solid foundation for party activity. Though the powers of the municipalities were restricted, they could provide the population with significant services in welfare and housing, the credit for which accrued to the party. In its turn, the party found in the municipal institutions employment for its activists and administrative experience for its leaders, present and future. The Communist municipalities created strong and lasting ties between the party and French urban society. For the first time, the Communists had a real stake in existing French institutions.

The party leaders had good reason to be satisfied with the elections. Their candidates had done exceptionally well. The trend toward polarization in the French electorate, apparent in the October, 1934, elections, had apparently been halted. The Radicals had held their own, and reactionary candidates had been defeated. In the much publicized Paris election, the liberal intellectual Paul Rivet was successful over the favored league candidate Lebecq. From the Communist point of view, the strength of the liberals was an encouraging sign, for it

[31] *Quatre Années de Luttes,* pp. 132–36.

meant that France was no longer repeating the electoral history of the Weimar Republic. The Communists had little reason to regret the United Front.

While the United Front had brought many important modifications in the Communist line, it had not affected the policy of "revolutionary defeatism." The Comintern had always been formal in its condemnation of aid to capitalistic countries at war, no matter who the aggressor. The Communists had only one fatherland, the Soviet Union. Outside the U.S.S.R., they were to attack the doctrine of national defense, to refuse to vote any military funds in parliament, and to fight "militarism." In the event of war among capitalistic countries, they were to incite the proletariat to civil war and revolution. They would thus be defeatists for the sake of the revolution.

In the early months of 1935, the French Communists remained as faithful to this policy as ever. Together with the Socialists, they organized a campaign against the introduction of two-year military service in the French army. During a parliamentary debate in March on national defense, Maurice Thorez affirmed categorically that his party "would not permit the workers to be dragged into a war said to be the defense of democracy against fascism." [32] Though the French Communist leaders were actively pushing signature of the Franco-Soviet Pact of Mutual Assistance (*L'Humanité* was even campaigning against the last-minute obstructionism of French Foreign Minister Pierre Laval), they were in no way prepared for the change in their own tactics which followed the signing.

The long-awaited treaty was finally signed on May 2. Originally, it was to have been only a part of a larger East European treaty system. In the hands of Laval, the treaty prepared by Barthou was drastically weakened. It lacked the

[32] *JO, Débats, Chambre*, No. 32 (March 16, 1935), p. 1038.

essential clause on automatic aid in the event of attack, and was linked only to the Franco-Czechoslovak defense treaty. As though the pact were not weak enough, Laval went out of his way two weeks after its signing to assure the Nazi leader Goering that it was no threat to Germany. The Soviet leaders had little reason to be satisfied with their alliance with France as it stood then. Yet they urgently desired it, fearing, according to diplomats in Moscow, a German attack in two or three years.[33] To be sure, they had not given up all hope of restoring good relations with Germany; the visit of a Soviet trade delegation to Berlin in July, 1935, provided an opportunity for discreet inquiries to German leaders concerning the possibility of improving German-Soviet political ties. But the Soviet advances were brushed aside then just as they would be in early 1937. In fact, until 1939 Hitler gave the Russians no reason to anticipate anything but war with Germany. Soviet interests, as defined by Stalin in his speech at the Seventeenth Party Congress in early 1934, were best served by adherence to the pact with France. At the very least, the alliance guaranteed that the Germans would not receive French support; at best, it promised the Soviet Union military aid from the state which men still believed at the time possessed the strongest army in Europe. The only other alternative for Russia was a highly dangerous isolation. Stalin's suspicion of the capitalist powers, reinforced by the bungling foreign policies of the Western states, did produce a strong isolationist trend in Soviet foreign affairs after 1936. But the Franco-Soviet pact was still preserved. The Soviet leaders, with the possible exception of Maxim Litvinov, certainly did not feel any devotion to the principles of collective security and cooperation with France. Given German hostility, their commitment to the French alliance is satisfactorily explained by political realism.

[33] Scott, p. 244.

Once the pact was signed, Stalin was quite willing to make the French Communist party pay the ideological price. At the request of Laval, in Moscow on an official visit in mid-May, the Soviet leader expressed in a public communiqué his "complete understanding and approval of the national defense policy pursued by France with the object of maintaining its armed forces at a level consistent with its security requirements." [34] At one blow, the Communist dogma of opposition to national defense had been demolished.

The Russians swallowed the pill easily. *Pravda* declared simply that "one must be strong to defend peace." [35] The Communist leaders in Paris, on the contrary, showed signs of befuddlement. Paul Vaillant-Couturier, editor-in-chief of *L'Humanité*, described Stalin's statement as a "clap of thunder." [36] All the Communists' powers of dialectical reasoning were brought out to show that black was white, that their opposition to national defense was unchanged. When André Ferrat, member of the Politburo, expressed the fear that the struggle against "French imperialism" would be halted, he was told by the party leadership that "our relations with our own imperialistic bourgeoisie are not modified." [37] Within a few days, however, it became clear that the old campaigns against civil defense, two-year military service, and the like, were things of the past. A week went by before an explanation was found to justify the new position. Proclaimed in posters sent throughout the country, the argument ran simply: "Stalin is right!"

Others were not so sure. The Socialist party, accused previously by the Communists of compromising with the French imperialists on the question of national defense, was now left

[34] Quoted in Jane Degras (ed.), *Soviet Documents on Foreign Policy* (London, 1953), III, 132.
[35] May 16, 1935.   [36] *L'Humanité*, May 18, 1935.
[37] Ferrat, *Lettre ouverte*, p. 8.

far behind by the new Communist position. Léon Blum, examining the consequences of Stalin's declaration, predicted that the former defenders of "revolutionary defeatism" would soon accept "the unconditional duty of national defense, and support of the governmental policy of rearmament [and] . . . the governmental thesis of security in armed force." [38] Despite vehement denials by the Communists, Blum's predictions were to prove in the main quite correct. The Communist party once again showed its prodigious ability to perform tactical and ideological somersaults.

Stalin's declaration in favor of French national defense opened a new phase in French Communist tactics. Originally, the popular front represented an attempt to create a mass antifascist movement uniting the petty bourgeoisie and proletariat. At the end of May, 1935, it suddenly became the watchword for a proposed political coalition to unite the Communist, Socialist, and Radical parties. The occasion for action was provided by a demand, made May 23 by the Premier, for special decree powers to meet a new financial crisis. On May 24, the Communists sent a letter to the Socialist party, calling for an agreement between the deputies of the two parties to fight this "anti-democratic" proposal and inviting other left-wing deputies to join in. The meeting of the Communist and Socialist deputies took place on May 28; it produced a common letter to the parties on the Left—the SFIO, the Socialist Republican party, and the Radical party—urging them to send delegates to a meeting to be held on May 30 to discuss the "conditions for a concerted action against the government's financial proposals." [39] This initiative, a step toward the possible creation of a new Left-Center majority, was in Léon Blum's words "even more" the work of

---

[38] *Le Populaire*, May 18, 1935.
[39] Quoted in Alexander Werth, *The Destiny of France*, p. 155.

the Communists than of the Socialists.[40] For the first time in its history, the Communist party was trying to play a constructive role in parliament. After the "united front from above," the time had come for the "popular front from above."

There seems little doubt that this change in Communist tactics was inspired by the new alliance between France and the Soviet Union and by Stalin's approval of French national defense. The latter action was of great importance for the French party and for the Comintern in general. It was the first indication that Stalin had decided to harness Comintern tactics to the specific requirements of his foreign policy. Until May, 1935, French Communist tactics had diverged considerably from Soviet diplomatic policies toward France, most notably on the question of national defense. After the signature of the pact, they paralleled with remarkable accuracy the evolution of Franco-Soviet relations, so much so that they provide one measure, imperfect to be sure, of Soviet intentions toward France.

It has been said, by Communists at the time and by others since, that the new tactics were the result of Communist success in the municipal elections, which encouraged the party leaders to seek political alliances.[41] It is quite possible that the Communist electoral triumph finally convinced the Comintern leaders of the general utility of the united front tactics, which were adopted by the entire world organization at the Seventh Congress in August. But this does not provide a

[40] Speech made at the Socialist convention in June, in *Compte rendu sténographique du XXXII Congrès national,* p. 224.

[41] Vassart, who had returned to France to participate in the electoral campaign, later gave this explanation (Lazitch, "Informations," p. 17). Thorez used the argument in an article in *L'Humanité* on May 15, when he first hinted that his party was contemplating new parliamentary initiatives. Georges Dupeux, author of an excellent study of the Popular Front, defends this point of view (*Le Front populaire et les Elections de 1936,* pp. 86–87).

satisfactory explanation of the new parliamentary tactics of the French Communist party, which had nothing to do with the old popular front or the United Front. The Communist leaders later proved that electoral success was incidental—though not unimportant in itself—to their immediate political goal of supporting a Radical government. Finally, the electoral interpretation does not explain why the Communist attitude toward the moderate Radical leaders who were still members of the National Union government, in particular Herriot, changed suddenly in late May from opposition and abuse to praise and support. At best, the municipal elections may have given additional encouragement to the Communist leadership to undertake parliamentary activity. But they were not the cause of this activity.

Soviet interest lay in strengthening the Franco-Soviet alliance, and the new tactics of the French party were conceived with this end in mind. The new center of French Communist attention was the Radical party. It was the strongest political organization backing cooperation with the Soviet Union. Its electoral manifestoes and convention resolutions continually defended the policy of *rapprochement* with Russia initiated by its president, Edouard Herriot. For the Soviet leaders, a French government under the direction of the Radical party presented much greater hope for the application of the newly signed treaty than one headed by conservatives, particularly of Pierre Laval's sort. Laval made no mystery of his low opinion of the Soviet alliance and of his desire for a reconciliation with Italy and Germany. After his visit with Goering in May, a Communist journal remarked that "you can have no confidence at all in him." [42]

The Radical leaders, especially Herriot, seemed to merit the Communists' confidence. Herriot had been instrumental in the

[42] *Correspondance*, May 26, 1935, p. 618.

preparation of the Franco-Soviet pact; he was to be treated from the end of May, 1935, until the very collapse of the alliance four years later with the greatest respect by the Communist party. Therefore, the Radical party appeared most capable of leading France in the direction of a firm alliance with the Soviet Union. Besides, it was unquestionably republican. The signature of the pact all but guaranteed Communist support of an antifascist government, of the sort a Radical, for example, would be very likely to form. Finally, the Radical party was obviously capable of leading a new government, since its group was the largest in the Chamber. From 1932 until 1934, its leaders had held the reins of power. They might well do so again, were they given new reasons to count on the support of a left-wing coalition in the Chamber. Beginning in late May, 1935, the Communist leaders set out to do everything in their power to convince the Radicals that these reasons existed. Their efforts were concentrated first of all on the Chamber of Deputies.

Their goal was very quickly made public. It was revealed on May 30 both in the Chamber and at the meeting of the left-wing parties represented in the Chamber. The meeting was an enormous success in terms of participation. All the parties contacted sent delegates. Interest in the initiative to regroup the Left was obviously high. The success went no further, however. The aims of the several parties were still too far apart for any agreement to be possible. The Radicals sought to attract the Socialists into a rather "do-nothing" government, while the latter demanded energetic measures to fight the economic depression. As for the Communists, they simply wanted to see the Radical party in power. Maurice Thorez said as much in person to Herriot during the Chamber debate later that day on the proposed "special powers." His party, he declared, "would be ready to bring you our support, President Herriot, if you or any other head of your party wished to lead a Radical government—since the Radical group is the most important of the left-wing groups in this Chamber—which would really apply the policies of the Radical party." [43] The Communist proposal was so sudden and unexpected that it apparently attracted no attention, and was ignored by Herriot himself. Yet in itself it was an astounding declaration.

The meager nine Communist votes in the Chamber gave Thorez no right to propose, before the cabinet crisis had even opened, that a Radical cabinet be formed. One can only imagine that he was under very strong pressure from above to try to obtain this result. While courting the Radicals, the Communist leaders also let it be known that they considered Socialist participation in a new left-wing government quite undesirable. They were incurably suspicious of the Socialists, and might simply have feared the results were Socialist leaders given positions of power. Their views were not shared, however, by the Radicals. Léon Blum remarked later that what the "inexperienced" Communists did not realize was that they were "pushing toward a situation which, in the minds of the Radicals, unavoidably entailed Socialist participation." [44] Much less did the Communist leaders realize that the coalition they were trying to create would within a year produce a cabinet with Socialist participation and under Socialist leadership!

The meeting of May 30 led to the creation of a very loosely knit organization to permit the left-wing parties to consult with one another. It was baptized the "Delegation of the Left" (*Délégation des Gauches*) after a similar political body formed in 1902. Its effectiveness depended entirely upon agreement between its two major participants, the Radical and

[43] *JO, Débats, Chambre*, No. 52 (May 31, 1935), p. 1741.
[44] *Compte rendu sténographique du XXXII Congrès*, pp. 224–25.

Socialist parties. The Communists had provided the impetus for the creation of this organization but their skeletal parliamentary force gave them virtually no voice in its decisions. Their initiative had come at the right time. The Socialists were interested in a regrouping of the Left. Within the Radical party, the minority favorable to a more dynamic policy was growing in strength, while the majority feared a disaster in the coming legislative elections should the Socialists remain in the opposition. But too much still divided these two parties for the Delegation of the Left to be able to take the effective action desired by the Communist leaders.

As was expected, the government of Flandin was unable to unite a majority in the Chamber in support of special financial powers. On the evening of May 30, the cabinet resigned, to be succeeded by the ephemeral government of Georges Bouisson. It in its turn was defeated on the very day of its presentation in the Chamber, June 4, again on the question of special governmental powers. In the course of the new political crisis, the Delegation of the Left met twice. Both times, it was deadlocked by the inability of Radicals and Socialists to agree on a political program. All that could be done was to appoint a committee to draw up a policy statement satisfactory to the participants. This did not at all satisfy the Communist leaders. They had sought once again to defeat the National Union, in Blum's words, "at all costs" and "to inspire in the Radical party sufficient confidence in itself to form a government." [45] But their own impotence in the Chamber permitted them only to propose, not to decide, and their proposal was ignored. Instead, on June 7 the crisis was ended by the formation of yet another government of National Union. Worst of all, the new Premier was Pierre Laval!

[45] *Le Populaire,* June 10, 1935.

The Communists were understandably bitter over the outcome of the crisis. "The program debated by the Delegation of the Left," declared Arthur Ramette in the Chamber on June 7, "could and should have succeeded." He accused the "Radical leaders" of having "yielded to the blackmail of the fascist leagues, to the pressure of the speculators," and promised the Radical deputies that "our constant effort will tend toward the achievement of this popular government." [46] Later, the blame was shifted to the Socialists. Their "conditions and demands" had "made the men of the Radical party back down before the responsibility of forming a government." [47] In reality, neither the Socialist nor the Radical leaders were probably ready for a left-wing government.

Even before Laval became Premier, the Central Committee had taken steps for the "development of the popular front," new style. Meeting on June 1 and 2, it approved the "contacts created on the parliamentary level" with the Radical party. But it also called for a "mass movement" uniting the left-wing forces in the country which would clearly serve as a pressure organization to guide the actions of the deputies. The aim of the movement was the defense of democratic liberties and of peace through "the development of loyal collaboration with the Soviet Union," the dissolution of the leagues, higher taxes, and so on.

Also, the Central Committee moved to break the deadlock over labor-union unification. It declared that the party was ready to make "the greatest sacrifices" to insure proletarian unity, by means of which the popular front would become "invincible." [48] Marcel Gitton put substance into this declara-

---

[46] *JO, Débats, Chambre*, No. 54 (June 8, 1935), p. 1806.

[47] *L'Humanité*, November 18, 1935.

[48] "Pour l'Unité de la Classe ouvrière et le Développement du Front populaire," *ibid.*, June 7, 1935.

tion of intentions when he stated that "there cannot be any sort of political groups [*fractions*] within the labor unions." [49] These *fractions* had been the instrument by which the Communists kept a form of political organization within the very unions they controlled. In December, 1934, the CGT had made the question of their abolition a test of the sincerity of the Communists' desire to achieve the unification of the two confederations. Though the CGTU representatives had made some concessions on the question of the "reintegration" of their confederation within the CGT, they had for six months balked at the renunciation of the *fractions*. [50] In March, the issue had been discussed in Moscow. Albert Vassart had argued that the political groups in the unions could easily be replaced by the factory cells as a center for Communist activity and leadership. For some reason, his suggestions were neither supported nor voted down in the Executive Committee. Instead, they were communicated to the French leaders for use "should the occasion arise." [51] Gitton's speech in early June was proof that the Comintern felt the proper moment had come. The "sacrifice" made on the question of the *fractions* was essentially one of prestige, important nonetheless as the sign that the Communist leaders were ready at last to accept the CGT's price for labor-union unification.

By the close of the Central Committee meeting on June 2, the Communist party had outdone itself in audacious initiatives. Its parliamentary representatives had set out to reverse the trend of the legislature toward Right-Center coalitions, and to push for the formation of a new Left-Center grouping. Its labor leaders had in effect sanctioned the end to a decade and a half of independent Communist labor activity in the

[49] "Il faut ouvrir la Voie à la CGT unique," *ibid.*, June 6, 1935.
[50] See André Delmas, *A Gauche de la Barricade*, pp. 53–61, for a firsthand account of the negotiations by one of the participants.
[51] Lazitch, "Informations," p. 15; also, Vassart, "Conférence," p. 24.

CGTU. Though labor unity was not yet a certainty, the CGT leadership could hardly refuse the new Communist offers. It was under strong pressure from union members to achieve unity and risked, like the Socialist party a year earlier, seeing a split in its ranks if it did not finally reach agreement with the CGTU. Finally, the Communist party had abandoned with little apparent difficulty the time-hallowed ideological principle of revolutionary defeatism in the name of the defense of the Soviet Union. A few Communists, primarily older party cadres, rebelled at such heresy and left the party.[52] But their departure created no public dispute and stirred no large-scale opposition within party ranks. On the contrary, the party entered the period of the popular front stronger than ever before.

[52] P. Broué and N. Dorez, "Critique de Gauche and Opposition révolutionnaire au Front populaire," *Mouvement social,* No. 54 (Jan.–March, 1966), pp. 96–98.

IV

The Political Coalition

The French Communist party became in a very real sense a part of the French political community after mid-1935. It showed a patriotic spirit, glorifying its country's republican past, expressing its approval of national defense, and accepting the existence of the French Empire. It was admitted as a member of a political coalition alongside highly respectable democratic organizations. Though its own centralized organization remained unchanged, it did soon open its ranks to a broader stratum of the French population. It pushed to great lengths its efforts to receive the support of an even wider cross section of social groups, including the Catholics. The response it received was highly encouraging.

Yet the party was not successful in its immediate goal. It had become active in French politics with the express aim of encouraging the creation of a Radical government. But it could not control the course of events it had helped set in motion. Before long, it found itself a member of an electoral coalition of all the left-wing parties in preparation for the national elections of the following spring. Brought together in what was officially known as the *Rassemblement populaire* ("Popular Rally"), these parties succeeded in drawing up a common program, similar in many ways to that suggested by Thorez in October, 1934. Though the Communists cooperated in this effort, it was not what they desired above all. The *Rassemblement populaire* gave them neither a Radical government—only the promise of one after the elections—nor the movement of the masses they had attempted to create with their popular front. Continued attempts to organize the masses were thwarted by the hostility of the Socialists and the Radicals. Ironically, only the slogan made a place for itself. *Rassemblement populaire* was not so successful a term as *Front populaire*, which rapidly supplanted the former as the title of the coalition (and as the designation of the coalition in all histories of the period, including my own—the term *Rassemblement populaire* will be used here to refer only to the committees of that name). The image of the "front" of the people, evoking memories of the heroism of World War I, was certainly closer to the mood of many Frenchmen than that of the "rallying" of the people. But the sense of militancy which the Communists sought to convey through the use of "front" was never embodied in the institutions of the Popular Front, which remained a very traditional political grouping of disparate forces. In the end, the Communist leaders would protest that the Popular Front was not a "petty parliamentary coalition" or an agreement uniting several parties, that it was really a vast movement of the French masses. But no one else would believe them. The Popular Front was to live, and to die, as a political coalition.

The Formation of the Popular Front

While attempting to bring together the parties of the Left in parliament, the Communist leaders took a new and audacious initative to create a movement with the support of all the left-wing forces in France. The theme they chose to emphasize this time was patriotism. Heretofore, they had completely rejected the French republican tradition and its symbols, especially the tricolor flag and the July 14 celebration. Stalin's declaration of approval of French national defense made it possible, even necessary, for the French Communist party to become a champion of republican unity and strength against internal and external foes. Bastille Day was close. The party leaders, through the intermediary of the Amsterdam-Pleyel Movement, called sometime in the last half of May on all the organizations which "defended peace and liberty" to come together on July 14, 1935, "under the tricolor" to declare their determination "never to separate before having definitely defeated fascism and reduced the danger of war." [1] Apparently, the response at first was weak. Finally, on June 17 representatives of Amsterdam-Pleyel, the Committee of Vigilance of Anti-Fascist Intellectuals, and the League of the Rights of Man decided to organize a "common celebration of a democratic July 14" and to send delegations to solicit the participation of the CGT, and of the Socialist and Radical parties. [2] The movement was taking on significant proportions. Should the Radicals agree to participate, the Communist leaders would have accomplished in the country what they had failed to do in parliament. Cooperation between Radicals, Socialists, and Communists in the preparation of a July 14 celebration would give considerable encouragement to a coalition of their forces in the Chamber.

Success depended above all on the cooperation of the Socialists. They had both the power and the respectability which the Communists lacked. Responding perhaps to the pressure from its left, the SFIO national congress, meeting from June 9 to 12, took an important step toward the creation of a movement uniting the left-wing forces of the country. It approved a motion calling for a "large popular movement to defend democratic liberties against attempted dictatorships, and the

[1] Revealed in an article by M. Octave Rabaté, the Communist secretary of Amsterdam-Pleyel, in the Movement's bimonthly newspaper *Front mondial*, dated "Last Half of May, 1935."
[2] *Le Temps*, January 9, 1936.

world of labor against the political, economic, and social effects of the capitalistic crisis." [3] Its action may well have been taken also as a result of the renewed agitation by the paramilitary leagues. In June, the *Croix de Feu* organized monster demonstrations which seemed to the Left to be dress rehearsals for insurrection. Laval himself was known to be sympathetic toward the leagues. In the face of the apparent danger, the Socialist and Communist parties resumed united action. Their municipalities signed agreements to resist the "fascist raids." The Communists abandoned completely the campaign against the SFIO leaders. In these circumstances, the Socialist decision to participate in the July 14 activities was no surprise.

The ease with which the Radical party was brought into the movement was much more unexpected. On July 3, the party's Executive Committee voted almost unanimously to join. The threatened split between liberal and conservative Radicals did not materialize. Daladier was more active than ever in pushing his party toward the left, but this time Herriot offered no resistance. The Communist leaders obviously were conscious of the potential hostility of the right-wing Radicals. They heaped praise on the entire Radical party, the "worthiest party" of France, and pleaded with the Socialists not to complicate the situation by introducing the thorny question of financial and economic policy into the July 14 movement. In fact, however, the Radicals had their own reasons for participating, partially electoral, partially political. They feared isolation in the coming elections if they cut themselves off from the Socialists, and were sincerely worried by the league agitation.[4] Nor were they alone in their support of the joint celebration of July 14. A total of forty-eight national organizations participated, including, in addition to the groups

[3] *Le Populaire*, June 13, 1935.   [4] Larmour, pp. 171–76.

already mentioned, the renegade socialists of 1933 and the two labor confederations.

The movement which they joined was officially called the "*Rassemblement populaire* of July 14." From the first, however, the term "Popular Front" was more commonly used. The Communists went along with this usage, though they occasionally pointed out that the movement they sought was to have direct popular participation and to be under the control of the masses in "democratically elected committees." The *Rassemblement populaire*, when finally organized in late June, was headed by a national committee made up of representatives from the participating groups. Final arrangements for July 14 provided for a giant demonstration, to be preceded by a meeting during which the audience would take an oath to remain united to achieve the dissolution of the leagues, the defense of democratic liberties, and peace. No one of liberal sentiment could take offense at these good intentions. Consequently, the July 14 celebration of the *Rassemblement populaire* forces was a great success. For the first time in French history, Communists and Socialists took part in the commemoration of the storming of the Bastille. A tremendous number of demonstrators, probably between 250,000 and 300,000, turned out to parade between the Place de la République and the Place de la Bastille on the east side of Paris. Many smaller demonstrations were organized outside Paris by local *Rassemblement populaire* committees.

The Communist party rallied round the tricolor flag with remarkable ease. There was at first a certain amount of confusion. Certain Communists in the July 14 demonstration demanded "All power to the soviets!" while others clamored "Daladier for premier!" Observers noticed that the red flags were more numerous than the tricolors. Still, party members gave evidence of real loyalty to French republicanism. In keeping with the new patriotic spirit, the official name of the party was soon changed from "French Section of the Communist International" to "French Communist Party"; the Committee against Fascism and War became simply "Peace and Liberty." Sometime in 1935, the party stopped its campaign for national independence movements among the colonial peoples of the French Empire. The argument, the same as that to be used after World War II, was that France was on the way to being governed by the "people," and that therefore the colonial peoples should accept a "fraternal union" with the French people for the sake of joint progress and resistance to common enemies. Thorez later stated the issue quite clearly when he argued that "the interest of the colonial peoples is in their union with the French people," since the "critical issue at present is the defeat of fascism." They should do nothing which might "encourage the activities of fascism." [5] This implicit condemnation of colonial revolts was a totally new policy for the French Communists, and put them in the position of supporting the Empire against such nationalist organizations as the Tunisian Neo-Destour. But at the same time, it rid the party of the last public vestiges of internationalism and antipatriotism. More than ever, it appeared the newest inheritor of the Jacobin tradition in French society.

The new tactics elaborated by the French party were of major importance for the entire Communist International. By July, 1935, the Comintern leadership had decided to apply the united front and popular front tactics throughout the world. Even the most recalcitrant parties, such as the Hungarian, had given their support by early July. The situation of the Chinese party had at last been regularized. During the flight from Kiangsi, the marchers had lost contact with Moscow. But by June, 1935, communication was apparently restored. Some-

[5] *La France du Front populaire et les Peuples coloniaux*, pp. 5–6.

time between then and the opening of the Congress in late July, Stalin accepted as leader of the Chinese party Mao Tse-tung, who had seized control during the Long March. The party in turn came out on July 15 in favor of a "united popular front of all fighters against Japanese imperialism and Chiang Kai-shek," in effect supporting the new tactics.[6]

The Comintern was thus able to proclaim a uniform policy shift at the Seventh Congress. George Dimitrov delivered the major report to the Congress, in which he supported both the united and popular fronts as applied by the French Communists. He omitted any mention of the "third period" or of "class against class," concentrating rather on the fascist menace and the tactics required to defeat fascism. He praised the French party for having "understood what was to be done *today*," [7] implying that short-range action and not long-range revolutionary goals was the most important task confronting Communist parties. He called both for mass antifascist movements uniting the working and middle classes, and—the principal innovation of the Congress—for agreements among the Communist, social-democratic, and bourgeois parties. The French example of supporting national defense was also made Comintern policy in the course of the Congress. Palmiro Togliatti urged Communists to support measures of civil and national defense necessitated by the threat of war from fascist countries, in particular Germany. His speech brought out clearly the new Soviet attitude toward the Comintern antiwar policy. Earlier, the Soviet leaders had proclaimed that the threat of war on their country came from capitalist imperialists, and had called on the Communists in all capitalist countries to follow tactics of "revolutionary defeatism." But the rise of expansionist German and Japanese states had altered

[6] Leibzon, pp. 86–91; John Rue, *Mao Tse-tung in Opposition* (Stanford, 1966), pp. 270–72.

[7] *Correspondance*, January 28, 1936, p. 144.

the situation. The countries opposed to Germany and Japan had become "objective" allies of the Soviet Union; their efforts to prepare militarily for war had to be supported by the Communists. Only in France and to a lesser extent in China was this defense policy carried so far as the political support of men or groups backing alliance with the Soviet Union—Herriot and the Radicals in France, Chiang Kai-shek and the Kuomintang in China. Still, the Comintern as a whole was of greater potential use to the Soviet Union than ever before. Its increased importance was recognized by the creation of the new office of General Secretary, given to George Dimitrov. In reality, Dimitrov was never more than a figure-head for the Soviet leaders. His title indicated not power but prestige, which he owed in part to the new Soviet foreign policy, in part to the success of the French Communist party in making the united and popular fronts seem feasible tactics for the Comintern.

Nonetheless, the French party leaders had more work to do. Dimitrov called on them to work especially to extend the influence of the Popular Front over the working masses, among whom he included the peasantry and the petty bourgeoisie as well as the proletariat. To achieve this goal, the "massive creation of elective organizations" was necessary.[8] In other words, the Popular Front had still to be made a movement of the masses as well as of political parties. Dimitrov did not explain, though, how the two movements were to be reconciled. This was a problem for the French Communist leaders to resolve.

In truth, a mass movement did not fit at all into a political coalition. The Communist leaders discovered this for the first time at the very moment the Seventh Congress was meeting. The French party had set out in late July on a campaign to

[8] *Ibid.*, August 20, 1935, p. 1035.

defeat the National Union government of Pierre Laval. Since political action had proved earlier to be ineffective, mass action was used. Laval had opened himself to attack by issuing in mid-July a series of decree-laws cutting the pay of state employees and workers by 10 per cent. Joining the general outcry from labor organizations, the CGTU went one step further by adding an appeal for demonstrations by the state workers when they would next receive their pay. At the same time, Jacques Duclos, probably the only French leader left in Paris during the Comintern congress, launched bitter attacks against Laval in the pages of *L'Humanité*. Spectacular coverage was given to the "ever-swelling wave of mass protest." On August 4, Duclos flatly declared that "the presence of Laval at the head of the government is a public menace," and that the Premier "must be chased out [of office]." On several occasions, he added that a "left-wing"—that is, Radical—government with a "left-wing parliamentary majority" could take Laval's place. On August 6, payday for the naval arsenals of Brest and Toulon, the demonstrations took place. In both cities, they degenerated into bloody riots. From many sides came accusations that the violence had been caused by Communists, Young Communists, and labor leaders of the CGTU. The demonstrations had created a political issue, but not that of the survival of the Laval government. The agitation threatened the frail ties between the Communist and Radical parties.

The Communist leaders realized the danger. On the one hand, they blamed all the trouble on "agitators" and "*provocateurs*" sent out by Laval to discredit their party and frighten the Radicals. On the other hand, they immediately sent out appeals for calm to the regional party secretaries in Brest and Toulon. Then, on August 16, the Politburo sent a letter to all regional secretaries "drawing their attention to the agitation in these two cities whose purpose was to divide the

Popular Front and provoke unjust accusations against the workers' organizations." [9] The party as a whole was put on its guard to remain disciplined and avoid disturbances.

With only this meager external evidence, there is no way at present of determining exactly who was responsible for the riots and why. All the signs point, however, to a Communist initiative which got out of hand. An order was given in Paris for demonstrations. The order was carried out, but in the process the workers took the action seriously and ultimately got out of control. Violence had certainly not been planned. Large demonstrations by the workers affected by the decree-laws might have started a nationwide campaign against Laval, leading to his defeat. But rioting might provoke a hostile reaction from the Radicals, break the fragile unity of the coalition, and destroy any hope of seeing a Radical at the head of the government. To prevent the Brest and Toulon disturbances from causing any political damage, the Communist leaders had to call a halt. They ceased their campaign for the immediate resignation of Laval and returned to more traditional methods of political maneuvering. Their first attempt to use mass agitation to influence the course of French politics had failed; not until a year later did they try again.

The presence of a sizable number of workers in the demonstrations was exceptional. Throughout 1935, the French proletariat remained apathetic, responding to few appeals for action. There was good reason for this situation. The economic depression, coupled with the disunity and weakness of the labor unions, left the proletariat very nearly defenseless against management. The Paris Association of Metallurgical Unions, part of the CGTU, complained in January, 1936, that "no [collective] contract exists. . . . Union rights are tram-

[9] *L'Humanité*, August 17, 1935.

pled underfoot, and most of the workers must join the union undercover." [10] With little to offer, the unions had few members: out of 250,000 metallurgical workers in the Paris region, 7,000 were members of Communist unions, while in the whole of France only 20,000 workers belonged to the national federation.[11] Yet this was proclaimed one of the "strong" federations of the CGTU! The fact was that the organization as a whole had little fighting strength and a low membership—certainly no more than 220,000.[12] The Communist decision in June to accept the CGT unity terms represented a gamble that the loss of a weak but dependable labor organization would be compensated by a more effective mobilization of the working masses in the future.

At the end of September, the CGTU formally accepted the conditions set by the CGT for its "reintegration" into the older confederation. The merger began in the months that followed. It was supervised by the non-Communist union leaders from beginning to end. In March, 1936, it had proceeded far enough to permit a "unity congress" to be held. The congress was under the control of the non-Communists, who possessed twice the voting strength of the Communists. It supported the old CGT policies, reaffirming the principle of confederal organization, forbidding the holding of political office, either in parliament or in the parties, by any of its officers, and continuing its membership in the non-Communist International Trade-Union Federation. The Communists meekly accepted these policies. Only on the question of the Popular Front did they show any heat. They feared trouble with the moderates in the coalition, notably with the Radicals, should the CGT adopt a radical reform program. Julien Raca-

[10] *Ibid.*, January 10, 1936.
[11] *Correspondance*, June 6, 1936, p. 673.
[12] This figure was given by Piatnitsky in *Internationale*, July 20, 1935, p. 973.

mond, the most respected of their union leaders, had argued earlier that the CGT should accept the modest plans of the Popular Front, with the "ambition" of "shaping, organizing, and animating" the coalition for "more decisive actions." [13] The Communists obtained partial satisfaction, since the congress "confirmed its membership" in the *Rassemblement populaire* while at the same time adopting a program for basic structural reforms.

The acceptance by the Communist labor leaders of the defeat of most of their proposals clearly indicated that the unification of the CGT represented for them not an end in itself, but a means to more important ends. The unified confederation stood as one more guarantee that "fascist" parties could not seize power in France. Perhaps more important was the fact that the CGT was a potentially powerful instrument for the achievement of greater Communist influence within the working class and the Popular Front. The old reformist leadership was in firm control of the central organs, but the confederal structure of the organization left ample room for maneuvering, primarily by means of strike agitation. The Comintern recognized this when it called for a "co-ordinated campaign in the unified labor-union movement" in France to "stop the capitalist offensive." [14] The CGT was for the Communist leaders a promising instrument for action.

Communist efforts to build up a mass political movement, however, brought little success. The party's difficulties were apparent in the campaign to defend Ethiopia against Italian aggression. In August, when the threat of war was already clear, the Politburo called on "the Socialist comrades" for joint action in support of Ethiopia.[15] The result was one ap-

[13] "Les Moyens d'Action du Mouvement syndical," *L'Humanité*, February 15, 1936.

[14] *Internationale*, April, 1936, p. 386.

[15] *L'Humanité*, August 17, 1935.

peal by the Co-ordination Committee for a public campaign in favor of Ethiopian independence, and, in Paris, one joint meeting on September 3. Following the invasion of Ethiopia on October 2, the Communist party launched an all-out campaign against the "fascist aggressors." On October 3, the Central Committee proposed demonstrations for the closure of the Suez Canal and for a complete embargo on commerce with Italy. French longshoremen were encouraged to refuse to load war goods bound for Italy, and "vigilance committees" were proposed to denounce arms shipments.[16] The campaign provided an excellent opportunity for the party leaders to measure the strong noncombative temper of the country.

Neither the Socialist-Communist Co-ordination Committee nor the *Rassemblement populaire* National Committee took any effective action. Maurice Thorez admitted later in the month that "the masses are not at all enthusiastic for military sanctions," and that "they have a tendency [*fonds*] to pacifism blended with egotism." [17] The new crusading spirit of the party did not even pervade the entire membership; there had been a time, just six months earlier, when Thorez had refused the support of the French proletariat in the event of an attack on France itself. To ask party members now to mobilize the working class in defense of a distant African country was to jump from one extreme to the other. The party leaders afterward confessed that there had been no "effective and generalized application of the proletarian sanctions against Italian fascism," and that their "excellent directives have not yet found a large practical application." [18] In reality, they could cite only one instance when dockers, in Marseilles, refused for a short time to load an Italian ship. They were faced with the obvious conclusion that the French

[16] *Ibid.*, October 3, 1935.   [17] *Pour la Cause du Peuple*, p. 12.
[18] C. S., "La Lutte contre la Guerre en France," *Internationale*, November, 1935, p. 1659.

4. At home in the factory: workers on sit-down strike, June, 1936. (*L'Illustration.*)

5. The "brigade of acclamations": Parisians greeting Daladier on his return from Munich. (*L'Illustration.*)

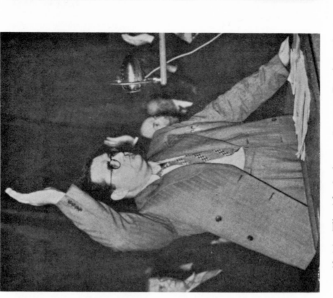

6 (*left*). The black sheep: Jacques Doriot, May, 1937. (*L'Illustration.*) 7 (*right*). Three generations of revolutionaries: demonstration in honor of the Paris Commune, May, 1936 (*foreground, young* Communists; *seated*, survivors of the Commune; *background*, Socialist and Communist party leaders). (*L'Illustration.*)

people were unwilling to set out on a crusade to halt fascist aggression. Frenchmen were sickened of war, and there was little that could be done to make them change heart.

The Communist leaders failed completely in their efforts to organize a "broad popular front." Their goal was still the creation of a "vast network of committees" open to everyone and outside the control of the political parties. Yet they could not develop the organization without the cooperation of the other parties in the coalition. Both Radical and Socialist leaders were hostile to the Communist proposals, fearing that the mass movement would come under the control of the Communists and would be used as a pressure group. Their opposition meant that the Popular Front as an organization would never be more than an association of political parties.

Even the choice of political allies was restricted more than the Communist leaders would have liked. They viewed parliamentary action purely in terms of immediate goals, and proclaimed that "the Popular Front cannot exclude anyone who wishes to join it in order to defend republican liberties and the peace." [19] They felt free to propose—timidly, to be sure—that such conservative parties as Flandin's Democratic Alliance be invited to participate in the Popular Front. The proposal was acceptable to the Radicals, eager for allies to the right as well as to the left, but was rejected by the Socialists and others as too compromising.

Despite the absence of any organization permitting popular participation, the Communist leaders went ahead with their efforts to attract the masses to the Popular Front. Their appeal went to the middle classes, the peasantry, and the proletariat, and included such disparate social groups as the intellectuals and the supporters of the leagues. Their most significant initiative was the change in the party's peasant policy. Previously,

[19] *L'Humanité,* October 26, 1935.

they had sought to organize the peasant proletariat, relying primarily on Renaud Jean's *Confédération Générale des Paysans Travailleurs*. In the fall of 1935, they abandoned the theme of class struggle in the countryside and turned to the defense of the interests of the entire peasantry. On September 18, *L'Humanité* devoted one entire page to a "Program for the Rescue of French Agriculture," including such moderate demands as price supports for farm commodities and easier credit. Renaud Jean even attempted to ally with certain conservative peasant organizations, but was rebuffed.

Indicative of the general tone of the campaign for mass support was an open letter in *L'Humanité* written by Marcel Cachin and directed to the followers of the leagues. In it, Cachin sought to convince the league members that their desire to make French society less "unjust" and the French nation less "divided" could be satisfied only by the Communist party, defender of "real reconciliation." [20] The Communist leaders were trying to remake the "image" of their party to make the Popular Front as attractive as possible to the greatest number of Frenchmen. In the spring of 1936, they would go so far as to appeal to the Catholics in France. Yet they had no way, outside of their own party, of organizing what mass support their campaign might have attracted. The absence of any organization allowing for popular participation and leadership meant that the Communists would never be able to capitalize on the growing liberal sentiments of many Frenchmen. The Popular Front never became a movement of the masses.

Instead, it was a real, working alliance between the left-wing parties. *Rassemblement populaire* committees, grouping the representatives of the various member parties, existed by the end of 1935 in great numbers throughout France. They carried on a modest but significant amount of political agita-

[20] *Ibid.*, October 6, 1935.

tion, and their meetings gained wide support among the population. Restricted in membership and action though these committees were, the local Communist leaders cooperated in their formation and in their subsequent activities. Examining thirteen years later the reasons for the inability of the party to create committees with popularly elected leaders, Joanny Berlioz admitted that few Communists pushed the mass movement. For the greatest number of party workers, it appeared that the masses would be brought into the Popular Front through agreements between the leaders of the national organizations. The grouping of active members of all the left-wing parties in the towns and cities served in their opinion as a means of "facilitating the *ententes at the summit.*" [21] For this purpose, the local committees of party representatives were adequate. The success of failure of the Popular Front would be determined by the leadership.

Despite these setbacks, the Communist party was in a stronger position than in previous years. After a long period of decline, the party was at last gaining members steadily. At the Eighth National Congress, finally held in January, 1936 (after a delay of almost two years), Marcel Cachin proudly announced that the official membership of the party was 74,400. This represented a gain of 45,000 over the 1933 figure. [22] With the good news for the party went good news for Maurice Thorez, at last named General Secretary. So self-confident were the Communist leaders that they immediately launched a campaign for 100,000 members. Were this figure attained, the party would be at a level never equaled since 1921. The drive for more members represented a policy change of great importance. The "revolutionary elite" of hard-core Communists, the stalwarts from harder years, were soon blended with, if not buried under, a mass of occasional

[21] "Une Leçon," *Cahiers du Communisme*, January, 1948, pp. 75–76.
[22] *Compte rendu sténographique du VIII° Congrès*, p. 36.

Communists and sympathizers from the middle as well as from the working classes. Symbolic of this change was the decision, announced at the Central Committee meeting in October, 1935, to open the doors of the party to members of the League of the Rights of Man, excluded by a decision of the Comintern in 1922. This, Thorez declared, would permit "peasants, civil servants, employees, [and] merchants" to join the party while remaining members of the League.[23] The Communist party was on the way to becoming a party of the masses.

At the same time, the Popular Front as a left-wing coalition was taking shape. The National Committee of the *Rassemblement populaire* was busy in the fall of 1935 with the elaboration of a political program suitable to its members. The idea had been suggested in late July, when the decision was taken to preserve the Committee itself. The Communist leaders appear to have been surprised by this burst of activity. Certainly, the idea of a program had been theirs to begin with. Thorez had been the first to suggest it to the Delegation of the Left in early June. What he had in mind then was a vague set of slogans which could be used to mobilize the masses around the Popular Front. Economic measures would hardly be touched on, to avoid "frightening" the bourgeoisie and particularly the Radical party. In the opinion of one Socialist leader, the "preoccupation" of the Communist party "to attract the greatest number of people into the Popular Front" had caused its leaders "to make the greatest number of concessions possible for the program, which they desire limited—we might even say, petty."[24] When Thorez finally presented in October his party's ideas on what the program of the Popular Front should contain, he emphasized "the immediate demands

[23] *Pour la Cause du Peuple*, p. 42.
[24] Jean Lebas, "Programme et Gouvernement de Front populaire," *Le Populaire*, July 7, 1935.

of all the categories of exploited men" and excluded any general program for basic economic reforms. As a "compromise" on nationalizations, he offered to accept a proposal for control of the armaments industry, but nothing more.[25]

Within the *Rassemblement populaire* Committee, significant discussion began after the presentation on October 2 of a tentative program for economic and social reforms drawn up by a subcommittee.[26] Not so radical as the CGT or Socialists would have liked, the program was still too strong for the Radicals and—by extension—for the Communists. Camille Chautemps, one of the liberals in the Radical party, felt it necessary to suggest on October 6 that all measures requiring long-term application and liable to create "needless controversies" be excluded from the common program. To this Marcel Gitton could only add that "this preoccupation was and remains the basis for the propositions made by the Communist Party." [27] The Communist delegates to the Committee made a point of supporting the Radicals virtually every time there was difficulty with the Socialists. The major point of contention was the question of the nationalization of industrial and financial monopolies and of natural resources. Though the tentative program presented October 2 made no mention of such measures, both before and after this date the Socialists and the representatives of the CGT pushed for their acceptance. The Radicals refused, joined by the Communists. Thorez later pointed with pride to this sign of moderation by his party, remarking that "it must be said . . . that the Communists were seen refusing to write into the program of the Popular Front the socializations which certain people urged." [28]

[25] *Pour la Cause du Peuple*, pp. 20–21.
[26] *L'Oeuvre*, October 5, 1935.
[27] "Le Discours de M. Chautemps," *L'Humanité*, October 8, 1935.
[28] *Ibid.*, July 9, 1936.

On the whole, the Communist position on economic policy was adapted to the desires of the Radicals as expressed at their congress in October. Interpreting rather freely these desires, Joanny Berlioz saw in the Radical economic program "more fiscal justice, . . . a correction of the injustices of the decree-laws, greater authority of the state *vis-à-vis* the financial oligarchy, control over the Bank of France, . . . price supports for farm products, etc." These measures were "modest," to be sure, but they "do not run counter to our propositions for a program of the Popular Front, and offer a basis for discussion." [29] With the combined support of the Radicals and of the Communists, they were to be much more than a "basis for discussion," for they became in fact the heart of the economic program of the coalition.

Such as it finally appeared in early January, 1936, the program of the Popular Front contained little to frighten the middle classes. Traces of the more radical proposals of the Socialists were few. There was at least a statement of principle on the need to restore the "purchasing power" of the people, with suggestions to reduce the work week, to introduce a large-scale public-works program and an unemployment compensation fund. Not a word was said of the need for "structural reforms," the battle cry of the Socialists and of the CGT. The victory of the Radicals and of the Communists was made clear in the Prologue, which declared that the program was "intentionally limited to immediately applicable measures."

The program itself did not go beyond chapter headings, all the suggested reforms remaining in reality vague proposals, the details of which would have to be worked out later. It was divided into three major units. "The defense of liberty" in-

[29] *Correspondance*, November 2, 1935, p. 1475.

cluded such measures as the dissolution of the leagues and the granting of union rights to workers; the "defense of the peace" blended the Socialists' call for a "disarmed peace," the Radicals' desire for "collective security in the framework of the League of Nations," and the Communists' concern to see the Franco-Soviet pact reaffirmed; "the economic demands" referred to the reforms deemed necessary to repress the "financial oligarchy" and to support the workers, peasants, and lower middle classes in France. There was promise enough in this cake for anyone who felt at all hungry. Vague though it was, no program like it had ever been seen before in France.[30]

No one seemed to know, however, what exactly the purpose of this program was. The Communists asserted that it was the "basis of common action for the masses."[31] Yet this was an illogical argument, one which the Communists themselves did not ardently defend, for the organizational framework of this mass movement did not exist. Both the Radical and the Socialist delegates to the National Committee of the *Rassemblement populaire* continually opposed all attempts to create new committees or to expand the old local committees to include individual memberships. At the same time as the

[30] The program itself can be found in all the left-wing newspapers, and in *Le Temps*, of January 11, 1936. There is no history of the negotiations for the program, and whatever minutes there were disappeared in 1940. My account is based on a variety of newspaper and magazine articles, notably: *Le Temps*, January 9, 1936; *L'Oeuvre*, January 21 and 22, 1936; *Le Populaire*, September 5, 1935; Jacques Kayser, "Le Parti radical-socialiste et le Rassemblement populaire, 1935–1938," *Le Bulletin de la Societé d'Histoire de la Troisième République*, No. 14 (April–July, 1955), pp. 271–93, and, by the same author, "Souvenirs d'un Militant (1934–1939)," *Les Cahiers de la République*, No. 12 (March-April, 1958), pp. 69–82. I also had interviews with M. Jacques Kayser and with M. Octave Rabaté.

[31] Jacques Duclos, *L'Humanité*, March 28, 1936.

program was agreed upon, the decision was made to preserve the local committees of the *Rassemblement populaire* as they had been formed before July 14, "in the image of the National Committee"—that is, including only the representatives of member organizations. Individuals as such, whether members of these parties or not, could not take part in the meetings of the committees, and all decisions had to be made unanimously. Further, it was the role of the National Committee to "animate and control the activity of the movement." [32] With these guarantees, there was little chance the Communists could use the Popular Front to create a mass movement.

The Socialists had no more success in making the program an electoral platform and program for governmental action. With the Radicals openly hostile and supported by the Communists, there was little the leaders of the SFIO could do. As early as November 15, the Radical delegate to the National Committee, Jacques Kayser, had obtained from it the assurance that the program would serve neither function. [33] Yet the Socialists were not willing to admit defeat. Convinced that the Popular Front had to be disciplined and united to be effective, they tried next to give the coalition a certain amount of control over the candidates of the member parties in the coming national elections. On March 12, 1936, Vincent Auriol presented the National Committee of the *Rassemblement populaire* with the draft of a letter to be sent to all the electoral candidates belonging to a member party. Each candidate would be asked to promise to "participate in a majority both disciplined and bound to the spirit of the Popular Front, and to support the government constantly by your votes." His answer would be "made known to the electorate," and cases of indiscipline would be brought to the attention of the par-

[32] Quoted in Dupeux, p. 93; the three conditions for the formation of local committees were cited in *Le Populaire*, June 11, 1936.
[33] Kayser, "Souvenirs," pp. 76–77.

ties.[34] The Radicals found Auriol's proposal unacceptable. They refused to be a part of any alliance which restricted their liberty in future political negotiations.

The Communist leaders regarded the new campaign by the Socialists as a dangerous threat to the unity of the Popular Front. In a special letter from the party Secretariat, published in *L'Humanité* on March 18, the Socialist proposal was termed "inopportune." The Popular Front, the Secretariat wrote, could be neither a "super-party" nor a "committee for electoral arbitration." Its proper role was to defend the interests of the masses—at which point the Secretariat launched another appeal for a network of democratically elected committees. Should the *Rassemblement populaire* Committee engage in electoral competition, it would risk provoking "clashes between the member parties or even dissension in their midst." The Communist leaders feared the reaction of the Radical party, in particular of Edouard Herriot. The Radical leader had at no time been a partisan of the alliance with the Socialists and the Communists. He had refused to accept the program of the Popular Front in its entirety, objecting to its financial provisions. To demand that he personally agree to participate in a "disciplined majority" behind a Popular Front government applying this very program might have any number of unfortunate consequences. It was much better, declared the Secretariat, for the National Committee of the *Rassemblement populaire* to "remain strictly within the limits of its activity as unanimously assigned to it by the organizations which are a part of it." [35] But this activity had

[34] The draft as accepted by the National Committee was published in *L'Ere Nouvelle*, March 16, 1936; the first draft exists only as a manuscript in the hands of its author, who kindly permitted me to consult it. Auriol exposed the reasons behind his proposal in *Le Populaire*, March 18, 1936.

[35] *L'Humanité*, March 18, 1936.

never been specifically delimited and had consisted in the past partly of launching a few appeals for meetings on a subject of immediate interest and partly of expressing a benign opinion on some burning issue. The Popular Front did not appear destined for an outstanding future.

The Communist party had acted as the faithful ally of the Radical party in all that touched on the coalition. After having accused the Socialist party of being the "lackey of the bourgeoisie," the Communist party seemed to have taken this role upon itself. The shoe was on the other foot now, with Paul Faure, General Secretary of the SFIO, accusing the Communists of being "timorous and opportunistic" during the negotiations for the program of the Popular Front.[36] Yet this was probably the price which had to be paid to keep the Radical party within the coalition. The Communist leaders had failed to achieve their popular front of the masses, but had at least preserved and even improved their ties with the Radicals.

Parliamentary Deceptions and Electoral Triumph

The Communist party was the junior partner within the coalition. Its power within parliament was still negligible. On the left side of the Chamber, the words which carried weight were those of the Socialists and of the Radicals. Strive though the Communists did to bring about the defeat of Pierre Laval, they found that his fate depended on others. As long as a majority of the Radical deputies preferred to give the Premier their support, his position was assured. Moments of bitterness might lead the Communists to call the wrath of the masses down upon the heads of these obstinate deputies, but to no effect. Laval continued in power.

All the while, the left-wing parties in the Chamber contin-

[36] Quoted in Maurice Thorez, *Fils du Peuple*, p. 99.

ued to meet in the Delegation of the Left. Meetings were held approximately once a month and were attended most assiduously by the Communist and the Socialist groups in the Chamber. The Radicals, not unnaturally, showed the least enthusiasm to see the Delegation take on an active role. In the fall of 1935, as in late May and early June, the chief problem remained the disagreement between Radicals and Socialists on financial policy. The regular parliamentary session began in mid-November, with the ever-touchy question of the 1936 budget the first major item for discussion. The Socialists and Communists were intent on defeating Laval on this issue, but not the Radicals. The Delegation met on November 20 and again on November 27, still without reaching any agreement. The Socialists made no secret of their sympathy for a program to fight the financial plight, including the devaluation of the franc. Many Radicals, on the other hand, continued to defend the policy of financial austerity, preferring it at least to a new cabinet crisis.[37] As a result, when the vote came on November 29, one-half of the Radical group supported the Laval government.

The Communist deputies were helpless. Their best efforts to convince the Radical leaders of the need to create a left-wing government were to no avail. The Radicals would take no action without the assurance of support for their financial program. The Socialists refused, and were thereupon accused by the Communists of putting too many "conditions" on their alliance with the Radicals. Joanny Berlioz blamed the "regrettable cautiousness of numerous Radicals" upon "influential Socialist comrades . . . and especially the leadership of the CGT," who "have not hidden their preference for a vague 'alignment of currencies' including undoubtedly an amputation of the franc."[38] Yet the Communist leaders, despite all

[37] *Le Temps,* November 21 and 28, 1935.
[38] *Correspondance,* December 7, 1935, p. 1733.

they did to minimize the financial question, could not themselves agree to support the Radical program. They promised
simply to back all measures "in the interests of the working
class." This imbroglio could only assure a longer life to the
Premier.

Surprisingly, it was at this moment that the Chamber of
Deputies finally took action against the right-wing leagues. In
the month of November, several bloody riots had broken out
between league members and followers of the Popular Front.
Rumors still circulated of a possible *coup d'état* by the *Croix
de Feu*. At the demand of the Socialists, a discussion of the
activities of the leagues was scheduled for December 6 in the
Chamber. It was thought that Laval would oppose the passage
of harsh laws against the leagues, and that he risked defeat on
this issue. To the amazement of observers, the discussion
turned into an appeal for "national reconciliation." In what
was probably a political maneuver engineered by Laval, a
reactionary deputy, speaking in the name of the *Croix de Feu*,
proposed the disarmament of all paramilitary organizations in
France. Léon Blum immediately accepted the offer on behalf
of the Socialist "self-defense" organizations, and suggested the
complete dissolution of all armed groups. Upon urging from
the conservatives, Thorez jumped up and declared that "the
Communist party associates itself with the declarations of M.
Léon Blum with regard to the groups of self-defense." [39] A
law was immediately passed for the dissolution of all paramilitary organizations.

The very next day, the Communist leaders began having
second thoughts. Though they had called repeatedly for action against the "fascist" leagues, the "national reconciliation"
in the Chamber was not to their taste. It occurred to them that
their party did not officially have a paramilitary group, that

[39] *JO, Débats, Chambre*, No. 72 (December 7, 1935), p. 2392.

Laval would not apply the law, and that the whole operation was probably a "comedy" organized by the Premier to protect his position. Thorez publicly ate his "brief words" spoken in a "moment of surprise caused by the words of the Socialist leader." [40] But the damage was done. Thorez's words had created "certain illusions" which brought a "relaxation of the vigilance of the masses" and even a "momentary hesitation in the progress of the recruitment" of the party.[41] Besides, Laval was still Premier.

The charmed life of this adroit politician continued on through December. At the end of the month, three Radical deputies sponsored a motion of "distrust" condemning Laval's foreign policy, and were defeated by the narrow margin of 296 to 276. Over 90 Radicals supported the motion, and only 37 backed Laval. But these few supporters were enough to save the Premier. The "working masses," Berlioz threatened, would have "accounts to settle with these eternal prevaricators" in the Radical party who continued to vote with the Center-Right coalition. Elections were approaching, and the time was past for hesitation between the Popular Front and the National Union.[42] As a rule, however, the Communist leaders did their best to accept the contradictions of Radical politics. Any gesture which might encourage a split in the Radical party was avoided. Open expressions of hostility at continued Radical support for Laval, such as Berlioz's threat to "settle accounts," were rare. Communist policy was "not to permit the destruction of the union achieved in the field of defense of liberty." [43]

Edouard Herriot, though the leading Radical participating

[40] *L'Humanité*, December 8, 1935.
[41] Berlioz, *Correspondance*, February 22, 1936, p. 223.
[42] *Ibid.*, January 4, 1936, p. 3.
[43] Duclos, "Que va devenir le Front populaire?," *L'Humanité*, November 30, 1935.

in the Laval government, was treated with particular kindness. As one astute French politician noted, hostility within the Radical party to the Popular Front had to be conciliated, for "if the Popular Front cannot extend itself to include the entirety of the Radicals, it will never govern France." [44] For the time being, the Radical party refused any initiative which might disrupt the National Union. Its national convention in October formally accepted participation in the *Rassemblement populaire* Committee, but did not break with the old coalition. Once again, the Communists bent over backward to "understand" this party, so "accustomed to the responsibilities of power." The Radical leaders, explained Joanny Berlioz, were reluctant to provoke a cabinet crisis because of a "lack of confidence in themselves," of a concern for "the inconveniences of ministerial instability," and of their desire to see a "common governmental program" set up "between the organizations participating in the Popular Front." [45] The Communists had done their best to achieve this compromise program, and had in large part succeeded. No one could say they tried to undermine the confidence of the Radical leaders. Time and again they had reaffirmed the viability of a Left-Center coalition which could move into power with no "inconveniences." What more could they do?

Ever since the abortive negotiations in late May and early June, the Communist leadership had made plain its desire to see Laval replaced by a Radical leader at the head of a liberal government. But, for lack of agreement between the Radicals and Socialists in the Delegation of the Left, nothing could be done. At a meeting of the leaders of the parties of the Popular Front on November 21, Edouard Herriot proposed a new solution, that of a government of "transition" which might include representatives of the Center and Left. In the event of

[44] Marcel Déat, "Faiblesses et Chances du Front populaire," *La République*, August 12, 1935.
[45] *Correspondance*, November 2, 1935, p. 1475.

the defeat of Laval, such a government would act as "care-taker" until the beginning of the new legislature, assuring democratic elections, but taking no measures to modify the financial policies of the previous governments. More basic policy decisions would be put off until after the elections. The Communist leaders apparently found the idea of a transition government, weak though this government would be, the best solution under the circumstances. Herriot's proposal received their full support.[46]

As the year 1936 opened, the reign of Laval appeared to be drawing rapidly to an end. More and more Radical deputies were abandoning the Premier on critical votes; by mid-January, a clear majority within their parliamentary group favored the withdrawal of their ministers from the cabinet. The impatience of the Communists grew with each passing day. After Laval received one more vote of confidence on January 16, Paul Vaillant-Couturier, editor of *L'Humanité*, suggested that "certain friends of M. Daladier" show "a little more activity" in uniting the entirety of their party against Laval.[47] The Premier had received that time the votes of 32 Radicals. The fall of Laval was imminent. Edouard Herriot finally decided on January 16 to resign from the government, probably because he felt the Radical party moving more and more toward the Popular Front.[48] On January 18, he stepped down as president of the party. He was succeeded the next day by Edouard Daladier, the Radical leader most closely associated with the left-wing coalition. Herriot's departure from the government was followed by the other Radical ministers. Laval had lost the necessary support to control the Chamber, and had to resign on January 22. The National Union was dead.

The Communist party, meeting at that moment in its na-

---

[46] Herriot, p. 611.   [47] *L'Humanité*, January 17, 1936.
[48] See Larmour, pp. 193–96.

tional congress, immediately came out in favor of a "government of transition." The delegates voted a motion stating that "if a left-wing government is formed" which effectively dissolved the rightist leagues and assured "normal elections" to the Chamber of Deputies in April, it would receive Communist support. To indicate their displeasure at continued Socialist efforts to achieve a "Popular Front government," the delegates expressed their "regret" to see "organizations claiming to represent the working class . . . multiply offers of ministerial participation." [49] The motion voted by the convention was on most points in agreement with the wishes of the Radicals; once again the Communists showed themselves more amenable to Radical policies than the Socialists.

Still, when the Radical Albert Sarraut formed his "transition government" on January 24, the Communists were not entirely pleased. Three conservatives had found places in the new cabinet. The Communists objected particularly to the presence of the conservative Pierre-Etienne Flandin at the head of the Ministry of Foreign Affairs. Arthur Ramette, speaking for his party in the Chamber on January 30, protested that "it would have been easy for the Radical Party" to "answer the hopes of the immense majority of the nation" by forming a "more coherent ministerial team," that is, with greater Radical participation.[50] At the very least, Sarraut's presence at the head of the government was better than that of Laval. If only to keep good relations with the Radical party, the new Premier deserved special treatment.

The Communist leaders therefore adopted an attitude of "wait and see." When on January 31 Sarraut presented his cabinet to the Chamber of Deputies, the Communist deputies for the first time did not vote with the opposition, preferring

[49] *Compte rendu . . . du VIIIe Congrès*, p. 378.
[50] *JO, Débats, Chambre*, No. 8 (January 31, 1936), p. 151.

to abstain. The Premier would be judged by his acts. Of particular importance was his policy toward the leagues and "especially" his foreign policy. Laval had never had the Franco-Soviet pact ratified by parliament. For the Communists, ratification was "indispensable." [51] In truth, the abstention of nine Communist deputies was little noticed. Thanks to the votes of the Socialists, brought reluctantly to support the new cabinet, Sarraut received a comfortable majority of 361 to 165.

The dislocation of the National Union marked the end of the "truce" which had reigned among the political parties in the old coalition, and which had existed *de facto* in the country following the "national reconciliation" of December 6. The hatred which still divided France was made apparent on February 13 by an unprovoked and criminal attack upon Léon Blum by members of the *Camelots du Roi*. In the days that followed, Socialists raided offices of the *Camelots*, severely injuring one member of the organization. On February 16, a giant demonstration was held in Paris to protest against the attack on Blum and to call for the dissolution of the leagues. All the parties in the Popular Front were represented. The demonstration had been authorized by Sarraut only on condition that there be as many tricolor as red flags. Neither the Socialists nor the Communists had any objection.[52]

Within the Chamber of Deputies, the end of the truce was marked by bitter debates. Discussion of the Franco-Soviet pact was an occasion for the Chamber to reveal its deep divisions between Left and Right. The more rabid conservatives showed a complete inability to distinguish between a foreign alliance and internal politics. Communism was their sole preoccupation. After a long-drawn-out debate, the pact

---

[51] *L'Humanité*, February 1, 1935.
[52] Jean Zay, *Souvenirs et Solitudes* (Paris, 1945), p. 199.

was finally approved in late February, with the Communist deputies voting in support of the government. The Sarraut cabinet was proving itself by its acts.

The real test, however, was yet to come. In a way, it was unfair that a cabinet which had been put in place as a "care-taker" for current affairs should be asked to make one of the gravest decisions on French foreign policy in the 1930's. On March 7, 1936, German troops began their occupation of the Rhineland. This flagrant violation of the Locarno Pact was the first serious test of the French commitment to the system of regional collective security. At first, the French govern-ment appeared ready to take action. The Communist leaders backed a policy of "firmness," and revived a slogan which had made its mark as that of the French nationalists: "Long live the union of the French nation!" But France remained inac-tive. On March 8, immediate French military intervention was refused by the Council of Ministers.[53] The Communists, in all likelihood, would have supported such action; they came out publicly for "sanctions," though they prudently stated that the measures taken should be economic and financial, not "military." [54] In later years, they would decry French inaction during the Rhineland crisis as a "capitulation" to fascism. Yet at the time they appeared to absorb the blow with great ease, making no issue of the Rhineland in the electoral campaign that followed. French passiveness during the March crisis may have disappointed the leaders of the Soviet Union, but it brought no change in the tactics of the French party.

[53] Edouard Bonnefous, *Histoire politique de la Troisième Répub-lique*, Vol. V: *La République en Danger: Des Ligues au Front populaire*, pp. 385–89.

[54] *L'Humanité*, March 11, 1936; in a dispatch from Moscow dated March 8, the French ambassador noted that "various Soviet leaders (*personalités*)" consider it "necessary" that "France react vigor-ously" (*Documents diplomatiques français, 1932–1939*, Series 2, Vol. I [January 1–March 31, 1936], p. 439).

On the whole, the first experience with a Radical cabinet was a disappointment for the Communists. Sarraut had let Hitler act with impunity. Within France, he took no action against the leagues. Sometime in early March, the party leadership felt it necessary to try to dissociate the Popular Front from the government. It sent a letter to the National Committee of the *Rassemblement populaire* declaring that "everyone" should know that "the *Sarraut Government is not the emanation of our movement.*" After the national elections, a new "left-wing government supported by the Popular Front" would have "entirely different" policies.[55]

The Communist leadership hoped to strengthen its position within the coalition through impressive gains in the parliamentary elections, held in late April and early May. Instructions sent to local Communist organizations called for a demonstration of " the force and influence of our party." They stressed the fact that "this influence will be measured by the *total number of votes obtained in the entire country.* The greater our influence, the more authority we will have to defend our propositions and to have them triumph."[56] In sheer quantity, the amount of material used as electoral propaganda was unprecedented, either for the Communists or for any other French party. Communist posters were everywhere. The country was flooded with 7,500,000 copies of nine pamphlets, followed up a few days before the elections by a booklet entitled *Communism, the Hope of the Country*, included in every copy of *L'Humanité*. The Communists were "going to the people" by every possible means, even using the state radio stations put at their disposal by the government for campaign speeches. With candidates active in every legislative district, urban or rural, votes could be expected to go to the Commu-

---

[55] Quoted by Berlioz, *Correspondance*, April 4, 1936, p. 419.
[56] *Les Elections législatives de 1936: Instructions et Conseils aux Régions, Rayons et Cellules*, p. 2.

nists if for no other reason than the ubiquity of their activity.

Communist electoral propaganda was modified to meet the new circumstances. The Communist party had always claimed to be the "voice of the oppressed," but its revolutionary panacea had appeared too remote to gain a wide following. This time, reform rather than revolution was the watchword. The campaign for mass support begun in late 1935 was greatly amplified. The party's electoral program promised to Frenchmen a "free, strong, and happy France." It called for such reforms as a forty-hour week, collective contracts, and a paid vacation for the workers; price supports for the produce of the peasants; and easy credit for the merchants. To finance these measures while at the same time "defending the franc"—devaluation, they cried, was anathema—the Communists proposed their usual "make the rich pay," with a progressive capital levy on fortunes of over 500,000 francs.[57] Something to receive and nothing to pay, such was the promise to the masses.

The Communist program declared the party to be the true defender of "national reconciliation" as well as the opponent of the fascists, "the dividers of Frenchmen." This was the sense of the first talk a Communist ever made on the French state radio network, on April 17. Thorez was chosen speaker for the occasion, launching at this time the slogan to be repeated invariably by Communist speakers in coming years— the *"main tendue,"* the "outstretched hand." To the Catholic worker, to the member of the leagues, to the veteran misled by authoritarian leaders, to every "son of the people," Thorez offered the "hand of the Communists" for a "reconciliation of the people of France." [58] The appeal to the Catholics created a

[57] *Recueil des Textes authentiques des Programmes et Engagements électoraux des Députés proclamés élus à la Suite des Elections générales de 1936* (Paris, 1939), pp. 16–24.

[58] "Pour une France libre, forte et heureuse," *L'Humanité*, April 18, 1936.

small scandal, and even provoked a reaction from conservative Catholic leaders. The Communist party was continuing to give proof of tactical audacity.

Within the coalition, the Communist leaders avoided any polemics with their allies. They did, however, offer on occasion some brotherly advice. Daladier was reported by conservative newspapers to have a "distant attitude" toward the Franco-Soviet pact, and to favor a *rapprochement* with Germany. The reporter for *L'Humanité* thought it would be well for the new president of the Radical party to deny these reports, "from which one might conclude that the position of M. Daladier on the question [of Franco-Soviet relations] is closer to the opinion of the Right than that of Radical leaders such as MM. Herriot, Delbos, Cot, Bastid, etc." [59] But Daladier said nothing.

The Communist leaders raised with the SFIO the old question of "Millerandism." Millerand had been the first Socialist to participate in a bourgeois government, for which he had been damned by many Socialists ever since. The Socialists had been debating the question of participation at virtually every national congress. Gradually, Léon Blum and other moderates had put across the point that Socialists might cooperate in the "exercise of power"—i.e., participate in a cabinet—without compromising their ultimate goal of seizing power for the proletariat. From the point of view of European socialism, the whole debate was anachronistic. Socialist parties were participating in governments in several countries. The Second International had since the war dropped its strictures on participation. Only the French Socialists continued the discussion, the sign perhaps of an ideological rigidity among many of the older members of the party.[60] For the French Communists to raise the issue in the election campaign of 1936 seemed the height of hypocrisy. After their intellectual somersaults on

[59] *Ibid.*, April 23, 1936.   [60] See Colton, pp. 66–67, 114–15.

questions as important as national defense, they were hardly in a good position to defend the Socialists against "class collaboration" and what they referred to as "Neo-Millerandism." Further, the Communist leaders did not seem to realize that both Socialists and Radicals anticipated, in the event of electoral victory, a coalition Socialist-Radical cabinet (Radical leadership was naturally assumed). Jacques Duclos argued on the contrary that "the proletarian parties" should remain "independent of the government while assuring it of their support." They could in this manner influence policies "in a democratic direction." This flexibility would be lost, he declared, if they participated in the government, for they would be obliged to accept "compromises." [61] The Socialists, however, gave no sign of agreeing.

Such as it was, the Popular Front struck a sympathetic chord in the hearts and minds of many Frenchmen. This new political formation, with its program already agreed upon, had much to offer to a people who needed much. In a time of depression and growing fear of war, peace and prosperity were attractive planks indeed. Born of antifascism, nurtured on the cooperation of the most important political parties, strengthened by a nationwide organization, the Popular Front had a dynamism its opponents could not equal. The general consensus was that victory would be on its side, with the Communists, aided by both the Socialists and the Radicals, certain to gain strongly. One political "expert" forecast a new Chamber of Deputies with 35 to 40 Communists, 108 to 112 Socialists, and 145 to 150 Radicals.[62] The political spectrum would merely be shifted more to the left.

The first ballot, held on April 26, upset predictions right away. The Communist vote soared to almost 1.5 million, 15

[61] "Le Gouvernement de Demain," *L'Humanité*, April 23, 1936.
[62] *L'Oeuvre*, April 20, 1936.

per cent of the votes cast and twice the party's 1932 vote. The Socialists just held their own, with 2 million votes (20 per cent of the votes cast). Most significant of all, the Radical vote fell to below that of the Socialists, to 1.95 million (19.5 per cent of the votes cast). The Popular Front had received the support of 54.5 per cent of the voting Frenchmen, a clear victory over the Right.

The great increase in Communist votes was obviously the result of the party's intensive campaign throughout France. Its vote advanced in every department save three. The gains were most significant in the regions with a large working-class population, such as the Lille, Paris, and Marseilles areas. Important gains were also made in several rural departments in southwestern France, hard hit by the agricultural crisis.[63] Electoral statistics indicate that the Communist voters were more socially diversified than before, though the real centers of party power were still the proletarian regions. The specific reasons for the increased electoral strength of the Communist party are hard to find; no intensive sociological studies of the 1936 elections have yet been made. It does seem clear that the depression was an important factor. Certain areas with a high rate of unemployment, such as the Paris region, also went much more strongly Communist than in earlier elections. The same cause was at work in depressed agricultural areas, for instance southwestern France.[64]

Yet the advance of the party was so general that it is impossible to explain it solely by such restrictive factors as economic decline or class appeal. One must also take account of the political climate of the country. The voters in the Midi, the Mediterranean coastal region, had traditionally voted

[63] Dupeux, pp. 127–28, and in particular the excellent graphs and electoral maps which accompany the book.

[64] See M. Labrousse, "Structures agraires et Résultats électoraux dans la Vienne," *Mouvement social*, No. 54 (Jan.-March, 1966), pp. 205–17.

"Red"—that is, for the most radical republican party. Before 1936, they had supported the Socialist and Radical parties, but in 1936 they shifted their choice in many instances to the Communist candidates. It is quite possible that many other voters in France supported the Communists for similar reasons. Revolution was still a symbol of progress for many Frenchmen who had no desire for a revolutionary change. It stood for real reform and for an end to sterile conservatism in French politics.[65] The Communists had, without a doubt, the best case for the title of revolutionaries. What they lacked was the mark of respectability, and this they obtained by their coalition with the Socialists and the Radicals in the Popular Front. Flanked by these two tried and true democratic parties, it seemed that the Communists were at last a part of the French community. For those who felt the desire to protest, for those too who felt that a change was in order in France, the party was now a good haven. Offering this time to defend democracy rather than to destroy it, to fight the depression rather than simply to seize power for the proletariat, the Communist party had infinitely greater appeal in 1936 than in 1932.

Since few of the seats had been filled on the first ballot, the second ballot was decisive in determining the composition of the new Chamber. Here was the real test of the Popular Front. On April 28, the leaders of the major parties of the Left signed a common declaration calling for the mutual withdrawal of candidates in favor of the leading candidate "proclaiming his allegiance [*se réclamant*] to the Popular Front."[66] Communist acceptance of this document was

[65] For a discussion of the reformist attitude of present-day Communist voters, see Charles Micaud, *Communism and the French Left* (New York, 1963), pp. 140–50.

[66] *L'Humanité*, April 29, 1936.

wholehearted in public; in the electoral districts, its application was less so. The party convention in January had declared that Communist candidates could in no case withdraw in favor of those 32 Radical deputies who had supported Laval on the vote of January 16. A list of the names of these renegades had been sent to all the local party organizations. During the quarrel in March with the Socialists over the nature of the Popular Front, this *vendetta* had been publicly buried. When the results of the first ballot were in, 14 of these Radicals led all the other candidates of parties in the Popular Front. In seven of the cases, the candidate of the Right stood a good chance of being elected if the vote of the Left were split; in the seven others, the contest was entirely within the Popular Front. The Communists' rule of thumb was to support those men menaced by the Right, and, March declarations notwithstanding, to fight the others.[67] In all, ten favored Radical candidates were opposed by Communists; in no case was the seat in jeopardy from the Right. Two other cases of Communist indiscipline occurred against candidates of a Communist splinter group. Compared to the Socialist record of 25 violations, and that of 22 for the Radicals, the Communists appeared to be the most disciplined of the parties in the Popular Front.[68]

When the returns from the second ballot of May 3 were in, Communist representation in the Chamber of Deputies had risen to the impressive figure of 72—62 seats more than in the previous legislature. Of these, 24 had been won from the Socialist incumbents—proof of the invasion of Socialist working-class fiefs by the Communist party—and 13 from the Radicals. In 20 of the 37 "steals" from the Socialists and Radicals, the Communist victor owed his seat to the with-

[67] *Le Temps*, May 5, 1936.   [68] Dupeux, pp. 133–35.

drawal of the candidates of the allied parties; a total of 41 seats
went to the Communists thanks to their alliance.[69] The Popular Front was for them an electoral bonanza.

They had less reason to rejoice at the situation among the
other parties of the Popular Front. A total of 378 deputies
could be counted for the Front as against 220 for the conservatives and moderates. Yet the Radicals had lost 51 seats, falling
to 106, while the Socialists had succeeded not only in filling in
the holes left by the 1933 scission, but also in gaining an
additional 16 seats, giving them in all 147 seats. The Socialist
party, as Léon Blum hastened to proclaim, was "the most
powerful group of the Popular Front majority, and of the
Chamber." The Socialist leaders wished to inform everyone
that *"we are ready to fill the role which is ours, that is to say,
to form and to lead the government of the Popular Front."* [70]
For the first time in the history of France, a Socialist would be
Premier. But the Communist leaders had struggled for almost
a year for a *Radical* cabinet, one whose foreign policy would
reflect support of the Franco-Soviet alliance. The elections
had deprived them of that objective. They may have found
the fruit of victory somewhat spoiled.

[69] J. W. Pickersgill, "The Front Populaire and the French Elections of 1936," *The Political Science Quarterly*, LIV (March, 1939),
82.
[70] "Le Parti socialiste est prêt," *Le Populaire*, May 5, 1936.

V

Under Socialist Rule

The elections of 1936 opened a new period in the history of the French Communist party and the Popular Front. The preliminary political and electoral maneuvering was over. The coalition of Communist, Socialist, and Radical parties possessed at last sufficient parliamentary strength and unity to control the government. The problem had become policy-making itself, the choice of alternative foreign and internal policies for the Popular Front cabinet. The Communist leaders had indicated by their actions earlier, when the Radicals seemed likely to assume power, that they were less interested in internal reforms than in a foreign policy based on antifascism, collective security, and strong ties with the Soviet Union.

They found the situation in May, 1936, more complex than anticipated, however, since the leadership of the Popular Front had passed into the hands of the Socialists. They looked on the SFIO as a dangerous rival for the allegiance of the proletariat and a defender of policies of international appeasement and nonresistance. The German occupation of the Rhineland had shown that France was not definitely committed to collective security and even suggested the possibility of a Franco-German understanding. The Communist leaders in France were undoubtedly under a heavy obligation to see that French foreign policy remain at the very least resolutely anti-German. Their own political ambitions led them at the same time to seek to expand their following among the working class. They began to push more ardently than before for social and economic reforms, and sought to increase their influence in the CGT.

They discovered that these tactics were difficult to apply. Their own initiatives reflected the desire to influence government policies, particularly foreign policy, without sacrificing the unity of the Popular Front, and to strengthen their support among the masses while avoiding serious social disorders. The balance was hard to find, however. The party was very successful in increasing its membership and solidifying its hold over a large segment of the proletariat, but not before it had inadvertently brought the country to the verge of civil war. The French workers, including apparently a considerable number of party members, were in a militant mood following the victory of the Popular Front. Their impatience became evident in the strikes and agitation of May and June. The Communist union leaders probably initiated the sit-down strikes, but intended to limit the movement to a select and manageable few. They were totally unprepared for the massive participation of over a million workers. The entire party had to be mobilized to help restore order.

The Communist leaders encountered even greater problems in their relations with the Popular Front government. They were unable to fix major policies or to change them once applied. They tried social agitation and then parliamentary maneuvering, but to no avail. In order to preserve their place in the coalition, they had to accept the effective leadership of the Socialists and the Radicals; their only alternative was to abandon the Popular Front.

The Mass Movement

At first, the Communist party sought to keep a distance between itself and the Popular Front government. When

asked by Léon Blum to participate in his cabinet, the party
leaders refused. Their attitude had been fixed by the declaration of Dimitrov at the Seventh Comintern Congress, and they
were not prepared to revise their view because of the unexpected results of the elections.[1] They had already stated that
they feared "anti-democratic compromises" should they be
bound by ministerial responsibility; they hoped that "independence" would permit them to "orient the policies" of the
government.[2] Indeed, they sought to influence Blum even
before his cabinet was formed. They called for the immediate
application of the social and economic reforms contained in
the Popular Front program. On a more serious note, they
indicated that they wished to see Edouard Herriot take a place
in the cabinet. "Would it be rash to conclude," *L'Humanité*
rhetorically asked, "that the cause of peace would best be
served by collaboration in the government between the Socialist leader [Léon Blum] and the man most representative of
Radicalism [Herriot]?"[3] The Communists also stressed frequently their desire to see the new government make a firm
commitment to the Franco-Soviet pact. Despite the importance of this goal, the Comintern leaders apparently did not
feel that the French party should take the risk of placing some
of its officials in the government. A year later, they admitted
their error by having the French Communists request participation—only to have the request turned down.

The French party leaders went about once more seeking to

[1] Dimitrov had foreseen Communist participation in an "anti-fascist popular front government" only if prerevolutionary conditions
existed (*Correspondance*, August 20, 1935, p. 1041). Thorez, in the
last edition of his autobiography, *Fils du Peuple,* claimed that he had
supported participation but that "the Politburo was of a different
opinion" (p. 121). His argument would be more convincing had he
not omitted it in all previous editions. It is possible that some
members of the Politburo favored joining the cabinet but unlikely
that the General Secretary was one of them.

[2] *L'Humanité*, April 23, 1936.   [3] *Ibid.*, May 20, 1936.

build up a mass movement in the country. With dogged perseverance, they launched again in May their proposal for "democratic committees of the Popular Front." Their local party officials issued appeals for the organization of such committees, but without success. More rewarding was the formation of subsidiary "front" organizations under direct Communist patronage. These groups, created in the name of every good cause from antifascism and antisemitism to art and nature, spread like mushrooms. One zealous German embassy official in Paris put together a list of sixty-two such organizations.[4] Amsterdam-Pleyel was still active in mobilizing left-wing intellectuals and liberals in support of peace. Its major operation in 1936 was the preparation of an international congress, the "Universal Rally for Peace," to be held in September in Brussels.[5] But it was never able to focus the vague desire for peace of its many European supporters on the precise issue of collective security.

The Communist party received a sympathetic hearing for many of the causes it defended. It could not, however, apply its discipline to the sympathizers and "fellow travelers" who had appeared in large numbers by mid-1936. Its relations with the intellectuals of the Left, recently studied by David Caute in *Communism and the French Intellectuals*, reveal this fundamental weakness. It enjoyed the favor of many leading French writers and scientists, including André Malraux, André Gide, Paul Langevin, and Frédéric Joliot-Curie. Its "Maisons de la Culture," an organization founded in 1934 to unite "pro-Communist cultural bodies," claimed in July, 1936, to have 45,000

[4] "Kommunismus in Frankreich," Auswartiges Amt, Politische Abteilung V, serial # 303, frame 186793–186800.

[5] J. Schleimann, "The Life and Work of Willi Muenzenberg," *Survey*, No. 55 (April, 1965), p. 77; Muenzenberg was the guiding force behind the "Rally," and used Amsterdam-Pleyel to mobilize support.

members, then, six months later, 65,000.[6] Yet the tradition of independent critical judgment remained strong among the intellectuals. After his trip to the Soviet Union in the summer of 1936, André Gide created a sensation by writing his book *Retour de l'URSS*, sharply critical of conditions in the "Socialist fatherland." Generally, the party's antifascist position was supported by left-wing intellectuals, but only so long as it did not entail the immediate prospect of war for France.[7]

The Communist leaders were interested above all in expanding their influence among the workers, who were less critical and more disciplined than the intellectuals. They proved their interest in the course of the sit-down strikes of May and June, one of the most important social movements in the recent history of France. Between May 7 and May 23, six strikes with worker occupation of the factories took place and all were successful. Two similar strikes were threatened but immediate management acceptance of union demands made them unnecessary. In all cases, the action occurred in the metallurgical industry, primarily in airplane factories. The plants affected were located in the provinces, and in the Paris region. In the week of May 22 to 29, the movement spread to almost all the metal-processing, aviation, and automobile factories around Paris. By May 29, an estimated 100,000 workers were on strike.[8]

[6] David Caute, *Communism and the French Intellectuals*, p. 44, n. 1.
[7] *Ibid.*, pp. 114–22.
[8] Several general studies of the movement have been made: Georges Lefranc, *Juin '36*, gives a selection of documents; Jacques Danos and Marcel Gibelin, *Juin '36*, though superficial, is the most nearly complete; Henri Prouteau, *Les Occupations d'Usines en Italie et en France, 1920–1936* goes deeper in a shorter space; Solomon Schwarz, *Les Occupations d'Usines en France de Mai et Juin, 1936*, gives an excellent day-by-day account of the events; Marcel Schulz, "Les Origines de la Crise ouvrière de 1936," *Le Musée social*, May 1937, pp. 121–39, June, 1937, pp. 153–65, July, 1937, pp. 185–200, analyzes various hypotheses as to the origins of the movement.

The Communist leaders were unquestionably pleased by these developments. The sit-down strikes in the metallurgical industry constituted the "co-ordinated campaign in the unified labor-union movement" called for by the Comintern.[9] But what role did the party, particularly its union officials, play in the spread of the strikes? Officially, it was only a spectator, but a very attentive one. Of all the Parisian newspapers, only *L'Humanité* followed the day-by-day evolution of the movement. Only in its pages were the lessons to be drawn from the successful conclusion of certain strikes spelled out for all interested parties. The victory of the first major strike, at the Bréguet aviation plant in Le Havre, was greeted by the Communist leader of the Metallurgical-Workers Federation as a "first and important example to be made known to all." [10] The second successful strike, at the Latécoère aviation factory in Toulouse, was pointed to by a Communist official in the Toulouse Union of the Metallurgical Federation as proof that a strike movement was "possible even in a period of economic crisis." The "basic condition for success" was the "organized struggle at the plant: the sit-down strike." [11]

The Communist newspaper's close attention to the strikes suggests that the party leaders had a hand in originating the movement and had a direct interest in its satisfactory outcome. In fact, they made no secret of their desire to see the metallurgical industry sign a collective contract with the Association of Metallurgical Unions of the Paris Region. But they left no trace of their role in the outbreak of the strikes, arguing at the time that the workers were solely responsible. Few facts can be cited against the claim that the movement began spontaneously, and they constitute only circumstantial evidence. A study of the history of the strikes reveals that the occupation

[9] *Internationale*, April, 1936, p. 386.
[10] *L'Humanité*, May 20, 1936.   [11] *Ibid.*, May 23, 1936.

8 (*left*). The intellectual and the proletarian: Léon Blum and Maurice Thorez (*with tricolor sash*) at the Bastille Day demonstration, 1936. (*L'Illustration.*) 9 (*right*). In search of a military alliance: Marshal Tukhachevsky (*on right*) and wife arriving in Paris on an "unofficial" visit, February, 1936. (*L'Illustration.*)

10. The birth of the Popular Front: the demonstration of the *Rassemblement populaire* in Paris, July 14, 1935. (*L'Illustration.*)

of factories did not occur in a haphazard manner. It was restricted throughout the month of May almost exclusively to the metallurgical industry, and was at first concentrated in aviation plants. According to a weekly magazine put out by the French management association, the owners of these factories had "urgent outstanding orders" with the government. Their rapid acceptance of the worker demands was partly due to the "intervention of administrative authorities and political leaders" who wished to see the orders filled.[12]

The Federation of Metallurgical Workers was one of the unions partially controlled by the Communists. It had begun an organizational drive that spring, and had conducted an especially active campaign for the celebration by the workers of May Day, not a legal holiday. Workers who had taken the holiday were dismissed at both the Le Havre Bréguet plant and the Toulouse Latécoère plant; their rehiring was the major issue behind the strike at the former factory, and at the latter was joined with the question of the right of the union to act as collective bargaining agent. The Communist organization in Toulouse was eager for some sort of action. On May 9, three days before the strike began, its weekly newspaper declared that the victory of the Popular Front depended primarily on "the action of the people, the massive pressure of [public] opinion, and even the activity of social struggles." [13] No other Communist publication that month came so close to calling openly for strikes.

When the sit-down strike movement reached Paris a few days later, the workers' demands had risen to include union recognition, a salary raise, and a paid vacation. The Paris union organization, the Association of Metallurgical Unions of the Paris Region, was highly regarded by the party. It was,

---

[12] *L'Usine*, May 21, 1936, p. 3.
[13] *La Voix des Travailleurs*, May 9, 1936.

in André Marty's words, "the spirit and the force of the Parisian proletariat and of our party." Its members possessed a "keen political shrewdness." [14] They were, that is, disciplined and reliable followers of party directives. A syndicalist magazine close to the union movement reported that the Association had acquired the reputation for being the "guinea-pig union" which tried out "experiments" in worker agitation.[15] One such experiment was the apparently unsuccessful attempt to start a sit-down strike on June 20, 1935, in the Bloch aviation factory in the Paris suburb of Courbevoie, one of the plants occupied by the workers a year later.[16] Taken altogether, these facts do seem to fall into a pattern. They suggest that the Metallurgical-Workers' Federation began the sit-down strikes on an experimental basis outside the Paris region. Then, having seen the effectiveness of the technique, it introduced the movement in Paris, where success would publicize the growing power of the proletariat. On the other hand, the concentration of the strikes in the metallurgical industry, the Communist influence in the Federation, the party encouragement to the occupation of factories, the reliability of the Paris Association of Metallurgical Unions, all may be purely coincidental to the spontaneous appearance and spread of the sit-down strikes.

It is clear, at least, that the Communist leaders set the major goal for the Parisian movement. The management organization of Paris metallurgy had refused in the past to accept the Association of Metallurgical Unions of the Paris Region as

[14] "La Situation générale en France," *Internationale*, July, 1936, p. 795. When this article was written (probably in late May), Marty was still in Moscow as French representative to the ECCI.

[15] *La Révolution prolétarienne*, No. 231 (September 25, 1936), pp. 11–12; it has recently been suggested that American Communists active in the CIO "inspired, directed, and controlled" the sit-down strikes of 1936–1937 (Sidney Fine, "The General Motors Sit-Down Strike," *American Historical Review*, LXX [April 1965], 695–97).

[16] *L'Humanité*, June 21, 1935.

legal bargaining agent for the workers. The Association could never become a strong organization without this power. Even before the wave of strikes began, its leaders had called for the signature of an industry-wide collective contract. On May 28, its Secretary underlined in an article in *L'Humanité* the "serious and corporative character of the strikes." The intransigence of management had created a "profound dissatisfaction" which was at last coming to the surface in the "present strikes." A "better understanding" of the situation in the factories would have permitted a solution to the problem "without forcing the workers to stop work." Implicit in this declaration was the promise that the strike movement would stop immediately were the limited demands of the Association satisfied. That very day, Premier Sarraut and his Minister of Labor initiated talks for a settlement. Jacques Duclos, one of those called in, came out of his interview declaring that his party wanted "first of all to avoid any disorder, then to obtain the opening of negotiations as soon as possible to achieve a peaceful solution to the conflict." [17]

So eager were the Communist leaders to obtain the regional collective contract that they accepted management's demand that the factories be evacuated before negotiations begin. They did so regardless of the workers' reaction. On the evening of May 29, the enormous Renault plant in Boulogne-Billancourt was emptied, despite the fact that no agreement at all was reached on wage increases for the plant employees. One Renault worker wrote later in a Trotskyite magazine that the evacuation had been achieved over "the protests of a part of the workers." [18] Within two days, only 10,000 strikers remained in Paris factories. A reasonable settlement appeared in sight; the Blum government would be able to take over power in an atmosphere of social calm.

The party leaders had done their best to restrict the sit-

---

[17] *L'Oeuvre*, May 29, 1936.   [18] *Que Faire*, July, 1936, p. 13.

down strike movement to limited action for well-defined purposes. They almost succeeded. Had the collective contract
been signed rapidly and respected by the workers, the party
could have gone into the new era of the Popular Front in a
strong position. It would have been assured of the backing of
a much more powerful Paris Association of Metallurgical
Unions which might, in case of need, be used as an instrument
of political pressure. Then, too, the method of the sit-down
strike, having proved its value, could have gradually been
extended into other parts of the labor-union organization,
such as the Building Trades Federation, where the Communists also had a solid foundation from the old CGTU.

It was easier to start a strike movement, however, than to
control it. Hopes had been raised and ideas suggested which
would be hard to still. Even among the Socialists, there were
those who proclaimed that "everything is possible." Marceau
Pivert, leader of the left wing of the SFIO, launched this
slogan on May 28. He foresaw the possibility of obtaining
many reforms quickly.[19] The Communist leadership disagreed. Marcel Gitton answered back immediately that social
and political moderation was necessary. The strikers simply
wanted "more human conditions" of work; management, if it
were "intelligent and comprehensive," would agree to negoti-
ate a rapid settlement. No "wave of the wand" could solve all
the problems at once. The program of the Popular Front
offered the best beginning. Governmental reforms such as
subsidies for public works and aid for the unemployed and for
farmers were both "possible and urgent." "Rash actions," on
the other hand, "could only lead to the alienation of an important part of the petty bourgeoisie." The Popular Front was
"responsible" for "the security of France" against "Hitler's
menace." This security would be "jeopardized" were the slo-

[19] "Tout est possible," *Le Populaire*, May 28, 1936.

gan "Everything is possible" spread about the country. On the contrary, the slogan should be: "Not everything is possible!" [20] But the workers felt differently.

After a calm weekend, strikes suddenly broke out everywhere on June 2. The metallurgical industry was hit anew and in regions previously untouched. Other sectors of the economy were seriously affected, including the chemical, textile, and wholesale food industries, while many regions of France previously immune now experienced their first sit-down strikes. For it was this method of action which was adopted everywhere. Entire federations were now applying it in orders for general strikes, such as that announced on June 6 by the Miners, whom no one could suspect of being Communist-dominated. Even the salesgirls in the large Parisian department stores "sat down" on the job. The strikes were by the end of the week an urgent national problem.

On June 4, Léon Blum took over as France's first Socialist Premier, under conditions to be envied no man. He immediately called on the country for calm. All the parties in the Popular Front coalition sent representatives to a meeting on June 5 of the Delegation of the Left, out of which came a call for the rapid end to the strikes. The Communist delegates had cooperated fully in the elaboration of this appeal. On June 7, Blum brought together representatives of the national management association and the CGT in an effort to arrive at a negotiated general settlement. A few hours later, management and labor accepted the so-called Matignon Agreements, granting the workers salary increases and recognizing the unions as bargaining agents for collective contracts.

Benoît Frachon, as a member of the labor delegation, was one of the signers of the agreements. In a front-page article in *L'Humanité* on June 9, he called on the strikers to resume

---

[20] "Tout n'est pas possible," *L'Humanité*, May 29, 1936.

work on the basis of the concessions already granted the CGT. In general, the Communist leadership in parliament and in the labor confederation supported the government's policy of social pacification. Though it did not—yet—condemn the strikes, its public declarations were all on the side of moderation. Marcel Cachin expressed on June 5 the "certainty" that the workers were "resolved to remain in agreement with their union organizations" and would return to work "as soon as their demands are satisfied." [21] But neither appeals to reason nor the signature of the Matignon Agreements was sufficient to bring the workers back to their jobs. The strikes continued to multiply, with a total of 1,105,000 workers occupying factories at "the most critical hours." [22] On June 10, the government finally decided to prepare for forceful action. It brought squads of special police, the *gardes mobiles*, into Paris and surrounding working-class suburbs and stationed them at principal intersections and near large factories. The Communist leaders were alarmed by these measures, and understandably so. The country appeared close to violence.

Yet the Communist party was partially responsible for the critical situation. Its union leaders had probably taken the lead in applying the new tactics of the sit-down strikes in May. Many Communists in union offices continued to play an important role in the movement. Charles Bourneton, Communist Secretary of the Association of Unions of the Nord department, claimed later that his fellow party members had been "the most active in leading" the strikes in that region. He added that it was not "exactly true" that they had "started" the movement—in all probability a sincere evaluation of the situation in the Nord department.[23] Once the strike move-

[21] *Ibid.*, June 5, 1936.
[22] Figure cited by the Minister of the Interior, *JO, Débats, Chambre*, No. 52 (June 27, 1936), p. 1607.
[23] Quoted in *Le Peuple libre* (Lille), October 30, 1936.

ment was under way, the Communist leaders were apparently unable in many cases to control their followers. The second strike of the Renault factories in Boulogne-Billancourt, begun on June 4, had according to an eyewitness been forced on the union by the workers.[24] The entire working force in the Paris metallurgical industry gave the Association of Metallurgical Unions of the Paris Region a great deal of trouble. The Association leaders tried, in a meeting on June 9 with delegates from the factories, to obtain the consent of the strikers to return to work on the basis of the Matignon Agreements. They were "jeered at" for their trouble. Eugène Hénaff, General Secretary of the Association, explained to the Communist Central Committee meeting of June 13 that the delegates had proven uncooperative since they "were far from being all members of the party and many of them were only 'loud-mouths' and 'smooth-talkers.' "[25] But many of them were probably Communists who were unwilling to obey orders from above. The French working class was on its way to paralyzing the economy in the best traditions of syndicalism.

As far as can be judged, the movement in June was not politically motivated, nor was it in any way under the control of political organizations. The Trotskyites, having just founded a party in early June, began beating the drums in their new newspaper for the formation of workers' militias and factory committees. The government closed down their publication after two issues! This was as close as anyone came to calling in public for a proletarian revolution. Individually, the Trotskyites were certainly urging the workers on. But no one has ever suggested that the tiny International Workers' party, as the Trotskyite party was called, could possibly have guided the course of the strikes. Outside of the Communist

[24] *Que Faire,* July, 1936, p. 19.
[25] Quoted by André Ferrat, a participant in the meeting, in his *Lettre ouverte,* p. 32.

and Socialist parties and the CGT, there were no significant worker organizations. The "radical Left" was divided and small.[26] The workers did not need the support of their political leaders. Their own class consciousness and solidarity assured adequate mobilization and unity of action. The June sit-down strikes were the closest thing to a spontaneous, nationwide proletarian movement France had ever seen.

The party leadership decided finally to take special measures to meet the critical situation. They were losing control of their followers and could see that the country was in serious danger of grave internal disorder. They began by obtaining from the secretaries of the party cells in the Paris region, brought together in a meeting on June 9, an expression of "confidence" in their policies. The next day, *L'Humanité* published an appeal to the workers to observe "vigilant rigor" against any "suspicious elements" seeking to upset the "tranquil discipline" in the factories. Finally, a special meeting of the party members from the Paris region was held on June 11 in order to give Maurice Thorez the opportunity to outline the new tactics. The General Secretary rejected completely any revolutionary hopes which the great strike movement might have raised within the party. "To seize power now," he declared, "is out of the question." He pointed out that the middle classes and the peasantry were not on the side of the workers. Showing the Comintern's concern for French unity, he warned that nothing must be done to "dislocate the cohesion of the masses." The strike movement had to be limited to the "satisfaction of demands of an economic character." Therefore, the workers "must know how to end [a strike] as soon as satisfaction has been obtained." Even "compromise" was necessary "if all the demands have not yet been accepted but if victory has been obtained on the most essential and

[26] Broué and Dorez, "Critique de Gauche," pp. 99–105.

important demands." He called on the metallurgical workers of Paris to end their strike and disavowed Communists who intervened in strikes.[27] The Communist party was thereafter unequivocally committed to the peaceful settlement of the conflict. Its motto, proclaimed in bold headlines on *L'Humanité*'s front page on June 14, was: "The Communist Party Is Order!"

From that moment on, the Communist leaders worked to end the strikes. On June 13, the Central Committee, presided over by the General Secretary of the Metallurgical Federation Ambroise Croizat, approved Thorez's call for an end to the strikes in order to avoid "campaigns of fright and panic." [28] The day before, the Paris Association of Metallurgical Unions had accepted a compromise settlement. This example was followed by several other major unions in the Paris region. Within a few days, the majority of strikes in the capital had been settled. Calm had been restored at last, thanks in large part to the authority of the Communist party among the Parisian workers.

In other parts of the country, however, the strike wave did not recede, and in some places, notably Lyon and Marseilles, it even swelled. In Marseilles, the strikes were at their worst on June 18 and 19. The leadership of the Communist party intervened personally to halt the strikes in that city. The effectiveness of their intervention was remarked by the Minister of the Interior, who declared later that the pacification of the disputes "coincided with the presence in Marseilles of Communist deputies, notably with the intervention of M. Maurice Thorez." [29] The combined efforts of the Socialist ministers, in particular Minister of the Interior Roger Salengro, the CGT leaders, and the major Communist union and

[27] *L'Humanité*, June 13, 1936.   [28] *Ibid.*, June 14, 1936.
[29] *JO, Débats, Chambre*, No. 52 (June 27, 1936), p. 1606.

party officials gradually brought the strikes to a halt. On June 26, there were 166,000 strikers in France, and, by early August, only 4,800.[30]

The Communist party had survived the wave of sit-down strikes in good condition. The membership had in the end obeyed the call to order from above. In the circumstances, its discipline was remarkable. Further, the party was not overly hurt by its efforts to halt the strike movement. The June strikes, nationwide and interprofessional, were undoubtedly spontaneous in inspiration and impetus. They exceeded in size anything the Communist leaders could have imagined or desired. Still, Thorez's virtual disavowal of the strikers on June 11 was for the leader of the party of the proletariat an appreciable sacrifice. Joanny Berlioz could point to this move later as proof that his party was a "governmental party." [31] The Communist party, though not directly involved in the government, had had to accept the responsibilities of its role as member of the ruling political coalition.

Nonetheless, the party leadership was able to preserve a semblance of leadership of the workers, which was more than the Socialist or CGT leaders could say. As a result, its position was potentially stronger than ever before. It could reach down to the workers in their factories thanks to the legal organization of factory delegates. In the opinion of André Marty, the delegates were "certainly the organism [*sic*] upon which the Popular Front will rest; they will be the best levers of action for the fulfillment of the program of the Popular Front." [32] He implied thereby that the labor unions could at last be mobilized for political campaigns. The Communist party had found a real mass movement.

The General Confederation of Labor was growing by leaps

[30] *Ibid.*, p. 1607; *ibid.*, No. 73 (August 7, 1936), p. 2476.

[31] *Correspondance*, June 20, 1936, p. 754.

[32] *Internationale*, July, 1936, p. 799.

and bounds. The legal recognition of its role as bargaining agent for the workers, plus the success of the June strikes, brought hordes of previously unorganized workers within its ranks. By mid-June, its membership was 2,500,000; by the end of the year it was 4,000,000. Unions which previously had been skeletal waxed prosperous: the Metallurgical-Workers Federation passed from 47,000 members at the end of 1935 to 833,000 at the end of 1937, the Building-Trades Federation from 33,000 to 342,000, and the tiny Agricultural-Workers Union from 5,000 to 48,000.[33] Within the CGT, the federations of state employees, heretofore dominant, were far outnumbered by the industrial federations. The moderation and political sophistication of the leaders of the state employees were to have less and less influence on the leadership of the Confederation. In the industrial federations, the massive influx of members had in many cases overwhelmed the old syndicalist *cadres*. The weakening of the former union organizations provided fertile ground for Communist organizational activity.

Theoretically, all partisan activity within the unions was banned. But the Communist union members always remained party men. Besides, they possessed an organization of their own, the party cell, in many factories, and could distribute numerous party periodicals, including a union weekly, *La Vie ouvrière*. The new union members were "available," and the Communist organizers were anxious to obtain their allegiance. Rather than educate the eager but naïve recruits, the party sought first to mobilize their votes in order to take control of the labor unions. Once in power, the Communists could easily modify the union statutes to assure their continued dominance, introducing the proportional vote, centralizing administrative control, encouraging the "direct democracy" of vote

[33] Prost, p. 198.

by acclamation.[34] Their opponents, the old syndicalists and reformists, were fewer in number, less quick to react, and less unscrupulous. Georges Dumoulin, non-Communist Secretary of the Association of Unions of the Nord Department and very active in union affairs, remarked sadly that many of his fellow non-Communists did not even have the energy to resist, preferring simply to "go along." "I find no movement of coherent resistance uniting reformists and revolutionaries prepared to struggle together for the independence of unionism." [35]

By the end of 1936, the Communists controlled the largest industrial federations, including the Metallurgical Workers, Railway Workers, and Building Trades. The departmental associations of unions in Paris (with 1,000,000 members) and in Marseilles, to name but the most important, were also theirs. Certain of the federations, such as the Miners and the Printers, did successfully resist this "colonization." They were soon a minority, however. The newly united Confederation escaped another scission thanks to the confederal structure of the organization, the conciliation of Léon Jouhaux, and a definite unwillingness on the part of the Communists to push their opponents too far.

The French Front

In the first months of the Popular Front government, the Communist deputies fully cooperated in the coalition. Their activity involved primarily support of the many bills introduced by cabinet members. There was much to do. By the end of the summer, the government had enacted an impressive number of economic and social reforms, including the forty-

[34] *Ibid.*, pp. 140–44.
[35] "Colonisation syndicale," *Syndicats*, April 22, 1937.

hour week for workers, a plan for public works for the unemployed, and for the peasants the Office of Wheat to assure them a minimum price for their grain. Blum treated the seventy-two Communist deputies as full members of the coalition, conferring every week with their leaders Thorez and Duclos. The Communists voted for all the government bills. They respected as well the unwritten rule that no member of the Delegation demand discussion in the Chamber of his bills without the consent of the other members. For novices in parliamentary ways, they performed rather well.

Yet their political effectiveness was hurt by the social agitation in the country. The sit-down strikes in particular created a growing feeling of discontent and even anger within the middle classes and peasantry, and also within the Radical party. The Communist leaders were concerned by this reaction, since it threatened their good relations with the Radical leaders. At the end of June, Jacques Duclos appealed for harmony to "that great republican, President Herriot," and to "those numerous Radical representatives and active Party members whose services to the Republic are without number." "The Radicals are right," he argued, in wishing to defend private property, to limit reforms, and to create a "national union" against the "bellicose ardor" of a "neighboring country [i.e., Germany!]"; the Communist party itself desired no more.[36] Proof that this was so came in early July.

On July 7, the Senate, stronghold of conservative Radicals, spent the entire day discussing the "shameful" violations of public order, especially the sit-down strikes. The Senators demanded, and received, a promise from the Minister of the Interior to "use all appropriate means" to prevent continuation of the strikes.[37] Everyone understood the declaration to

---

[36] "Les Radicaux ont raison," *L'Humanité*, June 27, 1936.
[37] *JO, Débats, Sénat*, No. 56 (July 8, 1936), p. 667.

imply the use of force, if necessary, to evacuate the occupied factories. The Communist leadership accepted the decision, though it earlier had objected to any limitation of the workers' right to strike. It made a real effort to halt the use of the sit-down strike and to stop the strike action completely. Benoît Frachon told the workers "frankly" that the "extension of the strike agitation, the continuation of the occupation of the factories, would be detrimental to their interests," then defined their interests as the preservation of the unity of the Popular Front.[38] Maurice Thorez, in a speech at a special party conference in early July, stressed the fact that the Popular Front was a "contract uniting the working and middle classes." Reforms had to be distributed equitably among these classes for the "welfare of our people." The Communist party, he concluded, was "in the service of the people of France." [39] For the sake of national unity, the Communist leaders ceased being the spokesmen of the proletariat alone and began speaking more and more of the interests of all the important social classes.

Significantly, their new posture did not seem to weaken the party's support among the masses. The elections of April–May had begun a period of extraordinary membership expansion. On July 11, the party membership had reached 187,000, and by August 6, 225,000, almost three times as great as in January, 1936. The insignificant Communist Youth League suddenly climbed to 78,000 members.[40] The party press throughout France experienced a similar growth, printing on an average between two and three times as many copies as before. This tremendous success was apparently an important factor in winning the old party stalwarts over to the

[38] "La Grève n'est pas le seul Moyen," *L'Humanité*, July 13, 1936.
[39] *Ibid.*, July 11 and 12, 1936.   [40] Ferlé, p. 65.

moderate policies of "national unity" and "service to the French people." One of the few who disagreed was André Ferrat, who broke with the party in July. He warned his comrades, in his last speech at the July conference, against the "intoxicating" feeling produced by the "immense wave of mass enthusiasm." He protested that popularity was no justification for opportunistic policies of cooperation with the bourgeoisie.[41] But he received no backing. It seemed that French Communists were for the time being content with participation in the Popular Front and massive support from the population.

The outbreak of the Spanish Civil War in mid-July did not at first substantially alter this situation. Rather, the Communist leaders responded to the violence south of the Pyrenees by developing even further their campaign for French unity. To be sure, they were not in agreement with Blum's policy of nonintervention, which sought to localize the Spanish conflict by blocking all outside aid to the belligerents. They argued that the fighting in the neighboring country was part of the international fascist crusade and hence a threat to the security of France. Though they did not call for direct French military intervention, they made it quite plain that they believed the Spanish Republican government deserved all the war matériel that France could provide. Yet their major concern in August was not with the Spanish question, but rather with a possible widening of the governmental coalition.

The example of the violence in Spain led many moderate Frenchmen to call for an end to internal divisions and strife in order to avoid civil war in their own country. The Communist leaders responded to these appeals with their own campaign for unity between friends and foes of the Popular

[41] Ferrat, *Lettre ouverte*, p. 13.

Front. They paid particular attention when the Radical Camille Chautemps suggested on August 2 that the parliamentary majority be "expanded" so that the government would
"represent more and more the totality of French interests." [42]
Two days later, Jacques Duclos, after having praised Chau-
temp's idea, asked if the time had not come for the formation
of a "Front of Frenchmen" (to become shortly the "French
Front") opposed to fascism and united in the "respect for
laws and in the defense of republican order." [43] The Communists never defined clearly what they meant by this new
"Front." They hinted strongly that they were thinking of a
political coalition including even the "republican Right."
Thorez, in a speech on August 6, described his party's suggestion as the answer to a "difficult internal and external situation." He outlined a program for the French Front consisting
of three main points: the "respect for laws," including the
Matignon Agreements; the "defense of the national economy," including aid to the middle classes and a high level of
production with job security; and the "liberty and independence of the country," based on principles of "indivisible peace
and collective security." [44] The program was an obvious attempt to satisfy the demands of the moderates.

Unfortunately for the Communist leaders, they could ac-
complish nothing without the aid of the Socialists, who in this
case refused to cooperate. On September 3, the SFIO leadership officially rejected the French Front, describing it as
"nothing other than an attempt at a national union." [45] Within
a year and a half, the Socialist party would reverse its position.
But for the time being, it remained firmly attached to the
Popular Front. With no aid from the Socialists and no indica-

[42] Quoted in *Le Temps*, August 3, 1936.
[43] "Le Front des Français," *L'Humanité*, August 4, 1936.
[44] *Ibid.*, August 8, 1936.   [45] *Le Populaire*, September 4, 1936.

tion of interest from anyone else, the Communists abandoned the new tactics in early September.

What were the Communist leaders trying to achieve by their "French Front?" In one sense, they were in full agreement with Blum. The Premier was searching to define a Spanish policy which would conciliate the conflicting interests and aspirations of liberal and radical Frenchmen. The Communists were in effect outdoing Blum by suggesting that conciliation be made the theme for all the policies of the government. There can be no doubt that they were concerned with the internal divisions of France. They appeared to recognize that the Spanish issue was extremely sensitive; they never insisted on aid to Spain in discussing the program for the French Front. Perhaps, therefore, they merely hoped that Blum would go even further in his moderation.

On the other hand, they may have thought to use the French Front as a means of removing the Socialist-led government. In parliament, the logic of the new Front implied an enlarged governmental coalition, which would likely have entailed the formation of a new cabinet, probably under Radical leadership. The continuation of the Communist campaign for the Spanish Republicans—comparatively moderate—still might be read as an effort to pressure Blum into resigning (an alternative the Premier had considered). The Communist press never mentioned in its attacks on the cabinet's Spanish policy the role of the Radical ministers, though their fear of Spanish involvement had been very important in the decision for nonintervention. On two counts—as traditional political conciliators and as supposed friends of the Soviet Union—the Radicals would have made desirable leaders of the French Front. But they never responded to the call. The attempt—if it really existed—was doomed from the start; the moderates were no more willing at that moment than they would be later to cooperate with the Socialists. The French parliament was a house divided, and there was little the Communist party could do to overcome the divisions.

"Planes for Spain!"

Suddenly, the Communist leadership abandoned its policies of moderation and national unity. The trouble began with a visit to Paris by Dr. Hjalmar Schacht, German Minister of the Economy and President of the *Reichsbank*. On August 26, a luncheon was offered in his honor, at which the French Premier and Minister of Foreign Affairs were present. In the course of the banquet, Franco-German political relations were discussed, though no agreements were reached. No sooner had the news of the banquet come out than Maurice Thorez sent a public letter to Léon Blum. Short but to the point, the letter protested that the reception of Schacht was "not in conformity with the dignity of our people." Blum immediately replied that the government of the Popular Front was quite capable of protecting the dignity of France, and that it would refuse no conversations, be they "economic, financial, or political," which might lead to an "overall settlement of European problems." The reply only upset the Communist leaders even more. Here was "proof" that the conversations with Schacht, these "disturbing secret meetings [*conciliabules*]," were "political." Germany was intent on forming a coalition of states for a "policy of war" against the Soviet Union. Was it "possible" that the government of Léon Blum might "head down this path in Hitler's tow [*à la remorque de Hitler*]?"[46] The Communists obviously feared as much.

In fact, the Comintern had just put the French party on its

[46] Both letters, and comments, are in *L'Humanité*, August 27, 1936; for a history of the Blum-Schacht conversations, see Colton, pp. 213–16.

guard against a Franco-German *rapprochement*. The Soviet leaders apparently did not feel enough confidence in the Blum government not to fear a "tendency" in French governing circles "to come to an understanding with the German aggressor." The French Communists had to show themselves the "most devoted defenders of the application of the Franco-Soviet Pact of Mutual Assistance." [47] It is not surprising therefore that their reaction to the cordial reception given Schacht was so hostile. The letter from Thorez to Blum could have created a diplomatic incident, and perhaps was intended to do so. In the days that followed, the Communist leaders called repeatedly on the French government to reaffirm its ties with the Soviet Union. Gabriel Péri, the foreign affairs correspondent for *L'Humanité*, advised Léon Blum to use "the next possible opportunity . . . to proclaim that France wants no one to imagine she is capable of loosening the ties which unite her with the USSR." [48] All the other French parties approved Blum's initiative, and both the Socialist and Radical leaders showed great displeasure at the Communist interference in the conduct of French foreign policy. But the Communist leaders continued for weeks afterward to ruminate bitterly over the treatment accorded the German financier. They apparently considered any political contacts with the Germans unacceptable. Blum's action may have been the immediate cause of a sharp change in Communist tactics in early September.

On September 2, Maurice Thorez delivered a speech whose message was unlike any he had given since the beginning of the Popular Front. He chose as his audience the 3,600 Communists of the Renault plant in Boulogne-Billancourt, assembled on only twenty-four-hour notice. He put great emphasis on the necessity for mass action. The workers had to remain

---

[47] "Front mira dolzhen pobedit' [The Peace Front Must Win]," *Kommunisticheskii Internatsional*, July, 1936, p. 10.

[48] *L'Humanité*, August 28, 1936.

"vigilant and attentive" in order to protect their social reforms and international peace. His most significant statement was an expression of approval of "the state of mind of those workers at the Bloch and Hotchkiss factories [metallurgical plants among the first to be hit by sit-down strikes in May] who wanted to start a strike to protest against the [Spanish] blockade." [49] In plainer language, Thorez was calling on the Paris Association of Metallurgical Unions to undertake strike action in support of the Spanish Republicans. On September 5, the factory delegates of the Paris Association were called together to approve a sit-down strike of one hour on September 7 "in order to protest against the blockade which is killing their Spanish brothers." Short strikes and meetings for aid to Spain occurred on September 5 and 6 in metallurgical factories in the Paris region. *L'Humanité* announced on September 6 that "the action is spreading and increasing," with the same goal inspiring the masses everywhere: the end of the "Spanish blockade." The means chosen to attain this end was the political strike.

The French Communists had undoubtedly been concerned over the fate of the Spanish Republic and its Popular Front government from the very outbreak of the civil war, seven weeks earlier. In fact, it is fairly well established that they were among the most ardent supporters of the Republicans throughout the three years of bitter fighting.[50] Yet, until early September, their ardor had expressed itself only in the form of moderate, verbal opposition to the government's policy of nonintervention. More energetic measures would have conflicted with the campaign for the French Front and with the policies of social and political restraint pursued by the party since late June. Before September 2, the unannounced motto

[49] *Ibid.*, September 4, 1936.
[50] Armstrong, *The Politics of Totalitarianism*, p. 39.

of the French Communist leaders was "France First"; then their priorities changed.

The reasons behind the change in tactics are still not clear. The simplest answer—hence the most tempting—is that the Comintern had finally decided that the Spanish Republic was worth the special attention of the French Communists. There was good reason to agitate for Spain just from the point of view of the Communist following in France. Support for the Spanish Republicans was widespread among liberals and so-cialists. Within the SFIO and CGT, a vocal minority was actively supporting aid to the Popular Front government in Spain. Pressure from below might well have been building up within the Communist party for more energetic measures.

At the same time, the Soviet government had also come to place less importance than in August on supporting French plans for international nonintervention. On August 23, it had accepted the Non-Intervention Agreement proposed by France and agreed to by the other major European states. On August 28, it had issued a decree placing an embargo on the export of arms to Spain. It had accepted this international agreement in order to conciliate the French government. But within three days of the issuance of the embargo decree, the Soviet leaders set about organizing the secret shipment of war matériel to the Republicans. In this, they were following the example set by Italy and Germany, both secretly sending important military supplies to Franco's rebel forces. According-ing to the former Chief of Soviet Military Intelligence in Western Europe, General Walter Krivitsky, the decision for the shipment of arms was taken on August 31; on September 2, he received instructions to organize these shipments from Western European countries.[51] September 2 was also the day

[51] *I Was Stalin's Agent*, pp. 98–99; the best critical analysis of this occasionally unreliable source is Hugh Thomas, *The Spanish Civil War*, p. 263.

Thorez called out the metallurgical workers. The coincidence
in dates is suggestive. But what was the Soviet Union trying to
achieve by intervening in Spain?

When necessary, the Soviet leaders were capable of sacrificing—and of making others sacrifice—ideological causes for
the sake of Soviet interests. But to what extent did they inter-
pret the international situation in the 1930's in terms of power,
and to what extent in terms of ideology? In January, 1934,
Stalin had declared that fascism was not the issue separating
Germany and the Soviet Union; but in mid-1934, the Comintern had set out on what appeared to be an antifascist campaign throughout Europe. Did the Soviet leaders in 1936
identify the threat to their country as fascism—they were certainly aware of the growing ties between the "fascist" countries, Germany and Italy—or as the territorial ambitions of
two sovereign states, Germany and Japan? Stalin continued to
hope that some sort of understanding with Germany was
possible; in late 1936, new contacts were made with German
representatives, though with no greater success than in 1935.
The problem of interpreting Soviet policy in Spain falls precisely within the limits of the issue of state interest versus
ideology. It was widely accepted that Franco's rebel forces
were "fascist," and that Germany and Italy had started aiding
Franco to promote the international fascist movement. To the
extent that the Soviet leaders saw Europe through this ideological prism, their actions in aiding the Spanish Republic
beginning in early September might have been motivated by
the belief that fascism did present a real threat in Spain. They
had every reason to wish to see the French government intervene as well. The French Socialist Premier had shown by his
conversations with Schacht that he did not have ideological
strictures against negotiating with the Germans. For the sake
of the international "front" against fascism, he had to be
pushed into the fight to defend the Spanish Republic. What

better instrument to attain this goal was there than the French Communist party?

Yet there may have been a strong element of realism in the Soviet Spanish policy and, consequently, in the French Communist campaign for aid to Spain. The Soviet Union may have supported the Spanish Republicans, thereby prolonging the Civil War, in order to embroil Germany in a conflict in Western Europe. In this manner, German pressure on Eastern Europe was eased. The same purpose would have been served by French aid to Spain, which would have had the further advantage of putting to rest—at least temporarily—Soviet fears of a Franco-German *rapprochement*. The "Schacht incident" could easily have reinforced Soviet fears that such an understanding was near. But French intervention on the side of the Republicans would inevitably have strained relations between France and both Italy and Germany. The Communist cry would be "Planes for Spain!" and "Open the frontier!" but no one, not Léon Blum and certainly not the Communist leaders, was so naïve as to believe the French government could stop at this. From the moment open support was given the Republicans, it would have to go as far as the aid given the rebels by the two fascist countries. Were Germany and France to find themselves at daggers' points in Spain, further Franco-German contacts would be impossible. The French Communist party, by calling for French aid to the Spanish Republic, may thus have been continuing its support of Soviet diplomatic goals. Perhaps both the struggle against fascism and resistance to Germany were factors behind the French Communist campaign. On the Spanish issue, the two were not incompatible.

It is at least clear that the French party was acting with greater daring in early September than the Soviet Union. The Soviet leaders had ordered Krivitsky to set up a clandestine organization to handle the transfer of arms from European countries, not from Russia. Moreover, they took special pains to avoid compromising the Soviet government, placing this organization under the aegis of the Comintern. In sum, the order for the arms transfer was probably a preliminary and subsidiary action. Another month was to elapse before Moscow resolved to send Soviet arms to Spain, a move accompanied by a public threat to withdraw from the Non-Intervention Committee if German and Italian shipments of arms and men to the Spanish rebels did not cease. Similarly, the decision to organize the "International Brigades" for Spain, in which the French Communists were to play an active role, was not taken until the end of September.[52] The Soviet leaders were avoiding action which might present risks for their country. But they were allowing the French party to run considerable risks, both for itself and for the Popular Front coalition. In the campaign begun in early September, the party leaders put aside their previous concern for French unity and their promise of loyal support to the government. Later, only the threat of the dissolution of the coalition would cause them to moderate their action. For the first time, they were organizing the metallurgical workers for a strike movement whose sole aim was to support a political campaign for aid to Spain. They were beginning a major political battle.

Their campaign was conducted primarily by the labor unions, in particular by the Association of Metallurgical Unions of the Paris Region. The first important move was the one-hour sit-down strike on September 7. Prior to this, the Association had sent a delegation to the Premier to offer "total support" for "any action aimed at aiding the legal government of Spain" and at raising the embargo. Blum replied in effect

[52] Thomas, pp. 263, 295–98. For interpretations of the cause of Soviet intervention in the Spanish Civil War, see Armstrong, pp. 38–39; Kennan, pp. 290–91; David Cattell, *Soviet Diplomacy and the Spanish Civil War*, pp. 32–37.

that his Spanish policy was none of their business.[53] Apparently some workers felt the same way, for the strike on September 7 was accompanied by confusion and discord. The figures published by the Minister of the Interior indicated that from 80 to 85 per cent of the metallurgical workers participated. Yet one non-Communist member of the union described the movement as a "masterpiece of disorganization." Disputes broke out between supporters and opponents of the nonintervention policy. Other workers went along with no idea why they were striking. "Two or three more experiments like this one," concluded the non-Communist, "and we shall say good-bye to our 200,000 members." [54] The Spanish issue was not so clear-cut as the Communist leaders presented it. A good case could be made for avoiding involvement. The evening before the strike, Blum had argued this case at length in his speech at Luna Park in Paris. Many of the Paris Socialists apparently felt the strength—or the emotional appeal—of his argument; many of the Paris metallurgical workers may well have sympathized with him as well.

But the Communist leaders, far from halting their campaign, kept up the pressure. Communist-controlled unions began sporadic strikes, whose justification was as much political as economic. Many workers had reason enough to wish to take action, for prices had already begun a sharp rise and layoffs had started hitting certain factories where the management was unable, or unwilling, to cope with the new welfare and wage expenses. The French economy generally was still in the doldrums. Yet the resulting worker agitation was accentuated by Communist action. According to one non-Communist member of the CGT Executive Committee, the Communist factory cells were "inciting" the workers to strike "in

[53] Quoted in *Le Temps*, September 7, 1936.
[54] *La Révolution prolétarienne*, No. 231 (September 25, 1936), pp. 11-12.

order to exercise considerable pressure on the government." [55]
Consequently, there were more sit-down strikes in September
than in any other month in 1936 save May and June. The
CGT leadership tried to exercise some control over the movement, warning all union members on September 18 "against
agents provocateurs who too often, under clever disguises,
incite them to impulsive acts which only result in condemna-
tions against themselves and against the regime." [56] But the
strikes continued.

Nonetheless, the Communist leaders found that social agitation in no way increased their political power within the
coalition. The government held resolutely to the nonintervention policy, turning a blind eye to the increasingly large secret
shipments of goods to the belligerents. Blum received the
support of most of the Socialists, and probably of the great
majority of all Frenchmen. Within the Delegation of the
Left, the Communists were in complete isolation on the Spanish question. When pressed during a meeting on September 9
to define his party's attitude toward the government, Thorez
declared that the Communist deputies would continue to vote
for the Blum cabinet. Two weeks later, they supported the
decision to devaluate the franc. They had no other choice,
since a hostile vote on their part would have meant the fall of
the government. Though the party leaders had promised
many times previously to defend the franc of the "common
people," they considered the survival of the Popular Front
coalition more important than this internal issue. Powerless to
alter the course of French politics, they fell back on demagoguery to justify their policies and to restore their damaged
prestige. Thorez explained in a speech on October 3 that

[55] Delmas, pp. 118–19.
[56] *Le Populaire*, September 19, 1936. This communiqué was never
published in *L'Humanité*, despite a direct request from Jouhaux that
it be inserted.

the Communist deputies had voted for devaluation only to avoid "a split in the Popular Front . . . , a change which would be a step toward fascism." He accused the government of "weaknesses, insufficiencies, even capitulations to the enemies of the people," and called for a more energetic reform program.[57] In the following days, Communist orators and newspapers throughout France echoed this theme.

Soon, the Communist leadership discovered that the use of political strikes threatened its relations with the Radical party. Protests from the CGT and Socialist leaders had no apparent moderating effect on its tactics, but Radical complaints did. Anticommunism had been stirred up among the Radicals by the suspected Communist role in the strikes and by the Communist campaign against nonintervention. By October it had become a "forceful mystique." [58] The national Radical congress was scheduled for the end of the month. Weeks before, Radical leaders began publicly warning the Communist party that the continuation of social agitation might result in a political crisis.

The Communist leaders responded to these comments, for they feared above all things a break with the Radical party. Rumors started to appear in *L'Humanité* in early October to the effect that the coming congress would recommend the withdrawal of the Radical ministers from the government, a sure prelude to a new shift of the party to the right. Once again the Communist party had to choose between the workers and the Radicals. Repeating their performance in June and

---

[57] *L'Humanité*, October 7, 1936; if one may believe the American Secretary of the Treasury, Henry Morgenthau, the Soviet government tried indirectly to sabotage the complicated financial operation behind the devaluation by dumping British pounds on the international money market (J. Blum, *From the Morgenthau Diaries* [Boston, 1959], pp. 173–75). If this is true, the Soviet leaders were obviously trying already to break the Franco-British *entente*.

[58] Larmour, pp. 214–15.

July, the Communists opted for the latter. The word went out in mid-October that strike action was to be discouraged. On October 17, the Central Committee was called together to hear Thorez emphasize the need to end the strikes in order to block "attempts" to use social unrest as an excuse to split the Popular Front.[59] Whether thanks to Communist control over the workers or to the natural unwillingness of the workers to occupy unheated factories in cold, rainy autumn weather, the strikes did virtually disappear by the end of October. The Radical congress saw quite a bit of anti-Communist oratory plus a real effort to expel the Communists from the coalition. But the delegates finally decided to continue their allegiance to the Popular Front. Communist relations with the Radical party were safe for the time being.

But the Communist leaders had not abandoned their campaign against the Blum cabinet; they had merely shifted the center of their attention from the social to the parliamentary arena. The Spanish issue was still uppermost in their minds. Their concern was certainly tied in with that of the Soviet government, more preoccupied with aid to the Spanish Republic in the last months of 1936 than it had been before and than it would ever be afterward. Large shipments of Russian military equipment began arriving in Republican Spain at the end of October, in time for the Battle of Madrid. The Soviet delegate to the Non-Intervention Committee implied that his country might withdraw from the Committee if other states continued to ship arms to Spain—a threat not carried out probably because, as in the case of the French Communists and the Radicals, the Soviet leaders felt that weak ties with France and England were worth more than open conflict over Spain.[60] They still continued to pour large amounts of war matériel into Spain, and the French Communist party pursued its attempts to reverse its country's policy of nonintervention.

[59] *L'Humanité*, October 18, 1936.   [60] Thomas, p. 310.

This time, the French Communist leaders sought nothing less than the fall of the Blum cabinet. They began their assault at a meeting on November 12 of the Delegation of the Left. The Communist delegates proposed a motion condemning French neutrality in the Spanish conflict and calling for arms shipments to the Republicans, then, failing to receive support from the others, refused to support any substitute motion. The Delegation was, for the first time, deadlocked.[61] A few days later, a Communist deputy made an official demand for general discussion in the Chamber on the question of "French foreign policy." The debate was set for early December. In late November, Léon Blum himself was forced to take note of the Communist campaign. At a meeting in Paris on November 27 organized by the Paris *Rassemblement populaire* Committee, the air was filled with cries of "Blum into Action!" and "Planes for Spain!" The Premier, one of the speakers that evening, acknowledged the attacks by stating that "the government of the Popular Front . . . cannot and will not live unless the parties and organizations belonging to the Popular Front remain united in its support." If it lost the confidence of one of the member parties, it would "cease to exist." [62] Blum clearly implied that he would resign if he felt the Communists were strongly opposed to his policies. Two days later, Thorez took up the challenge. He declared in a public speech that his party could never approve a policy of nonintervention in Spain since it was "contrary to the interests of our people." He stressed that *"the fate of the Popular Front is not restricted to the survival of one cabinet."* He expressed the certainty that a Popular Front cabinet could be found "with men applying resolutely the policies wished by the masses." [63]

---

[61] *Le Temps*, November 14, 1936.

[62] *Le Populaire*, November 30, 1936.

[63] *L'Humanité*, November 30, 1936. The italicized passage was prudently left out of this first account of the speech, but was filled in two days later "just for the record."

He was in effect inviting Blum to live up to his promise by resigning.

It is virtually impossible to discover the identity of the men whom Thorez wished to become the policy-makers. Supporters of aid to the Spanish Republicans existed in both the Socialist and Radical parties, but few had the stature to assume leadership of the French cabinet. The most likely candidate appears to be Edouard Daladier. President of the Radical party, a moving force within the Popular Front, he had long received the support of the Communist party. Though he, as Minister of National Defense, was one of the three most important members of the Blum Cabinet, his name was conspicuously absent from Communist attacks on the "Blum-Delbos Government." The Communist leaders, if one may judge by two isolated comments by Gabriel Péri, seem seriously to have thought that Daladier favored intervention in Spain. In late November, Péri wrote that "various sources" had assured him that there were in the Ministry of National Defense "very serious critics who share our worries [for the security of the country]." [64] Much later, after the Radical leader had become a lost cause, Péri bitterly remarked that "there was a time when M. Daladier . . . swore by all the gods that he had subscribed to this policy [of nonintervention] only grudgingly. He asserted that it was criminal to tolerate the Italo-German intervention." [65] In reality, opinion at the time differed as to where Daladier stood on the Spanish question. A recent study indicates that a number of Radicals thought him a supporter of the Republicans.[66] The Communist leaders may have been mistaken in their estimation of Daladier, but they at least were not alone in their opinion.

They did not even have the opportunity to test their ideas

---

[64] *Ibid.*, November 24, 1936.   [65] *Ibid.*, November 1, 1938.
[66] Larmour, pp. 207 and 292, n. 36.

for a new French government, for the Chamber debate on foreign policy did not turn out at all as they had expected. Both Thorez and Péri spoke on the first day of discussion, December 4, attacking the Premier and his Minister of Foreign Affairs Yvon Delbos for endangering the peace by appeasing the fascist powers. In the last speech the next day, Jacques Duclos proclaimed that his party should vote against the government, but would not in order to "leave the future open for a resolute shift in French policy toward the defense of peace." [67] The vote of confidence that followed gave 350 votes for the government, 174 against, and 78 abstentions, including all 72 Communist deputies. The Communist leaders had probably chosen abstention believing that it indicated a sufficient lack of confidence in Blum's policies without splitting the coalition. But their expectations of a cabinet crisis were very quickly disappointed. The coalition leaders decided immediately after the vote that Communist expressions of continued fidelity to the Popular Front should be accepted and the act of abstaining overlooked, since the missing Communist votes had been replaced by a roughly equivalent number of votes from the moderates. The cabinet did not resign. The events of December 5 had proved only that the Communist party was virtually powerless in parliament.

At that moment, the Communist leaders beat a hasty retreat. They minimized the abstention as a "passing disagreement" and expressed their confidence in the policies of the Blum cabinet. Their reaction indicated that political unity in parliament remained for them an absolute imperative. However, they were less willing to recognize the need for unity in the country, particularly with the Socialist party. They had obviously not forgotten their traditional goal of using united front tactics to undermine the support of the Socialist leaders

[67] *JO, Débats, Chambre,* No. 98 (December 6, 1936), pp. 3372–74.

among the masses. In the last months of 1936, Communist speakers took advantage of joint meetings with local Socialist organizations to attack the policies of the Socialist ministers, while Communist cells strove to attract Socialists in united action for aid to Spain, more reforms, and other projects opposed by the government. The campaign was not brought to a halt until one Socialist federation had in late December withdrawn from the departmental *Rassemblement populaire* Committee. Rather than risk a dispute which would certainly harm their relations with the Radicals, the Communist leaders stopped the attacks on the Socialists. Though they no longer appeared to care much for the fate of the United Front, they still desired to keep the Popular Front alive, in the country as in parliament.

The first seven months of power had revealed that the Popular Front was in certain respects more, in other respects less, a success than the Communists had hoped. It had struck a responsive chord in French society, as the elections and even the wave of sit-down strikes had shown. The strike movement was very much a product of the Popular Front. It could never have begun had not the left-wing electoral victory demoralized management and made the Sarraut government unwilling to use force against the strikers. It would not have spread so widely and so rapidly had the workers not felt that the creation of a Popular Front government meant victory was on their side. Their enthusiasm was so great that it soon forced the Communist leaders to withdraw their support. In a sense, thus, the Popular Front was too successful. Still, the Communist party benefited greatly by the new tactics in terms of expanded membership and electoral support. The identification of its interests with the popular desire for reform was more rewarding in the short run than its revolutionary program. On the other hand, it was forced to accept the inner logic of the Popular Front as a political coalition. Unity de-

11. The captured fortress: the Renault factory after the explusion by the police of occupying workers, November, 1938. (*Illustrated London News.*)

12. The makings of a riot: workers during the Clichy violence, March, 1937. (*L'Illustration.*)

pended on the acceptance of common policies, at least on important issues. The Communist leaders found themselves no less bound by this rule than the others. They had the further disadvantage of having excluded themselves from policy-making by their decision to stay out of the cabinet. Their sole advantage was that they could dissociate themselves more easily from responsibility for unpopular policies. But this was scant consolation for their inability to influence French foreign policy.

By the end of 1936, events in France and elsewhere had indicated that the popular front tactics were of limited applicability within the Communist International. The difficulties of the Spanish Popular Front suggested that these tactics were suited only for advanced democratic regimes in which there existed a consensus on the permanency of basic institutions and on the government's right to enact political and social reforms. The "Frente Popular" threatened the hopes of the reactionaries for a restoration of the old order by promising to strengthen the Republic and improve the lot of the masses. The continued power of the monarchists, the great landowners, the Church, and the army made the outbreak of civil war possible, even probable. The fact that the Spanish Communists thereafter assumed a major role in the Popular Front government does not mean that they were more successful than the French Communists. Their power was due to their ability to conduct a war fairly efficiently and even more to the importance of Soviet military aid. But this activity was a distortion of the popular front tactics and was made necessary only because these tactics had not worked as planned. Indeed, one might conclude that the Comintern committed a grave error in encouraging the creation of a popular front in a country neither socially nor politically ready for such a radical political formation. The Spanish Civil War immensely complicated Comintern activities and Soviet foreign policy.

Even in countries with strong democratic traditions, the popular front tactics had produced mediocre results. Political coalitions between Communist and other left-wing parties had been formed only in France, Spain, and Chile. In most advanced countries, the Communists were as isolated politically as before, though their reformist program and tactics had frequently won greater popular support. The French Popular Front, with all its limitations, was a comparatively successful, and at the same time exceptional experience in the international Communist movement.

VI

The Year of Deception

The French Communist party was much more effective as
the embodiment of certain political aspirations of Frenchmen
than as an instrument of Soviet foreign policy. Soviet interests
benefited hardly at all by the action of the French Communists. The party itself, on the other hand, flourished. As a
result of the united and popular front tactics, it had begun to
play an active role in local and national politics. By 1937, it
held over a tenth of the seats in the Chamber of Deputies, had
two senators, controlled a considerable number of municipalities, and, following the cantonal elections of October, 1937,
sent a large group of councillors to the departmental councils.
As it came to occupy a large place in the political life of the
country, its character changed. Its officials appeared to adjust
well to the life of politicians concerned with day-to-day business and with the intricate personal and institutional relations
of a complex society. Its greatly expanded membership reflected more than before the social diversity of France. Encouraged by the party's patriotic and even nationalistic
propaganda, many members believed that there was no contradiction between being good Communists and good French
patriots. Not only had the popular front tactics altered the
party's activities, they had changed the party itself.

"Loyal Support"

After the failure in December of the campaign against
Blum, the Communist leaders apparently reconciled them-

selves to the continued existence of the cabinet. The Premier benefited from their "loyal support" in parliament until he was forced out of office in June. The party did occasionally pursue disruptive campaigns in defense of the workers' interests, but in an erratic manner and for short periods of time. It ceased its action against nonintervention in Spain, and most of the time left the labor unions to their own business. Its policy reflected more frequently than not the point of view expressed by Marcel Gitton in early February. Gitton declared that his party would certainly like to see Blum "re-establish commercial freedom with Republican Spain"; still, "the present government . . . is the government that we desired." [1]

Serious difficulties did nonetheless arise with the Blum cabinet. They were the result of the financial crisis of the French state, which periodically lacked sufficient funds to pay the tremendous public debt. They were compounded by the weakness of the French economy, evidenced particularly by the inflationary rise in prices. By February, 1937, the increased cost of living had absorbed all the wage benefits granted the workers since mid-1936. But for the government, funding the public debt and protecting private investment seemed of more immediate importance than stimulating production and consumption. In mid-February, Blum called for a "pause" in wage increases for French workers and civil servants, then, in early March, sought to attract investment funds back into France by freeing the sale of gold, promising a budgetary policy of austerity, and other measures. The Communist leaders grudgingly accepted the "pause," but they protested against the March measures of financial orthodoxy. Their attitude was determined apparently by the fear that these measures heralded an abandonment of the alliance of the working and middle classes in the Popular Front in favor of

[1] *L'Humanité*, February 4, 1937.

the capitalists. They launched a new campaign for the complete application of the reform program of the Popular Front. On March 9, Thorez declared his party the defender of the masses who "will not let themselves be despoiled." He implied that the party leadership once again sanctioned strikes as one means of protecting the "vital needs" of the workers.[2] The party also picked up its struggle against "fascism," directing its attacks primarily against the French Social party of Colonel de la Rocque and the French Popular party, founded in 1936 by Jacques Doriot. The Clichy section of the Social party had planned for March 16 a private film showing in its suburb just outside Paris. The Communists seized on the opportunity to call the Paris workers to express their opposition to alleged fascist agitation in France.

The workers of Clichy, as of the neighboring suburbs, were among the most radical in France. In the late winter of 1937, their mood was bitter as a result of the rising cost of living and the evident weakness of the Blum cabinet. The political leadership of the town, divided between Communists and Socialists, decided to hold a joint counterdemonstration during the meeting of the French Social party to protest against the "fascist invasion of Clichy." The leaders cooperated with the Paris Police Prefect and the Minister of the Interior in preparing a route which would lead the demonstrators away from the movie theater where the followers of La Rocque gathered, and in front of which a police barricade was set up. But something went wrong. A crowd of some 8,000 people marched in the counterdemonstration that evening. The head of the procession, led by local Socialist and Communist officials, did get by the theater without incident, but not the last group of demonstrators; according to Léon Blum, it was cut off by "certain unidentified groups" and forced back upon

[2] *Ibid.*, March 10, 1937.

the barricade.[3] Fighting broke out between the demonstrators and the police, spreading quickly to the surrounding area. The violence redoubled when police reinforcements arrived. The demonstrators were armed with anything they could find, while the police made ample use of their firearms. Before the fighting was over, hundreds of police and demonstrators had been wounded, and six demonstrators were dead or dying of their wounds.[4] The social calm which the government had sought to achieve by proclaiming the "pause" was destroyed.

How did it all come about? No one has been able to answer this question. Léon Blum never explained what he described as the "obscure and mysterious point": the cause for the diversion of a part of the demonstrators away from the procession toward the police barricade.[5] At the time, the Communists and many Socialists maintained that the violence was a spontaneous outburst of worker discontent, ignited by "fascist provocations" and aggravated by police brutality. Others accused the Communists of secretly fomenting the fight in order to prevent the Blum cabinet from establishing good relations with French and foreign capitalists. The Communist leaders had certainly called for a heightened struggle against fascism a few days earlier, but there is no proof of intervention on their part that evening. Certainly a great deal of bloodshed later in the riot was the result of chaos and blind anger. Still, the origin of the disturbance suggests provocation by someone. An administrative report on the events was made but its results were never published. In early May, the Under-Secre-

[3] Report by Blum to the Socialist group in the Chamber on March 19, in *Le Temps*, March 20, 1937.

[4] The best firsthand accounts of the Clichy riot can be found in *Le Temps*, March 18, 1937; *Le Populaire*, March 17, 1937; *La République*, March 17, 1937.

[5] Speech before the Socialist National Council, April 13, in *Le Populaire*, April 14, 1937; see also his speech on March 23 to the Chamber, *JO, Débats, Chambre*, No. 33 (March 24, 1937), p. 1200.

tary of the Interior, the Radical Raoul Aubaud, affirmed that he "knew well . . . the secrets [*dessous*]" of the Clichy affair; he could not reveal "the names of the responsible persons" but did declare that "their aim was above all to weaken the authority and the prestige of parliament." [6] His sybilline declaration at least made clear that the cabinet believed some group responsible for the outbreak of the riot.

The Communists had no doubt that, as *L'Humanité* proclaimed in big headlines the day after the riot, it was all a "PLOT AGAINST THE PEOPLE" and part of "the offensive of the trusts." The newspaper demanded that the "fascists," La Rocque and Doriot, be put in prison and the "trusts" put in their place by the "complete application of the program of the Popular Front." In a speech on March 17, Thorez protested that "the government has shown too much weakness toward the enemies of the people." [7] His interpretation made Clichy very much a political affair.

The workers were called out to demonstrate their indignation. They were certainly angry at the events of March 16, which they blamed on the "cops" and fascist *provocateurs*. Their discontent did produce some sporadic demonstrations and a few short strikes. But the Communist-controlled Association of Labor Unions of the Paris Region itself organized a half-day strike on March 18. It justified the action by the need to "calm the indignation of the workers and to avoid a movement of spontaneous strikes." Jouhaux and the CGT leadership had supported the idea of an afternoon strike which would leave the transportation system unaffected. A public announcement by the Communist union leaders that the strike would come in the morning and would include both the buses and the subway forced the abandonment of these plans. [8] The

---

[6] Quoted in *Le Temps*, May 4, 1937.
[7] *L'Humanité*, March 18, 1937.   [8] Delmas, pp. 127–29.

Communists desired—and obtained—a temporary but total disruption of the economy of the city. The union leaders maintained that the strike was not directed against the government, "which must remain in power to act." [9] Their call for action squared poorly, however, with a policy of collaboration with "finance capital." In fact, the Clichy riot and the disturbances which followed provoked a sharp fall on the Bourse of French stocks and bonds and frightened away foreign investors. The Communist agitation, whether intentionally or not, contributed to the partial failure of the government's financial policies.

In parliament, on the other hand, the Communist leadership continued to place coalition unity above all else. It had expressed the desire immediately after Clichy to demand the dissolution of the Social and Popular parties and the arrest of their leaders. Its position received no support at all. Further, its campaign for more reforms was sharply attacked. Edouard Daladier, in a speech on March 21, declared that government initiatives were limited by the "possibilities of the French economy, which at the present time demands above all an increase in production." Implying that Radical desires had better be heeded, he warned that if his party withdrew its support, the Popular Front "could not endure." [10] By the time the Clichy question was brought before the Chamber on March 23, the Communist leaders had ceased their agitation. Jacques Duclos himself presented for the majority the motion of confidence in the government's handling of the riot. The campaign against fascism disappeared from the headlines of Communist newspapers, as did demands for the complete application of the Popular Front reform program.

But the problem of worker agitation continued to disturb Communist relations with the other members of the Popular

---

[9] *L'Humanité*, March 18, 1937.   [10] *L'Oeuvre*, March 22, 1937.

Front. Clichy was the signal for a wave of strikes, sporadic and apparently uncoordinated, in widely separated parts of the country. Discontent among the workers was sufficient to explain the origin of most of the strikes. Those which repeatedly hit the construction site of the World's Fair in Paris, and for which the Communists were frequently blamed, seem to have been due mostly to the instability of the employment of the workers. Their job completed, they knew very well they would go back to the enforced leisure of unemployment, the fate of the greater part of the workers in the crisis-ridden building trades. Publicly, the Communists called for the rapid completion of the Fair. Yet at the same time, in this and other centers of agitation, they took sides with the strikers and defended the workers' demands.

In certain strikes, party members must have gone even further, must have organized and led the action by methods perhaps similar to those used on March 18. Even the conciliatory Léon Jouhaux was upset. He warned at a meeting on April 13 of the National Council of the CGT that the working-class movement must not be used for purposes harmful to it or to the government of the Popular Front. In words stronger than any he had ever used before, he attacked what he called "a sort of daily repetition of a certain strategy by which certain elements seek to obtain the necessary knowledge for a hypothetical action." Unfortunately, Jouhaux, as was his custom, gave no details. He concluded simply that "it is indispensable that the discipline laid out by the CGT be observed by everyone." [11] He hoped devoutly to preserve the unity of the labor confederation, but even his patience had limits.

The Communist leaders were no more desirous of seeing a scission in the CGT than in the Popular Front. They immedi-

[11] *Syndicats*, April 22, 1937.

ately joined the chorus of voices warning the workers against
the effects upon the nation of "permanent unrest" and "rash
acts." Their union leaders intervened personally to prevent
strikes, though at times without success. The collective contracts for French industry were due to expire on May 31.
When the question of their renewal was brought up in early
May before the CGT leadership, Benoît Frachon joined the
others in accepting an automatic prolongation of the contracts
to avoid trouble with management. All that the government
requested, the Communist leaders seemed ready to grant. A
Socialist delegate to the Delegation of the Left remarked on
May 8 that they "at this very moment accept the 'pause' with
a sort of self-sacrifice." [12] A month later, Thorez even boasted
that the presence of his party in the majority "makes possible
the governmental stability," since it "does not indulge in the
game of ministerial massacre." [13] Party policy was still ori-
ented around the principle of "loyal support."

It is tempting to see the hand of Moscow guiding the
moderate policies of the French Communist party. In truth,
however, nothing is known of the relations in 1937 between
the French party and the Comintern. Fried was still in Paris,
but no information is available on the precise role he was then
playing. It is quite possible that the French leaders enjoyed a
large degree of autonomy in the making of day-to-day policy
decisions. One might thus see in their political moderation
evidence of their increasing political experience and sophistication. Their relations with the other members of the coalition
were correct and in certain cases even cordial. The one in-
veterate agitator, André Marty, was out of the country, busy
as an organizer of the International Brigades in Spain. The
remaining leaders—Thorez, Duclos, Gitton, and Frachon—

[12] Quoted in *Le Temps*, May 9, 1937.
[13] *L'Humanité*, June 12, 1937.

seem to have been content with their parliamentary reformist activity. Yet they remained above all disciplined officials within the Communist International. On an issue as important as relations with the Popular Front government, their actions had to follow policy guidelines laid down in Moscow.

Clues as to factors influencing Comintern instructions to the French party are rare. Only in the memoirs of Robert Coulondre, appointed French ambassador to the Soviet Union in late 1936, can one find mention of specific action taken which might have affected French Communist tactics. Coulondre accomplished a most unusual diplomatic mission immediately upon arriving in Moscow in early November. He had been charged by his government to warn Stalin of the grave consequences which continued Communist agitation in France could have on Franco-Soviet relations. He succeeded in communicating his message to the remote dictator. Stalin's answer was that the French government should be "strong and resolute with relation to [*face à*] Germany. Beyond this, it may conduct its internal affairs as it wishes." Using an example which would not have reassured the French Communists, he pointed out that the Soviet state had good relations with Turkey despite the fact that the Turkish Communist party was oppressed by its government. But to Coulondre's suggestion that the Soviet Union break its ties with the Comintern, he answered simply that the international Communist organization was "needed against Germany" as a factor in the "national defense" of the U.S.S.R.[14] There is no way of knowing whether or not Coulondre's initiative had any effect on the policies of the French Communist party.

It is even questionable whether the Soviet leader actually cared much for the fate of the Comintern as a whole. The Great Purge had already begun by late 1936 and increased in

[14] Robert Coulondre, *De Staline à Hitler*, pp. 31–40.

intensity throughout the first half of 1937. Despite Stalin's statement that the Comintern was useful in combating Germany, its Moscow organization was branded a "nest of spies" and was decimated by extensive arrests.[15] In the confusion that resulted, it is possible that no one paid much attention to the policies of the foreign Communist parties; perhaps these parties were simply called on to continue applying their long-standing policies. For the French party, this would have meant support of the Popular Front.

Perhaps, on the other hand, French Communist backing of the Blum cabinet was the result of a pondered policy decision in Moscow. French tactics were after all somewhat special, since they were closely associated with Soviet foreign policy. The Soviet leaders probably still valued their alliance with France sufficiently not to wish to jeopardize their relations with the French government. They were certainly more and more dissatisfied with French foreign policy. The clearest expression of their discontent came in an article in *Izvestiia* published on May 2, 1937, second anniversary of the signing of the Franco-Soviet pact. Using the example of the policy of nonintervention, the anonymous author accused the French of uniting with the British in seeking a "deal with the aggressor," that is, Germany. The Soviet Union, for its part, needed "neither pacts nor any kind of guarantees nor even collective security in general"; it could count upon its "strong" Red Army (the disastrous purge of the army was about to begin!) to assure the "annihilation of attackers." In effect, the Soviet leaders were warning the French that they were willing and able to do without the pact. Maxim Litvinov had first sounded

[15] Testimony of a Comintern official then in Moscow, Alfred Burmeister, *Dissolution and Aftermath of the Comintern: Experiences and Observations, 1937–47* (New York, 1955), pp. 3–5; see also Lazitch, "Stalin's Massacre of the Foreign Communist Leaders," Drachkovitch, pp. 139–74.

this theme in a speech in late November, 1936; certain of his statements were even reproduced in the May *Izvestiia* article.

Another indication that the course taken by French foreign policy did not please the Russians had been provided by Stalin's report to the Soviet Communist Central Committee in early March, 1937. The General Secretary had taken as his text the dogma of the "capitalist encirclement" of the Socialist fatherland. Making no distinction between democratic and fascist regimes, he had declared flatly that all capitalist countries were "waiting for an opportunity to attack it [the Soviet Union], . . . or at any rate to undermine its power and weaken it." [16] It appeared that Stalin rated the French Republic no higher than the Third Reich. Taken at face value, these statements suggested that the Soviet Union was moving from a foreign policy based on collective security to one of isolationism.

It is more likely, however, that the Soviet leaders meant their warnings to be read in Paris as mild threats of future action if the French did not mend their ways. One biographer of Litvinov has interpreted the Foreign Commissar's warnings to the French in 1936 and 1937 as "a reflection of a decision still in suspension in the Politburo, a forewarning of a course . . . which was in the cards if collective security failed." [17] Even Stalin's harsh statements to the Central Committee were given a moderate interpretation in an article in the Soviet theoretical journal *Bol'shevik*, written—significantly—by the Comintern leader Dimitry Manuilsky. He explained that the "capitalist encirclement" was the work of the "aggressive" fascist countries; the bourgeois parliamentary countries, on the contrary, showed a "readiness for friendly co-operation" with the Soviet Union. He then proceeded to defend the

[16] *Pravda*, March 29, 1937.
[17] Henry Roberts, "Maxim Litvinov," in G. Craig and F. Gilbert (eds.), *The Diplomats, 1919–1939* (Princeton, 1953), II, 373.

Soviet policy of collective security, the Comintern tactics of the united front, and even the moderation shown that spring by the French Communist party.[18] What Manuilsky was saying, in sum, was that Stalin's speech signified no change in either Soviet foreign policy or Comintern tactics.

The Soviet leaders had good reason to moderate the tactics of the French party. They had been held responsible for the social and political campaigns against the Blum cabinet. These aggressive policies had not produced satisfactory results and were, moreover, threatening good Franco-Soviet relations. Soviet interests lay therefore on the side of French Communist moderation and support of the Blum cabinet.

In June, 1937, the French Communist party extended even further its commitment to the government. Its immediate goal was to forestall the introduction of unpopular governmental policies. A new financial crisis had developed as the result of a sharp decline in the value of the franc on the international money market and new payments due on the state debt. On June 14, the government took the extreme measure of requesting approval by parliament of exceptional and virtually unlimited financial powers. Opposition came both from the conservatives, who feared higher income taxes and controls on foreign exchange, and from the Communists, who had wind of the cabinet's intention to raise indirect taxes. Shortly before the Chamber met on June 15 to consider the request, the Communist deputies issued a special announcement. They declared themselves unable to support the special financial powers, which would "compromise the attachment of the masses to the Popular Front"; they were ready, however, to "assume all the responsibilities in a reinforced government formed in the likeness of the Popular Front." [19] Without specifically

[18] "O kapitalisticheskom okruzhenii [Concerning the Capitalist Encirclement]," *Bol'shevik*, May, 1937, pp. 25–34.
[19] *L'Humanité*, June 16, 1937.

saying so, they were offering to participate in a coalition government similar to that proposed by Blum in May, 1936, on condition the government alter its financial policies.

In the circumstances, their offer was irrelevant and insignificant. The principal fight was between the conservatives and the government. The Communist leaders later admitted that no one had paid much attention to their proposal. Blum wanted Communist support on his terms, and said so during the debate in the Chamber. He stressed the fact that his cabinet was engaged in a struggle against an "assault of Finance." He had been faithful to the alliance with the Communist party, resisting the "secret pressures" for the exclusion of the Communists from the majority in return for "unlimited aid and co-operation [*toutes les commodités et toutes les facilités*]." Implicit in his statement was the warning that Communist opposition might lead to a shift in the majority to the right.[20] His words were effective. The General Secretary of the Comintern himself had two weeks earlier put the party on its guard against the "intrigues" of the "reactionaries" who sought a new right-wing government.[21] At the very end of the Chamber debate, the Communist deputies switched their position and voted along with the Socialists and Radicals for the government's proposal.

But the most difficult obstacle to enactment of the special powers was the Senate, the bastion of conservatism in the French state. The Senators had recovered by then from their fright of mid-1936 and were in no mood to accept radical financial measures from a Socialist-led cabinet. By June 20, it was apparent that their opposition was insurmountable; the resignation of the government was in the air. That evening, Jacques Duclos and Marcel Gitton personally assured Léon

[20] *JO, Débats, Chambre*, No. 53 (June 16, 1937), pp. 1980–81.
[21] George Dimitrov, "L'Unité de la Classe ouvrière," *L'Humanité*, May 2, 1937.

Blum of their party's "unconditional support" and "advised against the resignation of the government." [22] But they could offer no practical solution to the financial crisis. For Blum, the question was between resignation or a continued fight with the Senate followed, if unsuccessful, by the dissolution of the Chamber and new elections. His Radical ministers threatened, however, to withdraw from the cabinet if he persisted in opposing the Senate. He therefore tendered on June 21 the resignation of his government. [23]

The Chautemps Deception

The Communist leaders were clearly worried that the cabinet crisis would lead to their expulsion from the parliamentary majority. On the morning of June 21, *L'Humanité* proclaimed in big headlines that "THE COUNTRY DEMANDS A GOVERNMENT OF THE POPULAR FRONT AND NONE OTHER!" Three days later, Thorez was even more specific, warning in a speech in Paris that "the people of Paris will not permit a regression [*un retour en arrière*] which the financial oligarchy would like to force upon us." He reminded his audience that "if Paris, as a result of political centralization, dominates France, the workers dominate Paris in moments of unrest." [24] The Parisian proletariat was in Communist eyes a potent political force.

But the party also continued to offer its cooperation in government affairs. It repeated its proposal to delegate representatives to participate in the cabinet, and emphasized that it was on the side of "order" in the state and the country. But its

[22] *Ibid.*, June 23, 1937.

[23] Details on the resignation were given in a letter by Blum's Finance Minister Vincent Auriol in *L'Express*, No. 536 (September 21, 1961), p. 2; see also Colton, pp. 272–76.

[24] *L'Humanité*, June 25, 1937.

suggestions were ignored. Camille Chautemps, designated on June 21 to form the next cabinet, told Gitton and Duclos that "the time had not come" for Communists to enter the cabinet. Making the best of the Radical rebuff, Gitton declared later that "participation must not be made a question of prestige." His party was content to support a Popular Front government "even if we do not participate in it." [25] Chautemps did decide to retain the left-wing majority, in large part because the Socialists were adamant in resisting any "shift away from the formation of the Popular Front." [26] Their wishes, not those of the Communists, carried real political weight.

Once the Chautemps cabinet was in power, the Communist leaders resumed their policy of "loyal support." They had even more reason than before to do so. The Comintern leadership feared that the Chautemps cabinet "would inevitably form a transition to a reactionary right-wing government" unless the "political and organic cohesion in the Popular Front" be preserved.[27] It still viewed support of the Popular Front as the only viable policy for the French party. Then, too, Chautemps might seek to strengthen Franco-Soviet ties, a tradition of the Radical party earlier. The French Communists therefore went out of their way to support the new cabinet. They accepted with only a token protest Chautemps's orthodox financial measures of devaluation, budgetary restrictions, and higher taxes. They refused to associate themselves with the Socialist campaign against the Senate which developed in late June and July.

The party redoubled its efforts to assure social calm and stimulate higher production. Thorez told the workers in late

<hr>

[25] *Le Temps*, June 23, 1937.
[26] Declaration by the Socialist National Council, in *Le Populaire*, June 23, 1937.
[27] "Deux Ans de Lutte pour le Front populaire antifasciste," *Internationale*, September, 1937, p. 810.

July that they could "more and more identify their own
material and political interests with the cause of democracy
and of the Republic." [28] Government modifications of the
forty-hour week, taken to open certain bottlenecks in the
French economy, were quietly supported, though the Communist union leaders had earlier declared the forty-hour week
untouchable. Raymond Froidval, non-Communist Secretary
of the Federation of Building Trades, noted at the end of
October that the Communists in the unions had called on the
workers for "calm and discipline" and had denounced efforts
to start strikes as the work of "enemies of the people." Demands made in July for pay increases for the metallurgical and
building-trades workers of the Paris region were not pushed.
"Despite the dissatisfaction [among the workers] and the long
wait, there has been no [strike] movement . . . because it was
not desired." [29] Chautemps was being given even more support
than Blum earlier.

Perhaps part of the explanation for Communist moderation
was also, as Froideval suggested, the desire of the party leaders
to make the cantonal elections of October an electoral
triumph. Social restraint was necessary if a large number of
votes were to be won. The Communist party spared no efforts
during the electoral campaign and presented more candidates
to the district (*arrondissement*) and departmental councils
than any other party. The issues defended by its candidates
were no different from earlier campaigns, running the gamut
from "the defense of the old people" and aid for peasants to
the "union of France." The Communist leaders were trying to
repeat their formula for success used so effectively in the
national elections of 1936.

The first ballot of the cantonal elections, held on October
10, was a manner of victory for the Popular Front. While the

[28] "Toujours unis," *L'Humanité*, July 25, 1937.
[29] *Syndicats*, October 28, 1937.

significance of the myriad of local elections was in fact very small in regard to national questions, a picture was obtained of the over-all electoral support of the parties as compared with 1936. In terms of percentage, the Communists and the Socialists maintained their positions, the former with 14 per cent, the latter with 21 per cent of the total vote. The Radicals showed their strength in local affairs by climbing from 16 to 20 per cent.[30]

The second ballot posed great difficulties for the coalition. The Socialists had expressed the determination to withdraw their candidates only for those who definitely supported the program of the Popular Front, a measure designed to weaken the right wing of the Radical party. The Radical leaders naturally rejected the idea of any selectivity being exercised by another party on their own candidates. The issue was fought out in the week preceding the second ballot, but no satisfactory solution was found. The Communist leaders defended in public the position of the Radicals. But in practice, the Communist candidates confronted with a choice between a Socialist and a Radical hostile to the Popular Front usually chose the former. The results of the second ballot gave the Communist party a sizable increase in its representation on the local councils, though left it far weaker still than either the Radical or Socialist parties. It possessed 107 councilors, compared with over 500 for the Socialists and over 1,000 for the Radicals. It still did not have an important political base in the countryside.

The party membership was growing too, though not as rapidly as in 1936. By the end of 1937, it numbered 302,000, four times as many as in January of the previous year. The great influx of members represented a wholesale renovation of party personnel, but did not break with the old tradition of instability of membership. It seemed as though the commit-

[30] *Le Temps,* October 12 and 14, 1937.

ment to the party was born of an enthusiasm which waxed and waned, a tendency which would indicate that the true image of French communism should be a mood, not a party. Still, this instability should not be exaggerated. The party organization, with its schools, its study programs and instruction pamphlets, was capable of rapid assimilation of new members. In addition, the party was now supported by a powerful network of labor unions, out of which came many of the party members and cadres. The growth of membership in 1936 was in large part a result of the growth of the CGT; the monthly rate of increase of the membership of the two organizations was almost identical that year (see Graph 1). This

Graph 1. Rate of membership expansion of the CGT and the Communist party, 1936

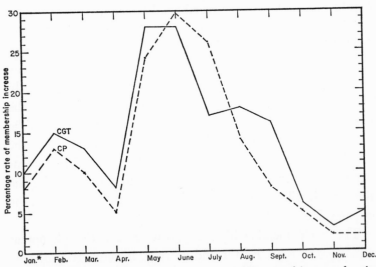

* January figures represent the average monthly rate of increase for the periods October 31, 1935–January 31, 1936 (CGT) and June 30, 1935–January 31, 1936 (CP).

Sources: Antoine Prost, *La C.G.T. à l'Epoque du Front populaire* (Paris, 1964), p. 41; Annie Kriegel, "Le Parti communiste français sous la Troisième République (1920–39): Evolution de ses effectifs," *Revue française de Science politique* (February, 1966), pp. 26–27.

suggests that a fairly constant proportion of union recruits were going into the party. Perhaps the increase in labor-union consciousness among the workers produced a heightened interest in the party. The result was an expansion of the party organization within French industry. The factory cells increased from 600 (20 per cent of the total) in 1934 to 4,000 (40 per cent of the total) in late 1937.

The increased attraction of communism represented something new in the outlook of the French proletariat. It was a break with the syndicalist tradition, which had denied the utility of worker participation in politics. Unfortunately, there is no evidence from the 1930's which would help explain the behavior of these new party members from the working class. Perhaps they saw in communism the hope of the future. But on the other hand, they may have interpreted communism in traditional French terms. Twenty years later, workers sympathetic to communism identified the party with French revolutionary ideals. In a study of CGT cadres in the city of Grenoble, Charles Micaud found that their "mental image" of the party was that of a "party of protest and of progress, in the tradition of French Jacobinism, a democratic party that is forceful in its defense of the underprivileged." [31] If this "image" was present in the mid-1930's—as I believe it was— the major explanation for the great increase in Communist membership would lie in a sort of reactivation of the Jacobin tradition among hitherto politically apathetic Frenchmen.

In social composition, the party remained heavily weighted toward the major industrial regions of France; one third of its total membership was from the Paris region. Still, it was no longer the exclusively proletarian party of pre-popular front years. In a speech to the national party congress in late December, 1937, Marcel Gitton remarked that the party had

[31] Micaud, *Communism and the French Left*, p. 148; see also Kriegel, "Le Parti communiste," pp. 10–12, 32–34.

"changed greatly." Its "essential base remains the working class [but] it includes in its ranks thousands of peasants, people from the middle classes, men from the liberal professions." [32]

The new party differed from the old also in terms of the ideological and political commitment of the new members. Interviews after the war with ex-Communists from France, Italy, England, and the United States indicated that the popular front tactics altered significantly the character of the parties in those countries. Though the data is not broken down by individual party during the popular front period, it is at least suggestive of developments in the French party. It shows that the new members were less active than recruits from earlier years, devoting less time to Communist functions. They were generally less interested in Communist ideology and more concerned with "agitational goals," notably antifascism and improved living conditions, and with the satisfaction of personal, nonpolitical needs. [33] This trend would appear the natural result of the party's greater interest after 1934 in reform activities and the struggle against fascism. The leadership of the French party was in fact concerned with the declining militancy of its followers. Thorez, in his speech before the national congress of December, 1937, attacked the "spirit of excessive confidence, of boastfulness, even of petty-bourgeois complacency" which existed among the rank and file. [34] Thanks to the popular front tactics, the French party had found strong support among the masses. But it paid a price for this success. Many of its members considered their activity as Communists to be the realization of the republican ideals of "liberty" and "equality." Their allegiance was to

[32] *La grande Famille communiste,* p. 25; extensive statistics on party membership can be found in *Deux Ans d'Activité au Service du Peuple,* pp. 103–5.

[33] Gabriel Almond (ed.), *The Appeals of Communism* (Princeton, 1954), pp. 106–7, 149–50.

[34] Thorez, *La France du Front Populaire,* p. 83.

their party *and* to "Jacobin" France. Though the central core of leaders continued to identify communism with the interests of the Soviet Union, the membership to a large extent did not. Perhaps some disagreed; many others were probably unaware of any contradiction between loyalty to France and sympathy with the ideals of the Soviet Union.

In order to retain the large mass of working-class supporters, the party leadership was obliged to defend their interests. Throughout most of 1937, it had avoided raising issues on which conflict might have arisen with the government. It did so probably for the sake of good Franco-Soviet relations. But it was in effect taking sides against the more radical—hence from its point of view more politically dynamic and valuable—workers by not actively opposing nonintervention in Spain and by accepting a "pause" in wage raises and social reforms. The cantonal elections had provided immediate justification for moderation until late October. Suddenly, at the end of October the party began a militant campaign for aid to republican Spain and support of the interests of the workers. The cause or causes for this sudden change remain a mystery. For some reason, the protection of the Soviet alliance was no longer felt to justify a policy of complete social and political restraint. Perhaps the Soviet leaders were already hostile toward Chautemps as a result of his coolness to the Franco-Soviet pact. Perhaps the French Communist leaders believed the strength of their party necessitated more demonstrative action than in previous months. Their agitation was not so extreme as to disrupt the economy or, until January, split the coalition, but it seriously worsened relations with the other members of the Popular Front.

Part of the campaign was an attack on the government's Spanish policy. Efforts were made to engage the Socialist party and the National Committee of the *Rassemblement populaire* in the action, but they failed to produce anything besides an irate letter from the Socialist leadership protesting the unilateral and disloyal Communist initiative. As a matter of fact, the French government had in late October secretly opened its Spanish frontier to the passage by night of arms for the Republicans.[35] The Communist leaders almost certainly knew of this move. But they desired a public commitment from the French cabinet in support of the Spanish Republic. On October 30, the Paris Association of Metallurgical Unions proposed a twenty-four-hour strike of all Paris workers to demand "the opening of the Spanish frontier" and to protest against the "slowness of arbitration and the high cost of living." No support was found for this radical measure; even the Communist-dominated Association of Building-Trades Unions took no action. In the end, the Metallurgical Unions simply called a one-hour sit-down strike on November 10. The action had to be considered a failure either as an effort to arouse the masses or as an attempt to influence French foreign policy. The economic demands were too vague to stir up interest among the workers and the strike too limited to have any impact on the government. The Communist leaders were sorely mistaken if they believed that, as Benoît Frachon wrote in late October, mass action could "bring again to life in our country a realistic foreign policy." [36]

The Communist party showed its opposition to Chautemps most clearly by its action in the Chamber of Deputies. Its speakers argued for the complete application of the Popular Front reform program, paying no attention to the government's desire to continue the "pause." Serious trouble arose when the Communist deputies refused to allow the Delegation of the Left to act as mediator in a dispute between the Union of Civil Servants, demanding a long-delayed salary increase, and the government. Chautemps asked the Delegation in mid-November to try to find a compromise settlement satisfactory to both parties. The Socialists and Radicals agreed, but not the

---

[35] Thomas, p. 502.   [36] *L'Humanité*, October 23, 1937.

Communists, who supported the demands of the Union. Chautemps forced the issue finally by presenting his own proposal to the Chamber and making approval a question of confidence in the government. At that, the Communist deputies moved over to the Premier's side. The party leaders explained their vote for the government by the lack of support for the workers from the other members of the Popular Front and by their own desire to preserve the unity of the coalition. They made it quite plain that the blame for the abandonment of the civil servants lay with the Socialists and the Radicals.

They continued in December their policy of supporting the agitation of the workers until threatened by the Premier with the end of the Popular Front. That month, wildcat strikes broke out in several factories in the Paris region in protest against the dismissal of workers. Tension rose when the government declared its intention to use force to evacuate factories occupied by strikers. On December 23, police action against strikers at the Goodrich tire plant resulted in a spontaneous demonstration by workers from surrounding factories. As a result, the police were withdrawn. The Communist officials from the area gave their full support to the defiant Goodrich workers and *L'Humanité* proclaimed the next day that the defeat of the police was a "success of solidarity." Chautemps responded by giving the Communist union leaders the choice of obtaining the evacuation of the factory or provoking the resignation of the cabinet. He warned that the very existence of the Popular Front depended on their reaction. He received satisfaction immediately. The Goodrich plant was evacuated, following which a Secretary of the Paris Association of Labor Unions publicly called on Chautemps to take note of the action. "Yes, Mr. Premier," he wrote, "the Popular Front must continue to exist, and, better still, to grow stronger." [37]

[37] *Ibid.*, December 27, 1937.

A few days later, a new dispute broke out between the Paris municipality and its employees. The city council had refused on December 27 to grant a pay raise to the workers. The Communist councilors had prudently abstained from voting on the issue. But on the evening of December 28, at the very moment when union representatives were discussing a compromise settlement with the Minister of the Interior, the Communist leader of the municipal-employees' union called a strike for the next day, December 29, including all Paris public transportation and public power. The city awoke paralyzed that morning. The surprise and disapproval were general. Even the few Communist deputies remaining in Paris during the party's national congress appeared embarrassed. They issued on December 29 a communiqué expressing a very weak "sympathy for the workers in private industry . . . and for those in the public services." It is impossible to determine from the evidence available whether the strike was undertaken on orders from the party leadership—away at the congress in southern France—or was the sole action of the union leader. It did end that very evening, thanks to promises given the strike leaders by the Socialist ministers that the city workers would receive satisfaction.

Two days later, the Communist party abandoned its policy of compromise. The party congress ended December 30. The next day—no coincidence, surely—the Communist leadership exploded with anger in the pages of *L'Humanité*. Large headlines proclaimed—falsely—that "the Radical and Socialist Government [!] Was Forced to Abandon the Use of Coercive Measures Demanded by the Fascists," referring to the possibility of the use of the army to run public transportation, by the "Unanimity of the Movement and the Solidarity of the Working People!" The Secretariat declared its "complete solidarity" with the municipal workers, and announced the party's readiness to "support unreservedly the social action of the workers." The Executive Committee of the Paris Association of Labor Unions accused the Chautemps cabinet of having acted in a manner "incompatible" with the interests of the Popular Front and warned that a general strike might be called if the forcible evacuation of factories were not stopped. This beating of the drums was irrelevant to the case of the municipal workers, since the strike had ended a day earlier. Rather, it put Chautemps on his guard that the Communist party was henceforth opposed to his policy of economic and social stability. The strike had become a political incident.

Chautemps decided to force the issue into the open. The Chamber reconvened after its New Year's recess on January 12. The next day, the Premier came before the deputies to request a vote of confidence in his policies of "social peace and public order." He declared that he could not govern with a majority in which there occurred the "disconcerting spectacle" of "colleagues fighting outside [the Chamber] policies they have approved here." The Communists had expected the showdown; *L'Humanité* had predicted on the morning of December 13 that there would be "important political explanations" that day. The Communist Arthur Ramette announced at the end of the Chamber debate that his party's deputies would abstain on the motion of confidence; he declared that they were not going to vote against the motion "simply to avoid breaking the Popular Front." The party leadership was apparently trying again their maneuver of a year earlier, hoping to force the replacement of the Chautemps cabinet by another Popular Front government. But the Premier surprised them by interrupting Ramette's speech to state that he gave full "liberty" to the Communist deputies to vote against his cabinet, in effect expelling them from his majority. Léon Blum later affirmed that Chautemps wanted a "shift" of the governmental majority toward the center. The Premier hoped for a coalition which would extend from the moderates to the Socialists and would exclude the Communists.[38] But he overlooked the continued fidelity of the Socialists to the Popular Front. Shortly after he had placed his "ban" on the Communists, the Socialist ministers resigned from the government, stating that they were opposed to a split in the majority. Chautemps then announced the resignation of the entire cabinet. A new cabinet crisis had begun.

The Communist leaders had probably decided to play the dangerous game of "ministerial massacre" for the sake of the Franco-Soviet alliance. They seemed during the cabinet crisis to be more concerned with French foreign policy than with the defense of the workers, the ostensible cause of their refusal to support Chautemps. The comments of Gabriel Péri in his daily column in *L'Humanité* constituted a sharp indictment of French relations with the other major European countries. "The essential moves of French policy," he wrote, had been "subordinated to the consent of London," and had "never taken account of the opinion" of Moscow.[39] The Communist obsession with British domination over French policy, evident earlier in 1937, had grown stronger since then. Péri even blamed British "Conservatives and bankers" for having "inspired" Chautemps's move against his party. He accused the British of having pushed the French government into nonintervention and into the "pause," and now of seeking, among other things, the exclusion of the Communists from the coalition, a French foreign policy "less and less in harmony with the spirit" of the Franco-Soviet pact, and "deals" with the German and Italian governments.[40] Once again the Communists revealed their deep fear of a French understanding with Germany. This time, they fixed the blame for French policy directly upon Yvon Delbos, the Minister of Foreign Affairs. He was the man who bowed to all the wishes of the Foreign

[38] "La Revanche de la Réaction," *Le Populaire*, August 10, 1939.
[39] *L'Humanité*, January 19, 1938.
[40] "La Crise française et l'Europe," *ibid.*, January 16, 1938.

Office. Even his tardy attempt to shore up French alliances in Central Europe, in the course of a trip taken in December, 1937, had been a failure. "To save the peace," Péri concluded, it was obvious that "the minister with a record as deplorable as that of M. Yvon Delbos must not return to the Quai d'Orsay." [41] For the first time, the Communist party had called for the ouster of a leading Radical in the government as a result of his handling of French foreign policy.

This action may have been directly related to the worsening of Franco-Soviet relations in late 1937 and early 1938. The Soviet leaders were more concerned than ever that the French had turned their backs on the Franco-Soviet pact. Andrei Zhdanov said as much at a meeting of the Supreme Soviet of the U.S.S.R. on January 17, 1938, when he asked point-blank "if this Pact exists or not." [42] Zhdanov, already one of the most powerful leaders in the Soviet Communist party, was certainly acting as the mouthpiece of the Politburo. The discontent—one might even say anger—he expressed with the French alliance was justified. The Russians were still waiting for the reinforcement of the alliance by a military pact, a test of French intentions as well as a guarantee of French aid in the event of an attack upon Russia. Two months earlier, in the course of a trip made to the Soviet Union, Léon Jouhaux had been received by Stalin, Molotov, and Voroshilov, to hear them complain that "the indispensable mechanism of the Pact [the military accord] has still not been set up. The French government should say if it wishes to apply this Pact or not." [43] Delbos's trip through Central Europe had only

[41] *Ibid.*, January 15, 1938.

[42] *Izvestiia*, January 18, 1938. Zhdanov was reported to be at that time a member of the subcommittee on foreign affairs of the Politburo, exercising "special responsibility for Comintern . . . affairs." Merle Fainsod, *How Russia Is Ruled* (Cambridge, 1955), p. 282.

[43] Told to Paul Reynaud by Jouhaux in a German prison camp during the war, and noted in Reynaud, *Mémoires*, II: *Envers et contre Tous*, 163.

heightened Soviet dissatisfaction. He had stopped off in Berlin to talk to Neurath, the German Foreign Minister; he had spent several days with Polish leaders in Warsaw, and had talked to Roumanian officials in Bucharest. But he had not gone to Moscow. According to a report by the well-informed German ambassador to Moscow, Schulenburg, he had turned down in November a personal invitation from Maxim Litvinov to come to the Soviet capital, putting Litvinov "in a huff." [44] The unwillingness of the French Foreign Minister to visit Moscow to talk with Soviet leaders may well have been the immediate cause of Zhdanov's outburst in mid-January in the Supreme Soviet. The Russians had good reason to be displeased with the Chautemps government, and with Yvon Delbos in particular.

But was there a connection between opinions in Moscow and actions in Paris? No direct evidence exists to prove that there was. Still, the coincidence of dates is intriguing. It is quite possible that the Soviet leaders (perhaps Zhdanov himself), exasperated by Delbos's snub and by the general course of Franco-Soviet relations, should have called on the French Communist party to take action to modify the foreign policy of the French government. The German ambassador to the Soviet Union held this view. He informed Berlin later that Moscow had attempted "to interfere in the French cabinet crisis . . . and to bring the removal of Delbos." This action had been taken, he asserted, "in part" as a result of Litvinov's "irritation" arising from his unsuccessful invitation to Delbos.[45] If true, it would indicate that the Soviet leaders were still intent, despite numerous signs of isolationism, on preserving their alliance with France. They had probably held the French party in check until November at least partly in the hope Franco-Soviet relations might improve. Having been disappointed in these plans, they then apparently turned to

[44] *German Documents*, D, I, 1144.   [45] *Ibid.*

direct interference in French affairs in order to achieve the same result. But their efforts were wasted.

Thus the Soviet leaders had little reason to be satisfied with the Popular Front or with the French Communist party. Throughout the entire year of 1937, the Soviet Union and France had drifted further and further apart. Gabriel Péri's analysis of French policy was essentially correct; the Radicals did seek British support above all else, and neither they nor the British cabinet leaders desired an effective Soviet alliance. It was a rare Western statesman who could, as Winston Churchill did, overlook ideological quarrels and concentrate on the German menace. Churchill told Ivan Maisky, Soviet ambassador to Great Britain and representative of the Soviet Union to the Non-Intervention Committee, that "it's not worth while worrying one another [over Spain]. We need all the unity we can get on the main question. . . . Hitler is equally dangerous to you and to us." [46] This was basically what the French Communists were trying to get across to French leaders. But they were unable to do so. In a way, they were prisoners of their own ideology; all they said was interpreted ideologically, when it was not actually framed in ideological terms. Gabriel Péri was one of the most astute analysts of foreign affairs in Paris, but only Communists read his articles. Besides, most Frenchmen wanted to hear of peace, not war; no amount of propaganda or parliamentary maneuvering, no degree of labor agitation, could change their mood.

[46] Maisky, *Spanish Notebooks,* trans. Ruth Kisch (London, 1966), p. 73.

VII

The Popular Front Abandoned

The French Communist leaders clung to the Popular Front in the Chamber only until they found a satisfactory alternative. When other members of the coalition suggested in 1938 broader parliamentary majorities which still included their party, they immediately accepted. In so doing, they indicated that their first obligation was to an effective French government able and willing to resist Germany. Their second obligation was their continued participation in political life. They quickly put aside the Popular Front after they thought their needs had been met. Only when they found that the new formation had in fact adopted an unacceptable foreign policy did they seek to recreate the old political ties. But it was too late.

The Slow Transition

By opposing the Chautemps cabinet, the party leaders were accepting grave risks in order to defend the Franco-Soviet alliance. But it is hard to see just how they thought to achieve their end. As events during the cabinet crisis proved, their political influence was nil. None of their demands were heeded. Their strictures on Delbos's conduct of foreign policy passed unnoticed. Their appeals for a "cabinet in the likeness of the Popular Front," that is, with Communist participation, were ignored. They were not even sure for a time that they would remain in the majority. For two days, Georges Bonnet tried to set up a Center coalition excluding the Communists, but failed because of Socialist opposition. Blum then attempted to create a government of *"Rassemblement national"* to include the conservative Paul Reynaud in addition to moderates and representatives of the old coalition—the motto was "from Thorez to Reynaud." The Communists accepted unhesitatingly the offer to join. Their demands for a government of the Popular Front were forgotten and their earlier proposal for a "French Front" revived. The problem of their collaboration in a government with moderates and conservatives was dismissed with a verbal wave of the hand. *L'Humanité* simply remarked that "one should not determine one's attitude by the shape of head or the name of men." [1] But Blum was unable to obtain the cooperation of the conservatives; he was unable even to create a complete Popular Front government when the Radicals turned down the idea of working with Communist ministers. In the end, the Communist leadership could do nothing to prevent Chautemps from returning to form a government made up entirely of Radicals, including Delbos again, and some dissident socialists. The Communist deputies grudgingly gave him their support, for there was nothing else they could do. They, and everyone else, expected the second Chautemps cabinet to be little more than a "transition" to a broader, more conservative coalition. The important political decisions were still to come.

In the meantime, the party leaders made a new attempt to create a mass movement in support of their political program. The "popular front from below" appealed to them as a means of reaching a broader cross-section of the population than

[1] *L'Humanité*, January 17, 1938.

their party alone could touch. But they could do little without at least the acquiescence of the other Popular Front parties; unfortunately for them, the Radicals and Socialists remained inveterately suspicious of all suggestions tending to remove part of the control of the Popular Front from their hands. In February, 1938, the Communist party resorted once again to unilateral action. In the country, new efforts were made to form "popular front committees" with popularly elected leaders. One attempt was even made to create in Paris a central organization for the movement. The Paris Association of Labor Unions tried in mid-February to call together the parties in the Popular Front for the preparation of a "popular front congress" in March. "The time has come," explained the General Secretary of the Association, "for the popular will to make itself strongly felt to defeat all opposition and to revive the policy of bread and liberty." [2] But the local leaders of the other parties did not understand the "popular will" in the same way and refused to participate. Nothing more was heard of the proposal. The Popular Front remained as much as ever a political coalition.

By the end of February, it was on its last legs. Chautemps sought in the weeks after his return to power to find the grounds for the establishment of a broader majority, but reported to the Delegation of the Left that he found only "objections, suspicions, and fears" on both the Left and the Right of the Chamber. [3] The Communist leaders were not opposed to the idea, provided they had their place in the new political formation. But opposition was fairly general to their entry into a cabinet; even their continued presence in the majority created difficulties. This problem, and others, thwarted all Chautemps's efforts. By early March, he had lost all taste for power—perhaps in part because his intelligence

[2] *Ibid.*, February 22, 1938.
[3] Quoted in *Le Temps*, February 26, 1938.

services had warned him of the imminent German invasion of Austria. On March 10, he resigned. The period of transition appeared to be over.

The March cabinet crisis started out as a repetition of that of January. Léon Blum tried first to create a full Popular Front government in spite of the hostility of the Radicals to Communist participation. The Austrian crisis, public knowledge on March 11, came as a sudden and very unpleasant surprise. Blum responded by making a new appeal for a government of *"Rassemblement national."* The Communist leaders supported his proposal as eagerly as in January. Again the opposition of the conservatives defeated the suggestion. On the evening of March 12, Blum succeeded in creating, as a last alternative, a coalition Socialist-Radical government similar to that of June, 1936. The one notable change was the replacement of the discredited Yvon Delbos by the more energetic Joseph Paul-Boncour as Minister of Foreign Affairs. But most of the political leaders in parliament looked on the second Blum cabinet as a temporary expedient useful only to dispel the last Socialist illusions about ruling France.

The Communist leaders apparently shared the general feeling of indifference toward the policies of the new government. They criticized the hesitation Blum showed in preparing new financial measures, declaring that a democracy must show itself "resolute and strong." Their comments indicated that they were already preparing their position on the next cabinet, which they desired stable and energetic in the face of foreign threats. Joanny Berlioz expressed the desire of his party that France be given a "government which governs." He added that "the men who will compose it are of less importance than its program of national recovery and of struggle against warmongers and agitators." [4] Taken alto-

---

[4] *Correspondance*, April 8, 1938, p. 454.

gether, the party declarations suggested that the leaders hoped for a moderate government of unity to replace Blum.

At the same time, the Communist leaders sought to profit by the presence of Blum at the head of the cabinet. They had neglected the Spanish issue during Chautemps's second period in power, despite the fact that the Premier had in January closed the Pyrenees frontier to the secret passage of arms. But they had little reason to conciliate Blum. They therefore sought to pressure the new government into intervening directly in the Spanish conflict. The cabinet did in fact discuss the possibility of sending French forces into Spain if Germany and Italy did not stop aiding Franco. A well-orchestrated campaign in the pages of *L'Humanité* backing aid to Spain accompanied the discussions within the government, indicating the Communists knew what was at stake. The party leadership almost certainly knew also that the Blum cabinet decided on March 17 to organize extensive shipments of military supplies to the Spanish Republicans. But the campaign continued. Marcel Gitton even objected to the "rumors" circulating that "the French government is . . . sending matériel." He contended that "absolutely nothing is being done." [5] In other words, the Communist leaders wanted a public avowal from the government that it was aiding the Republicans.

It is not at all clear just what they sought to gain by this action. The survival of the Spanish Republic was obviously not the issue. They seem to have anticipated some beneficial results from an open renunciation of nonintervention. One possible effect would have been strained relations between France and England. Chamberlain was in full control of English foreign policy by March, 1938. His goal was the re-establishment of good relations among England, France, Italy, and Germany. The Soviet leaders were profoundly disturbed by

[5] *L'Humanité*, March 24, 1938.

his actions; in July, *Izvestiia* declared that "the cause of peace" was endangered primarily by the foreign policy of England. The cabinet in London was trying to do everything "to disarm France's foreign policy . . . and to transform her into a submissive 'second-rate partner' who will easily be dragged into a 'four-power pact.' " [6]

By the spring of 1938, the Soviet leaders apparently hoped for little more from the French government than continued opposition to Germany. In all likelihood, they no longer expected to see the actual implementation of the Mutual Security Pact. In late March, Litvinov told the American ambassador to Moscow Joseph Davies that "France had no confidence in the Soviet Union and the Soviet Union had no confidence in France." [7] In order to avoid a Franco-English *entente* with Germany, the Soviet leaders had to try to undermine the good relations between France and England. One means to this end was to push the French cabinet into supporting openly the Spanish Republicans, an action certain to upset Chamberlain. At the same time, French intervention might easily have worsened Franco-German relations, since Germany was still supporting the rebels. The Soviet leadership had apparently decided that the Spanish conflict was most useful as a means of keeping Hitler tied down in Western Europe.[8] French aid to the Republicans would have led to greater German involvement in Spain. Both the fear of English influence over French foreign policy and the desire to worsen relations between France and Germany can explain the action of the French Communists. Perhaps also their campaign against nonintervention was one more effort to attack the Socialist leadership at a time when no risk was involved, the Blum cabinet being condemned anyway to a very short life. There is no way at

[6] *Izvestiia*, July 16, 1938.
[7] Joseph Davies, *Mission to Moscow* (New York, 1941), p. 291.
[8] Thomas, p. 503.

present of knowing what the real reasons were. Blum himself simply ignored the issue in public. His Spanish policy remained unaffected by Communist wishes.

On the more serious matter of French defense production, the Communist leaders had much less freedom of movement. Their policy had returned after mid-January to one of social restraint, though not of abandonment of the interests of the workers. The metallurgical industry in the Paris region was very important for the country's rearmament, being engaged in the production of essential war matériel such as planes and tanks. The workers in the industry were without a collective contract in March. The old contract had expired on February 28 and labor and management representatives had been unable to draw up a new agreement. The Association of Metallurgical Unions of the Paris Region had prepared for a strike on March 7, then had delayed action by setting a new deadline, March 20, for signature of the contract. March 20 came and went with no agreement. The workers were becoming restless and discontented.

Apparently, the union leaders wished to avoid a general strike which would have serious consequences for the economy and the defense effort. A CGT delegation, including Communists, had on March 14 agreed to Blum's proposal to relax the forty-hour law for the sake of increased production. Yet the metallurgical workers were pushing strongly for action. The union decided therefore to take limited measures which might spur settlement of the dispute but would not cause serious economic harm. According to a worker who headed the Socialist organization in the Citroën automobile plant, the union leaders on March 24 informed the workers in the factory that they could strike but that "public opinion must be led to believe that the movement was not planned." [9]

---

[9] *Juin '36*, May 1, 1938.

The following day, several other sit-down strikes broke out in Paris metallurgical factories. The evidence available leaves little doubt that it was the Communist union officials who had prepared all the strikes.[10] Publicly, however, they emphasized repeatedly their own lack of responsibility for the "spontaneous" movement. They did not give their official approval until March 30, the day before Blum called in both union and management to try to resolve the conflict.

But Blum failed to achieve a settlement, while the workers in the other unaffected plants became increasingly unruly. The union leaders multiplied their efforts to keep the strikes under control, but with increasing difficulty. On April 5, they at last approved a gradual widening of the strike movement which, in the words of another non-Communist worker in the industry, was "on the point of escaping their control."[11] Finally, just after Blum resigned as Premier on April 8 the union called a general strike in the industry for April 11. At the expense of a serious interruption in metallurgical production, the union officials had learned that spontaneity made poor tactics.

The Failure of Unity

The Communist leaders abandoned with no apparent regrets the second Blum cabinet. They proclaimed their continued fidelity to the Popular Front, but refused to follow the example of the Socialists in protesting against the conservative Senate. On April 8, Blum resigned as a result of the opposition of the Senate to his financial project. Edouard Daladier was

[10] See *Syndicats*, June 22, 1938; also, *ibid.*, July 13, 1938; also, "Quand les Grévistes ne dirigent pas leur Grève," *La Révolution prolétarienne*, No. 270 (May 10, 1938), p. 2; also, *La Grève de la Métallurgie parisienne* (Paris, 1938), pp. 7–9.

[11] "Quand les Grévistes," p. 2.

immediately chosen as his successor; the Radical leader put together a government of unity consisting of moderates and Radicals and excluding the Socialists. The Communists greeted him with some suspicion but not hostility. For them, he was something of an unknown value; he had backed the Popular Front at its birth but had moved to the right since 1937. He created the impression of being a strong leader, but had occasionally stated a hope of reconciliation with Germany. Thus, his decision in setting up his cabinet to replace Paul-Boncour, committed to collective security and the defense of Czechoslovakia, by Georges Bonnet as Minister of Foreign Affairs was taken as a bad sign. Still, Gabriel Péri remarked that his party "did not wish to stir up further dissension" by raising the issue of foreign policy before the new cabinet had proved itself.[12] Then too, Daladier's first policy statement, stressing the need for national defense, sounded a theme which appealed to the Communist leaders. They therefore overlooked his neglect of the question of the Popular Front and supported his government.

They seemed to have decided to give Daladier their provisional backing during his first months in office. Their union officials in the Paris metallurgical industry halted the strike before any general settlement had been reached, arguing that "the prolongation and extension of conflicts cannot avoid having their repercussions on the economy and the security of France."[13] They accepted with what amounted to a spirit of resignation Daladier's financial decree-laws in May, which among other things raised taxes 8 per cent across the board and further weakened the forty-hour law.

Their self-sacrifice was a political liability for the party. Their handling of the metallurgical strike had had damaging effects on the union. The confusion surrounding the strike

[12] *L'Humanité*, April 18, 1938.   [13] *Ibid.*, April 13, 1938.

and the meagerness of the settlement led to "severe losses" of membership. Other Communist-dominated unions were also on the decline.[14] Trends within the party were even more alarming. The recruitment of new members was at a standstill; it was reported that certain Paris sections of the party had lost one-third of their members. For the first time since early 1936, the call went out for a new membership campaign.[15] As for the Communist Youth League, it had lost by the end of October one half of its 1936 membership, falling from 100,000 to 50,000.[16] The evidence before the party leaders indicated that their support from the working class was declining drastically. In part, the loss of support was an inevitable result of the disillusionment following the great hopes of 1936. More specifically, the party, like the SFIO and the CGT, was suffering from its support of the government's conservative labor policies. The effect on the party was serious, so much so that at the end of May the party leaders abandoned their policy of political moderation.

The theme for the new campaign was the "dissatisfaction of the masses" with the Daladier cabinet. The party took upon itself the responsibility of defending the social and economic policies desired by the people. The emphasis was on parliamentary agitation, not strikes. Gone was the tolerance shown Daladier's financial program, gone also the respect for the wishes of the majority in parliament. After a recess of two months, the Chamber of Deputies reconvened on May 31. The Communist deputies had their program ready. The popular social reforms still to be enacted were resurrected, the request by the state employees for a pay raise defended, aid to Spain pushed, all within three days of the opening of the new

[14] *Syndicats*, May 25, 1938.
[15] "Au Recrutement, Camarades!," *L'Humanité*, June 23, 1938.
[16] *Une Année de Lutte pour le Pain, la Paix et la Liberté: Rapports du Comité Central*, p. 101.

session. By the middle of the month, the exorbitance of Communist demands had tried the patience of everyone involved. Daladier made his discontent known on June 15, when he sharply criticized those "supposed friends" of the government who waged a campaign for "demands known to be inapplicable, but which are brandished for electoral purposes." [17]

Just as this warning was being sounded, the Communist leaders learned that Daladier had closed the Pyrenees frontier to the passage of arms to the Spanish Republic. The news came as no real surprise, for on May 26 the French delegate to the Non-Intervention Committee had agreed to the restoration of international controls on arms shipments to Spain. Still, the action was one further indication that the French government was still very much within the British sphere of influence. Instead of heeding Daladier's call to order, the Communist deputies engaged in a parliamentary free-for-all on June 16. They interrupted Chamber debate to demand immediate discussion on the Spanish question, then, failing in that, returned later in the day with new petitions for immediate discussion of social reforms no one else could support. The next morning Daladier suddenly announced the closure of the parliamentary session.

The party's aggressive tactics in parliament were paralleled by a worsening in its relations with the Socialist and Radical parties. Its speakers blamed the Socialist deputies for the absence of new social reforms. Its local organizations expanded their efforts to create a "united front from below" by seeking organizational ties with Socialist party members. These attacks on the Socialist organization and leadership had begun even before the action in the Chamber. In early May, the Socialists had refused to consider a proposal for united action until the Communists had ceased their campaign against the

[17] *Le Temps*, June 17, 1938.

SFIO. In late June, they rejected a new offer for united action, explaining in a public letter to the Communist leadership that "day after day, with an obstinacy worthy of a better cause, you foment distrust and hostility against the Socialist party."[18] The United Front was in fact dead. The Popular Front continued to exist, but had lost its power. Daladier preserved the fiction of relying on the coalition, but ignored it in making his policies. Meetings of the National Committee of the *Rassemblement populaire* were filled with bitter debate, but did not produce an open split among the member organizations. No one was yet willing to assume the onus for ending the existence of what had once been a noble dream.

The Communist leaders, for their part, refused to admit that the dream no longer moved the masses. In June and July, they turned more and more to the argument that, in the words of Thorez, "the Popular Front is not, as certain people wish, a simple electoral coalition, it is a union of the workers and peasants of France."[19] They apparently hoped to compensate for the evident ineffectiveness of the Front in parliament by mobilizing the masses. But they were unable to do so. A campaign for aid to the Spanish Republic met with a monumental apathy on the part of the workers. A meeting in Paris on July 6 had to be canceled for lack of an audience. The only issue which could move the workers was the defense of the social reforms of 1936, particularly the forty-hour law, and Daladier had been careful not to raise the question—yet—of the abolition of this law. A few attempts were also made to organize "Popular Front congresses," which were completely ignored by everyone else.

In this unstable political situation, the Communist leaders took no drastic action. They appeared content with the preservation of an uneasy *modus vivendi* in their relations with the other members of the coalition and with the government.

[18] *Le Populaire*, July 1, 1938.   [19] *L'Humanité*, July 18, 1938.

There were no noisy campaigns following the closure of the parliamentary session. Moderation was still the watchword for the workers; strikes were infrequent and unimportant throughout the summer. The Delegation of the Left continued to unite the representatives of the left-wing parties in meetings which accomplished nothing but at least proved that everyone, Communists included, preferred unity over conflict. In reality, Communist policies depended entirely upon the actions of the government. If the party temporized at this moment, it was because Daladier was doing the same.

From the point of view of the Communists, both in the Soviet Union and in France, the Premier was in mid-1938 a losing, but not lost cause. His foreign policy was headed down the wrong path. He had closed the Spanish frontier. His cabinet had turned down a suggestion made in early May by Maxim Litvinov that Franco-Soviet military conversations be begun. According to Joanny Berlioz, "members of the cabinet" had "vigorously opposed the recommendations of the French General Staff for a more intimate technical collaboration with the Red Army." [20] With these black marks against Daladier, the Communist leaders were unwilling to accept any more unpopular policies. Their union officials were not disposed to approve greater sacrifices by the workers in order to increase industrial production. After much delay, the Federation of Metallurgical Workers refused to accept a government proposal to lengthen the work week, even in certain specific factories working for the national defense.[21] Politics was not absent from this decision. As the Communist leadership would later reveal, it was willing to accept any and all demands upon

[20] *Correspondance*, July 30, 1938, p. 902. The French cabinet's opposition to Litvinov's proposal was revealed in Coulondre, pp. 142, 153.
[21] Testimony by Daladier, in *Les Evénements survenus en France de 1933 à 1945: Témoignages et Documents*, I, 20.

the workers under certain conditions, chief of which being that the "appeasers" leave the cabinet. But in the summer months, nothing was decided.

Munich was still simply the name of a German city; the social reforms of 1936 were untouched in their essentials; the Popular Front was still respected in word, if not in deed. Until Daladier had fixed his position on the basic problems of foreign and internal affairs, the Russian and French Communists would wait. In the Soviet Union, Litvinov implied in a speech on June 23 that the next move was up to France, declaring that "the responsibility for further developments" in the field of "collective cooperation" did not belong to his government.[22] In France, the Communist party was for the time being willing neither to impede nor to aid Daladier's policies.

The first serious difficulties arose over Daladier's social policies. On August 21, Daladier declared that France had to be "put back to work" by a general easing of the forty-hour law. He did so without consulting either his dissident socialist Minister of Labor or the SFIO leaders or the CGT. His action thus implied a clear break with the former policies of the Popular Front. Within the Chamber of Deputies, the Communist leaders reacted in a fairly mild manner, accepting a compromise resolution from the Delegation of the Left. But following the Premier's decree allowing supplementary hours beyond the previous limit in all branches of French industry, they decided to support once again strike movements.

They could count on the discontent of a sizable proportion of the proletariat at the partial abandonment of the Popular Front social reforms. By the clever use of inflammatory headlines and aggressive calls for resistance, they tried to turn this discontent into action. Strikes already under way were given a publicity they had not enjoyed before in the Communist

---

[22] Quoted by Schulenburg, in *German Documents*, D, I, 921–22.

press. Strikes to come were announced unofficially even before all the preparations had been made. The party fought compromise solutions which avoided social conflicts. When the non-Communist leaders of the Miners Federation agreed to an extension of the work week in the mines, they were attacked as lackeys of Daladier. The miners were called upon to reject the agreement and to refuse to work any extra hours. As a direct encouragement to the spread of social agitation, the Paris Association of Building-Trades Unions called a general strike for September 19. One non-Communist labor leader from the CGT remarked that the Communist party looked "dismayed when a conflict is settled" and "desirous that others appear very quickly." [23] By starting their movement of social protest, the party leaders appeared oblivious to the mounting international crisis over Czechoslovakia.

Perhaps they thought the crisis would never lead to war. They were ardent defenders of the "integrity" of Czechoslovakia and of the application of the Franco-Czech Mutual Assistance Pact. They greeted Chamberlain's first voyage of conciliation to Berchtesgaden with dismay, and Daladier's acceptance on September 18 of the plan for the secession of Sudetenland to Germany with indignation. This, they declared, was nothing other than "capitulation," which "compromised" the security of France and the peace of Europe. [24] They turned once again to the Delegation of the Left for support in their policy. "No one," affirmed Duclos to the assembled delegates on September 21, "would understand how Mr. Chamberlain could go a second time to take Hitler's orders without a declaration having been made by the groups of the majority on the defense of Czechoslovakia." With this introduction, one resolution was presented calling for a dele-

[23] "Pas de Combinaisons politiques à propos de la Défense des 40 Heures," *Syndicats*, September 7, 1938.

[24] *L'Humanité*, September 20, 1938.

gation to be sent to Prague to express the determination of the French people to respect its agreement and a second defending the territorial integrity of Czechoslovakia. In sum, Duclos was asking the Delegation to take a position diametrically opposed to that of the cabinet. Both resolutions were defeated.[25] Nothing the party did impeded in the slightest degree that policy of conciliation with Germany it feared the most.

Suddenly and unexpectedly, Hitler himself came to its aid. By refusing on September 22 the plan presented by Chamberlain, he brought Europe within a hair's breadth of war. The next day, the Czechs declared a general mobilization; a day later, the French ordered a partial mobilization; on September 27, the British mobilized the fleet and declared a state of emergency. In this new situation, the Communist leaders reversed tactics completely. They supported wholeheartedly the decision for mobilization. The strike in the Paris building trades was halted on twelve hours' notice at the orders of Arrachart, leader of the Federation, following the announcement of partial mobilization on the evening of September 24. He told the strike committee that the Sudeten crisis obliged the workers to stop the strike in order "to take up arms against fascism." [26] Communist union officials announced that the workers in the aeronautical factories in Paris agreed to work extra hours for the defense effort. In that "hour of firmness," as *L'Humanité* termed it, the Communist party was ready for war.

Then came Munich. It must have been a staggering blow. In one day all that the party leadership had been fighting had been made history. France had come to an agreement with Germany and at the expense of a third power; a new Four-Power Pact had been signed; the principle of collective security had been violated; a treaty for mutual assistance had been

[25] *L'Oeuvre*, September 22, 1938.
[26] Quoted in *Syndicats*, September 28, 1938.

torn to shreds; the Soviet Union had been ignored in the elaboration of the most important European treaty since Locarno. The vocabulary of the French Communist leaders was scarcely rich enough in maledictions to curse the agreement at Munich. It was the "greatest treason a republican government had ever committed against peace," and a "breach of promise"; it was "scandalous," "criminal," and much more. But few Frenchmen listened. The Communists later admitted that they were "swimming against the current" in opposing Munich. The French people had "given a great sigh of relief" at the news of the settlement.[27] *L'Humanité* bitterly saluted the masses who cheered Daladier on his return to Paris as the "brigade of acclamations" and asserted that only "simpleminded optimists and friends of Hitler see [in Daladier] the savior of peace."[28] But the Communists were alone in their recrimination. The situation in the Chamber resembled that in the country. On October 4, Daladier presented parliament with a request for approval of the Munich settlement and another for special financial and economic powers. On both issues, the Communist deputies voted an unequivocal "No!" On Munich, they were joined by two other deputies against 535, and on the special powers, by five deputies against 331. But on the latter vote, the Socialist deputies for the first time since 1936 abstained. The majority of the Popular Front was broken.

The Communist leaders clung to the myth of Popular Front unity. They had nothing besides the organizations created around the coalition—the Delegation of the Left and the National Committee of the *Rassemblement populaire*—with which to exercise some political influence. By the fall of 1938, the Delegation of the Left was inoperative. The National Committee, however, still met. In October, the Radical Exec-

[27] *Correspondance*, October 8, 1938, p. 1143.
[28] *L'Humanité*, October 2, 1938.

utive Committee, obviously at Daladier's urging, decided to break the last ties with the Communist party. It accused the party of having "deliberately withdrawn" from the coalition by its opposition in recent months to the cabinet's policies. The Radicals hoped that a majority of the delegates from the member parties in the *Rassemblement populaire* Committee would unite to expel the Communist from their midst. But no one else on the Committee beside the Radicals saw the need for such action. The Communist leaders rejected with indignation the Radical accusations. In a letter sent to the National Committee on November 2, they reaffirmed their resolution "to maintain solemnly" their membership in the organization.[29] Finally, on November 10, the Radical delegate withdrew from the Committee. The Popular Front was formally dissolved. It was the only way out. The Radical and Communist parties defended contradictory policies in the name of the Popular Front. In a way, no one was right, for the coalition had never definitely defined its goals. In 1938, almost everyone sought to replace the Popular Front by a new political formation. Daladier succeeded, with the hesitant approval of the Socialist and Communist parties. Thus in reality all the members of the coalition were responsible for the end of the Popular Front. It was an exercise in futility for the Communist leaders to try to defend the old alliance in October.

After Munich, their primary concern was to defeat Daladier. The Executive Committee of the Comintern had issued a call to "replace the governments of national treason and shame in the countries menaced by foreign fascism by governments ready to fight back against aggressors." [30] The French Communist party set out to force the Radical Premier out of office. It sought to do so principally by waging a campaign against the government's financial and economic policies. On Novem-

---

[29] *Ibid.*, November 11, 1938.   [30] *Cahiers*, November, 1938, p. 728.

ber 1, the conservative Paul Reynaud became Minister of Finance and two weeks later the Popular Front reform program was largely abandoned. Using the decree powers, Reynaud fixed the work week at six days, with a maximum of forty-eight hours of work. Taxes were raised, the public works program stopped, and the personnel of the state railways cut.

The Communist party cried out immediately against the "decree-laws of misery," making the issue its principal charge against Daladier. The choice suited the mood of the CGT and many workers, but was in real contradiction with the party's expressed aim of strengthening France against "aggressors." Paul Reynaud was himself one of the strongest opponents of appeasement in the cabinet. In fact, the Communist leaders stressed several times that they might reconsider their position were the government's foreign policy changed. Speaking before the Central Committee on November 21, Thorez offered the "maximum effort" of the working class for a program of national recovery, the "first condition" of which, however, being "the departure from power of the men of Munich." [31] But Daladier preferred to fight.

The principal arm in the struggle against the Premier was the CGT. The Communist union leaders could probably have taken over the Confederation, had they wished. Their power was such that, at the Nantes Congress of November 14 to 17, they held a majority of votes. Yet they did not try to force their own policies upon the non-Communists. They perhaps feared a scission if they overextended themselves and in any case had more to gain by cooperation from everyone. They were particularly interested in mobilizing the CGT for action against the decree-laws. Eugène Hénaff, leader of the Communist-dominated Paris Association of Unions, proposed to

[31] *L'Humanité*, November 25, 1938.

the congress that the working class be called out "in a general movement of limited duration, and, if it is necessary, [in] a wider movement which would make the enemy retreat as in June, 1936." [32] He was in effect proposing a nationwide general strike.

The Communist proposals met with general agreement among the delegates. A non-Communist labor leader had even made the suggestion for a general strike before Hénaff spoke out. Most of the union leaders believed they could repeat their performance of February 12, 1934, and that in any case, they could no longer acquiesce in the application by the government of conservative social and economic policies. The time had come to fight. [33] The Congress therefore approved a motion for the "collective cessation of work" as part of the "necessary action" against the decree-laws, but left the details of the action up to the CGT Administrative Committee. The next day, November 18, Benoît Frachon reminded the National Confederal Committee that "the principle of the general strike has been accepted," warned of "grave deceptions" if there was any delay, and called for an immediate decision on the matter. [34] But Jouhaux and the other non-Communists were not to be hurried. Not until a week later did the Administrative Committee take action. Again the Communists acquiesced, victims now of that unity for which they had sacrificed so much in 1935.

While the CGT leadership dallied, the Communist union leaders pushed ahead with their own plans. On November 21, the first day the decree-laws were applied in French industry, a wave of sit-down strikes broke out both in the Paris region and in the department of the Nord. Most affected were the

[32] *Ibid.*, November 17, 1938.
[33] See Delmas, pp. 163–64; Mowdi, "Impressions de Militant," *La Révolution prolétarienne,*" No. 284 (December 10, 1938), p. 9.
[34] *Le Temps,* November 20, 1938.

metallurgical factories and the mines. By the middle of the week, upward of 100,000 workers were involved. In part, the strikes were certainly the spontaneous expression of the discontent of the workers. No less certain is the role played by the Communists in certain cases. On November 24, the Citroën, Bloch, and Renault plants were occupied. The party was clearly throwing its big guns into the battle against Daladier. But the Premier was ready to do the same. No less than 2,000 police were sent to clear the Renault factories of strikers. They found on entering the plant barricades of oil drums and of trucks loaded with scrap iron. From behind these shields, the workers hurled steel bars, crankshafts, and pieces of cast iron at the invaders; the police used tear gas bombs in return. After four hours of fighting, all the strikers, approximately 25,000, were expelled and 300 were arrested.[35] The Communist fortress, in which the party counted 7,500 members in December, 1937, had been taken. The other factories were evacuated with no resistance. Only the general strike remained to decide the fate of the Daladier cabinet.

The following day, November 25, the CGT Administrative Committee called on all French workers to participate on November 30 in a twenty-four-hour general strike, the sole aim of which was to protest against the decree-laws. The non-Communists on the Committee had insisted upon this restrictive clause. In fact, the entire strike bore their stamp. It was to remain strictly within the limits of the law, with no occupation of factories, and work was to be resumed without fail December 1. A strike directed against governmental pol-

---

[35] Daladier gave a sketchy account of the battle in the Chamber of Deputies on December 9, in *JO, Débats, Chambre*, No. 58 (December 10, 1938), p. 1710; *Le Temps* gave more detail on November 26, 1938. According to a non-Communist worker in the plant, the fighting was begun by the strikers against the recommendation of their union officials. *Juin '36*, December 2, 1938.

icy, yet termed "legal" and declared five days in advance, could only appear a contradiction in terms. The Communist leaders had striven for this decision. They had even obtained on November 24 an advance agreement to participate from the Federation of Railway Workers, a decision of great weight in obtaining the approval of the Administrative Committee.[36] They presented the action as nonpolitical, nonviolent, "orderly and powerful, for republican laws against illegality." Nothing more was said of the necessary fight against the "appeasers of Munich." Yet they continued to insist that Daladier had to resign, thus admitting that for them the strike did have a political aim. The confusion of political and social motives weakened the movement before it began.

The difficulties grew greater as the strike date approached. Daladier refused all offers of mediation, preferring a showdown over what he thought was a Communist-inspired action directed against himself. On November 28, he ordered the requisitioning of the railroads, of the subways and buses, and of all public services. Workers and employees thus affected were required to report to work or suffer possible prison penalties. The labor unions whose members were under government orders to report to work acquiesced in the action; not even the Communist-controlled Federation of Railway Workers offered any resistance. With public services and transportation untouched, the general strike could not possibly have a powerful impact on the population and the government. But no one within the CGT suggested that the strike be annulled.

It should have been. November 30 went down as a black day in the history of the French labor movement, and as a red-letter day in the political life of Edouard Daladier. To be sure, there were strikers, particularly in private industry. The

---

[36] Delmas, p. 182.

Paris metallurgical industry reported 50 per cent of the workers absent; the mines which had not been requisitioned were empty. From industry to industry, the record was uneven, but, on the whole, could not compare at all with that of February 12, 1934. Interestingly enough, the strike was most successful in the non-Communist unions, among the longshoremen, the printers, and the miners. In the sectors of the economy touched by the requisition order, there was no strike. The railways functioned normally, as did the public transportation in Paris, the public utilities, and the post offices. The general strike did not seriously disturb the life of the country and was therefore a failure. The CGT had been dealt a defeat which only the war would efface. The workers left it in droves; its membership fell from 3.5 million in 1938 to 2.5 million in August, 1939, and the greatest part of the loss came in the weeks after the strike.[37] Daladier emerged the victor, gaining rather than losing strength as a result of the encounter.

The Premier's victory over the CGT marked the end of Communist hopes to alter French foreign policy. The party leaders enjoyed neither political influence in parliament nor, after the failure of the general strike, the force they once possessed through the manipulation of parts of the labor-union movement. They continued to apply the popular front tactics until September, 1939; in fact, however, it made little difference what they did. By the late spring of 1939, the Soviet leaders had begun a major revision of their foreign policy which would lead to the German-Soviet pact and to the abandonment of the popular front tactics. They had sanctioned these tactics in order to further Soviet interests; their hopes had been disappointed. The French Communist party had failed completely as an instrument of Soviet foreign policy.

[37] Prost, pp. 47–48.

But many Communists had lost sight of the continued dependence of the party leadership on the Comintern. They assumed that the party had definitely adopted the French republican and patriotic traditions. They sincerely believed in the justice of supporting the republican regime and defending the country against foreign attack. They were totally unprepared in September, 1939, for the Comintern order ending the popular front tactics and reintroducing revolutionary defeatism. Even older party members from the pre-1934 days balked at the idea of betraying their country because Soviet power interests dictated an alliance with Germany. As a result, the party almost went to pieces.[38] Only an inner core of leaders and active members remained unquestioningly faithful to the Soviet Union, but they were sufficient to preserve the organization. Without them, the party would not have survived as a disciplined Comintern section. Had the leadership not been so obedient, the party might well have supported French national defense in spite of the Soviet alliance with Germany. It would thus have repeated the performance of the French Socialist party in 1914. But the Communist form of "internationalism" turned out to be stronger than that of the Socialists. The key appeared not ideology—it absorbed too easily national traditions—but organization. The Comintern had succeeded in forming a Communist elite in France whose whole life was bound up in the activities of the vast network of Communist operations. They kept the network functioning; without it, they would have been lost. Their faith in communism was buttressed by its continued existence. When Mau-

[38] Evidence on this subject is extremely rare. P.-L. Darnar, who remained in the party until late September, 1939, found the Paris organization literally falling apart (personal interview); Auguste Lecoeur, then Secretary of the party federation of the Pas-de-Calais Department, later asserted in his memoirs that "the cadres of the party, from the Central Committee to the section committees, were severely shaken" (*Le Partisan* [Paris, 1963], pp. 106–7).

rice Thorez was told in early October to desert from his army unit and to go into hiding, he left.[39] He obeyed apparently with as much speed as he had earlier obeyed the order for mobilization. But for him, highest allegiance went to the Comintern, not to the French state. In this loyalty and discipline lay the secret of the survival of the French Communist party in 1939.

[39] Rossi [Tasca], *Les Communistes français pendant la Drôle de Guerre*, pp. 74–77.

VIII

*The Communist Party
and the Popular Front*

The French Communist party never successfully freed itself from the influence of French political traditions. The
revolutionary tactics of "class against class" had completely
isolated the party within the political system of the country.
Its labor unions could mobilize only a very small minority of
the proletariat. Its own membership was so reduced by 1933
that it deserved to be called a sect, not a party. It is remarkable
that, under these conditions, there still existed among the rank
and file a feeling of loyalty to the democratic institutions of
the Third Republic. The "class against class" tactics had been
introduced in 1927 specifically to break the continued hold of
republican traditions on the party. The extremist policies followed after 1929 had rejected "opportunism," that is, united
action with other proletarian or bourgeois forces, under any
circumstances. But the events of 1934 proved that many Communists were prepared to defend the Republic against an
apparent fascist danger, in spite of contrary orders from the
Comintern. The failure of the "class against class" tactics as a
revolutionary program suggests that it was unsuited to the
French political climate. The totalitarian organization and the
strict controls from Moscow were not sufficient to create in
France a strong movement completely opposed to the political
values and institutions of the country.

It was thus fortunate for the Communist leaders in Paris that the Comintern allowed them to participate in a new form of "united front from above." Had they not joined the anti-fascist movement in 1934, their party would probably have undergone a scission with Doriot at the head of a large group of dissidents. They could claim no credit for the reversal of policy in Moscow, for they had consistently adhered to the extremist tactics. Their unwillingness to take any new initiatives was an indication to what extent the French leadership had adopted the mentality of bureaucrats, whose sole duty was to execute orders. They showed also bureaucratic inflexibility in their first timid attempts to apply the new tactics in May and June, 1934. At that moment, the subservience which the Comintern had instilled in the personnel in its sections was a distinct liability.

The party leaders showed real improvement in their political capacity a year later. While they could claim no part in the creation of the antifascist movement, they did play a key role in the first moves which led to the formation of the Popular Front coalition. They initiated the discussions which led to the first political contacts between the left-wing parties in late May, 1935. They set in motion the negotiations which resulted in the tremendous *Rassemblement populaire* of July 14. Their willingness to ignore quarrels of the past for the sake of political unity contributed significantly to the adoption of the Popular Front program, without which the Front would have been no more than a weak electoral coalition. After a moment of confusion, they adopted with little difficulty the patriotic slogans of their country. The Communist party had finally made the French republican tradition its own.

In the years following, the French Communist leaders showed in their actions a certain degree of political maturity. It is very difficult to determine how much initiative they were actually exercising, and how much control Moscow wielded

over their decisions. One may at least assume that the broad
guidelines of policy were always set by the Comintern but
that the French leadership probably determined day-to-day
tactics. The general pattern of Communist support for the
policies of the Popular Front governments was thus the result
of instructions from Moscow. But, for example, the problem
of supporting or rejecting Blum's financial project in June,
1937, was apparently in the hands of the Communist parliamentary leadership. The eleventh-hour decision to vote for
the bill was certainly the wise move, for the Communist
position in the majority was already uneasy at that time. The
development of the sit-down strike movement in May and
June, 1936, is another instance of Communist moderation in a
critical situation. It is likely that the movement was begun by
Communist labor-union officials. They soon found that by
introducing the tactics of the sit-down strike they had set in
motion a wave of strikes over which they had little control.
The threat of violence finally forced the party leaders themselves to seek to halt the strikes. For the sake of national unity,
they accepted in effect to oppose a powerful proletarian
movement. Their call for order was, with a few exceptions
and some hesitation, obeyed by the membership. It was a
remarkable display of discipline.

The disillusionment which crept like a blight over the Popular Front, in parliament and among the workers, had only a
little to do with Communist agitation. The pernicious effects
of the depression distorted and undermined all the reforming
efforts of the government. The coalition was plagued by the
differences of opinion separating Socialists and Radicals. The
timidity of the Radical party in economic and social matters
weakened the Popular Front from the start. It was in truth
only a reflection of the widespread conservative sentiment in
the country in the 1930's. This mood acted as a brake on
progress in all fields, in politics no less than in industry.

The desire of other Frenchmen to break this hard mold of immobility is certainly one important reason for the wide support given the Communist party during the Popular Front period. The party's activism promised the full use of the new member's energy and talents, while its new reformism seemed to guarantee that the activity would not be expended on a vain pursuit of the millennium. Communist propaganda emphasized antifascism and the need for greater social justice. It was thus only natural that it should attract many who were concerned with the improvement, not the overthrow, of France's democratic society.

Still, one would have to conclude that the party was not successful as a source of new ideas for the improvement of the French state and society. The creative proposals, such as those for economic planning, came from within other political movements, notably the SFIO and the Radical party. Blum's economic reforms of March, 1938, inspired by Keynesian theory (and elaborated with the aid of a young Radical economist named Pierre Mendès-France) met with Communist hostility. The Communist millenarian ideology stood in the way of the acceptance of any significant measures for economic reform. All the party could offer were the old reforms on taxing the rich and giving to the poor, of defending the franc and protecting the peasantry. Ironically, the most dynamic party in France was incapable of real political leadership. It, too, turned out to be a defender of immobility.

Yet the party was different from the others. Its organization was totalitarian, not democratic. At no time was an effort made to alter the Stalinist pattern of hierarchical discipline. Policies were executed, not discussed; leaders were obeyed, not chosen. Only a very few Communists dared call for internal party democracy, usually when they were dissatisfied with the policies then being applied. Thus on important policy issues, the party leaders enjoyed much greater freedom of movement than did the leaders of the other parties. In addition, they were free to use methods of political action incompatible with normal democratic procedures. Their occasional use of strikes for political ends between 1936 and 1938 undermined the authority of the Popular Front and contributed to its downfall.

Their continued attacks upon the Socialist party were not only unscrupulous but petty as well. The issues of the day—economic recovery, political stability, external security—were far too important to be subordinated to maneuvering against one's political rivals. Yet the Communists could not shake off their obsessive desire to weaken the SFIO. They adhered to the United Front after 1935 only out of necessity. Without the aid of the Socialists, the Radicals could not have been held to a left-wing coalition. Further, only the alliance with the SFIO gave the Communist leaders some voice in parliamentary deliberations. Within the limits of political necessity, the Communist leadership felt free to turn to its advantage all the difficulties of the Socialist party.

The governments of the Popular Front were occasionally fair game also. Demagoguery was no monopoly of Communist speakers. They used it to a degree, however, rarely attained by other politicians. Eager to assume the role of "voice of the people," they made promises which could never be kept, and demanded reforms which the government could not enact. The party's concerted campaign in June, 1938, in favor of expensive economic and social reforms succeeded only in disrupting the activities of the Chamber of Deputies. It seemed at times that the party leaders were interested less in furthering reforms than in spreading their own renown as defenders of the interests of the masses.

There was another side to the coin, however. After the summer of 1936, reforms became less and less the order of the day in parliament. The program of the Popular Front was not applied in its entirety; major reforms promised earlier did not become law, and others, such as the public-works program, were seriously vitiated. In fact, the Communist leaders suffered a series of major parliamentary defeats. They had placed an anathema upon devaluation of the franc, and had sworn up and down that no representative of the people could accept this pernicious means of "making the poor pay." Yet devaluation came in September, 1936, and the Communist deputies, after a weak display of opposition, voted for it. A few months later, in February, 1937, they again had to eat their words when confronted by Blum's decision to declare a "pause" on salary and wage increases. They approved the "pause," and approved as well Blum's demand, made in mid-June, 1937, for special financial powers. On basic policy matters the Socialist and Radical leaders had the last word. The same story was repeated while Chautemps was Premier, and even during the first months of the Daladier government. Despite the fact that, from the fall of 1936, the economic, social, and financial policies of the several cabinets of the Popular Front were essentially conservative, the Communist party remained with the majority.

Seen in this light, Communist demagoguery is more understandable. Within the coalition, the Communist leaders were making real sacrifices. None of their proposals for reform were made law. Far from using the coalition for their own ends, they were in fact being used themselves for ends set by the Socialists and the Radicals. Their propaganda campaigns were in large measure a form of compensation for the acceptance of policies they disliked. For the sake of the unity of the Popular Front, they accepted what in fact was a subordinate position within the coalition.

They were no more accustomed to the role they had to play in their relations with the French proletariat. The successful strikes of May and June, 1936, marked a profound change of mood of the workers; the apathy of earlier days was replaced by an aggressive militancy. The workers were no longer willing to accept a position of inferiority under management and were ready to fight for what they felt were their rights. This new attitude worked in part to the advantage of the Communist party, for it heightened the political consciousness of the workers and made them much more responsive to political slogans and movements. The political strikes organized by the Communists were the most spectacular sign of the heightened "availability" of at least an active minority of the proletariat. Yet this same militancy created new and serious problems for the party. Before mid-1936, the Communists could with reason speak of themselves as being the "vanguard of the proletariat." Afterward, they could not say as much.

They found themselves torn in fact between conflicting forces. On the one hand, the workers pushed ahead with their demands for greater social justice; on the other, the Popular Front governments, which the Communists were committed to support, sought desperately to restore social calm and to raise production after June, 1936. The conflict was very real, for, as has so often happened in France, social calm had to come at the expense of social justice. The necessity for increased production, all the more urgent since it was the basic condition for French military rearmament, outweighed in the eyes of the government the complete satisfaction of the needs of the workers. The Communist leaders could not possibly satisfy both sides at the same time. Now and then they sided with the workers, simply because to do otherwise would have meant a serious loss of political strength. In May, 1938, all the signs pointed to a decline of Communist support among the workers due to the party's approval of the conservative economic and social policies of Daladier. To stop this trend, the party leaders abandoned their public support of Daladier's policies in favor of a campaign for social reforms. Yet it is significant that in this case, as in others, a rise in Communist demagoguery was not accompanied by the encouragement of strike action. On the more important issue of social calm and increased production, the Communists were most often on the side of the government.

This was true from the very beginning of the Popular Front governments. The decision of the party leadership in early June, 1936, to work actively for an end to the wave of sit-down strikes and for a resumption of production indicated a fundamental policy commitment. For the sake of internal order and national defense, the party was willing to exercise restraint upon the working class. Key industries which played an important role in French production—and military rearmament—suffered least of all from strikes throughout the period of the Popular Front. Between June, 1936, and March, 1938, the Paris Association of Metallurgical Unions, Communist-dominated, did not call one major strike. Indications of discontent among the workers in this industry were disregarded and contracts were signed which did not give satisfaction to the workers. Even the strike wave of March and April, 1938, appeared more the work of aggressive metallurgical workers than of their union leaders, who had attempted to create only a limited strike movement. Given this general policy of social restraint, it was natural that strikes could and did break out in Communist-controlled unions without the approval of the union officials. At times, the Communist party let such strikes run their course. At other times, it called publicly for a halt to the strikes, and even directed its union leaders to work personally for compromise settlements. The fact that these conciliatory moves placed the Communists in a position of semiopposition to the more militant workers did not alter their policy.

Occasionally, however, the party tried to mobilize the workers for its own ends. The labor-union movement was a tempting arm to use in moments of political conflict. When worker discontent coincided with Communist militancy, political strikes were quite feasible. But too often Communist use of the unions had no relation to social issues. In the general strike of November, 1938, the Communist union leaders were less successful in mobilizing the workers than the non-Communists. They paid then for having mixed politics with labor affairs.

They had done so primarily to aid the Soviet Union. There can be no doubt that all the party did in the years 1934–1938 was in harmony with Comintern policies. The Communist leaders did not remain faithful to the Popular Front for so long, nor restrain angry workers so often, because they themselves preferred to do so. These policies had been at least outlined by higher authorities whose major concern was the salvation of the Soviet Union, not of France. One can say today that the fate of the two countries was bound together in the 1930's, and that the French Communist party was advocating certain policies which should in fact have been followed by its government. Yet this judgment throws little credit upon the party leaders. They had abandoned their earlier revolutionary intransigence upon the orders of Moscow. They later ceased their reformist moderation when told to do so. To be sure, they sought also to further the interests of their own party through electoral maneuvering and propaganda campaigns. But their major social and political policies can be satisfactorily explained only as a product of the diplomatic interests of the Soviet Union.

Their acceptance of the United Front with the Socialist party was probably the result of a re-evaluation in the Soviet Communist party of the dangers of German fascism. By mid-1934, Hitler's anticommunism was taken seriously as a menace to the Soviet Union. Soviet foreign policy was involved to the extent that it too was being realigned to meet the German threat. The Comintern's international antifascist campaign was thus a defensive action in support of the Soviet Union, much as the extremist "class against class" tactics of 1929–1933 had been. The difference lay in the identification of fascism, not the bourgeois capitalist regimes in general, as the prime enemy.

The revision of French tactics in mid-1935 was a marked change in this pattern. The French party was called on to take offensive action which was political, not revolutionary. Its goal was at the least the firm commitment on the part of the French government to resist German expansion, and at the most the creation of solid and enduring French ties with the Soviet Union. Antifascism was equated with anti-German policies. The Communist leaders sought to bring the Radicals into a left-wing coalition clearly to encourage the creation of a Radical government strongly in favor of the Soviet alliance and resolutely opposed to fascism inside and outside France. Their continued pursuit of these two goals as late as 1938 is an indication of the importance Soviet leaders placed on the French alliance. Their policy of "loyal support" throughout most of 1937 seems directly related to this issue. Their attack on the Chautemps cabinet in January, 1938, was probably another attempt—by very different means—to alter French policy toward the U.S.S.R. Had the Russians given up all hope for the Franco-Soviet alliance, they would surely have not had the French Communists act so vigorously.

But in no respect was the French Communist party able to aid the Soviet Union in the years of the Popular Front. France never supported any sort of international movement against fascism. The majority of the population desired peace, and were ready to go to great lengths to avoid a holocaust similar to that of 1914–1918. The policy of nonresistance and appeasement followed by the government between 1935 and 1938 was a true reflection of this mood. Nor did the party have any success in its efforts to strengthen the Franco-Soviet alliance. Neither its participation in the Popular Front nor its support of the Radical party proved effective. Not even violent propaganda campaigns accompanied by labor agitation brought satisfactory results. The French government did not become a firmer ally of the Soviet Union in the years between 1936 and 1938. Quite the contrary, it slipped away from the alliance, and there was nothing the Communist leaders could do to stop the unfortunate drift.

On the other hand, the party did not harm the alliance. Communist political activity in France during the Popular Front did not create any new enemies of the Soviet Union. Those who did not favor the Mutual Assistance Pact or who looked upon it with skepticism, such as Daladier, had held these views long before the Communist party entered the political arena. French foreign policy was not made by rabid anti-Communists who feared the proletarian revolution above all things; it was made by average Frenchmen whose principal defect was a lack of foresight. The French Communist party had little place in their view of the world and was quite unable to change it.

Could the party have done any better? In truth, its possibilities for action were meager. The choice was basically between more coercion and more cooperation. The only means of coercion was in the action of the masses. The "popular front of the masses," with mass participation and democratically elected leaders, might have been useful. But it never received the necessary sanction of the other parties in the coalition. The only instrument of mass pressure left was the labor-union movement. Labor strikes were a potent weapon, at least in theory. In practice, the few times they were used for political ends were sufficient to reveal that they did not sway the government in any positive manner. They were only useful as a source of political and economic disorder. As such, however, they worked contrary to Communist goals, for they weakened both the French state and the French economy and thereby lessened France's value as an ally of the Soviet Union. More coercion thus was not a feasible alternative.

More cooperation was possible. The Communist leaders could have been better partners in the coalition. They made a definite error in turning down Blum's offer of participation in the new Popular Front government in May, 1936. They admitted as much when, a year later, they offered to participate in this same government. But then it was too late. Participation might not have assured them of a greater role in the making of decisions in the field of foreign policy, but it would at least have given them a greater voice during the preparation of policy. Further, they could have supported the Socialist-led governments much more actively than they did. They seemed congenitally averse to granting wholehearted support to the Socialists. It was so much easier to cooperate with the Radicals, who did not pretend to be true Marxians or to represent the working class. The Communists still did not place total confidence in the Radical leaders, who were known to be less committed to the Popular Front than the Socialists. As a result, the party oscillated between the Socialists and the Radicals, relying first upon the former and then upon the latter, until finally, in October, 1938, it could rely upon neither. At the same time, its occasional attempts to use strikes to force the government to change policies alienated everyone. To be sure, greater moderation appears in retrospect a sterile alternative as well. Only a few leaders in the coalition, notably Léon Blum, Joseph Paul-Boncour, and Edouard Herriot, were committed to a foreign policy of collective security. All one may conclude, therefore, is that the Communist party did not explore all the possibilities of cooperation.

One should not underestimate the French Communist leaders as political tacticians. On certain basic issues, they showed a realism and flexibility worthy of the best of politicians. Their unexpected proposal at the end of May, 1935, for a coalition of the left-wing parties did offer a way of ending the rule of the conservatives in the National Union, and of Pierre Laval in particular, and of bringing the Radical party to power. They were naïve in their assumption that the Radicals could be so easily wooed from the National Union, but not in their belief that only through the union of Socialists and Radicals could a left-wing government be brought back to power. The Communist leaders showed real flexibility of tactics also in accepting in 1938 the necessity of coalition governments with the Center. To strengthen the Franco-Soviet alliance and support French resistance to Germany, they were ready to accept any allies. Until 1938, however, the Popular Front was the only promising political formation in which they could participate. By early 1938, it was apparent that France was in great need of a government of union. They therefore supported Daladier's cabinet because it did seem to embody that political "authority" which they realized France desperately needed. They did see the risk involved. Yet the political "princes" in France were agreed upon Daladier, and political realism dictated Communist acceptance.

Ironically, then, one can conclude that the Popular Front was more successful for the French Communists than for the Russians. Despite political defeats, the French Communist party found profit, popularity, and honor in the role of defender of French liberties. On the basis of meager evidence, it does appear that the party was consciously associating itself with the French Jacobin tradition. Party propaganda put off the day of proletarian revolution and stressed the need to right injustices immediately while protecting French republicanism. The party cadres do not seem to have prepared actively in any way for the revolution. There was opportunism in these policies, dictated by Soviet interests. Yet the masses did not see this. For the socially or intellectually disaffected, Jacobinism was a myth which interpreted the world about them and provided a goal for action. To the extent they identified the Communist party with this tradition, they were translating the Communist ideal for a new society into the images of an old political dream.

The great upsurge of party membership in the wake of the expansion of the labor unions in 1936 indicates that a significant proportion of the new union members felt the necessity to combine politics with union affairs. Their influx into the party brought communism into the working class on a massive scale for the first time. The political activism of these workers suggests that the old syndicalist prejudice against politics was disappearing. But what was taking its place? It is a truism of French political history that the working class has been attracted to radical movements as an expression of its revolutionary socialist ideals. But the rise of the Communist party in the 1930's indicates a somewhat different interpretation. In 1936, the party was in theory still the champion of the proletarian revolution and an arm of the Third International; in reality, it was an active partner in a reformist political coalition defending the Republic and the immediate interests of the masses, and had cut its most conspicuous ties with proletarian internationalism. The triumph of the strike wave that year produced massive enrollments in the CGT and the Communist party. Yet the Socialist party, revolutionary too in theory, profited much less. Between the two Marxian parties, the workers preferred the one which was youngest, and had had in the past the least contact with parliamentary life. Their action seemed to reflect the influence of tradition, but not that of pure revolutionary idealism. The Communist party had fused most successfully the ideals of proletarian revolution and Jacobin republicanism, and the two together provide perhaps the key for its success among the French proletariat. It appears that French communism in the 1930's made its peace with French political traditions. The Popular Front brought together communism and the Third Republic and created a new Jacobinism.

Selected Bibliography

The problem of interpretation in French Communist history is paralleled by the problem of sources. Scholars are just beginning to study intensively the fields of recent French history and of Comintern history. The results so far are quite spotty. In France, only the book by Georges Dupeux, *Le Front populaire et les Elections de 1936*, affords a study in depth of the Popular Front in its formative years. Georges Lefranc has written a general history of the Popular Front (*Histoire du Front populaire*). Edouard Bonnefous has brought out a detailed political history of the years 1930–1938 in the fifth and sixth volumes of his work, *Histoire politique de la Troisième République*. In the United States, William Scott, in his book *Alliance against Hitler: The Origins of the Franco-Soviet Pact*, provides a good introduction to Franco-Soviet relations in the period 1930–1935; Peter Larmour's study, *The French Radical Party in the 1930's*, has interesting insights to offer into the development of the Radical party. The closest thing to a political history of the Popular Front is contained in Joel Colton's biography of Blum, *Léon Blum: Humanist in Politics*. On the whole, these works are suggestive, not definitive.

The situation is far less encouraging with regard to Comintern history. There is still no satisfactory study of the history of the Comintern. The book edited by Drachkovitch and Lazitch, *The Comintern: Historical Highlights*, contains essays and documents on various relevant topics. A recent Soviet study by Leibzon and Shirinia, *Povorot v Politike Kominterna* (The Change in the Policy of the Comintern), introduces important new material on Comintern history in 1934–1935, and suggests that Soviet scholars may at last be able to produce original research in the area. The history of the French Communist party in the 1930's is still unexplored territory, whose contours are largely obscured by the bitter passions of the past. Robert Wohl's excellent study of the origins of the party, *French Communism in the Making*, stops at the mid-1920's; Angelo Tasca took up the story from September, 1939, in his work *Les Communistes français pendant la Drôle de Guerre*. In the field of general histories of the party, only Jacques Fauvet has been able to keep a certain balance in his treatment of the 1930's (*Histoire du Parti communiste français*, Vol. I). Thanks to the French historian Annie Kriegel, we at least possess a very good historiographical survey of the problems of research in this field ("L'Historiographie du communisme français," *Mouvement social*, No. 55 (October–December, 1965), pp. 130–42).

Archival sources are virtually nonexistent or still inaccessible. French government archives are shut for another twenty years. The Comintern archives are closed to all except a chosen few of the Marx-Engels Institute; the French party's archives are similarly restricted. The German Foreign Office kept a file on "Communism in France" which is occasionally entertaining but rarely reliable. Almost all that was of interest in private archives—the papers of the League of the Rights of Man, and of the Socialist party, those of Socialist leaders such as Léon Blum and Vincent Auriol, those of ex-Communists such as André Ferrat—was seized by the Germans in 1940 or destroyed. No one has yet found a trace of the papers taken to Germany. What is left essentially are newspapers. They are not to be disdained. In a country where a free and inquiring press has been active for a long time, their information is frequently both reliable and significant. The Bibliothèque Nationale has complete collections of all the major newspapers, and of many minor ones. Further search in municipal libraries, such as that at Saint Denis, is rewarded by the discovery of such gems as Doriot's *L'Emancipation de St. Denis*, a great fund of information on the dispute within the party leadership in 1934. A weekly newspaper like *Syndicats*, written by non-Communist labor leaders with the express purpose of publishing information on the struggle between Communists and non-Communists in the CGT after 1936, throws light on an essential part of Communist activity. Extreme left-wing periodicals, such as *Que Faire*, in which André Ferrat wrote after 1936, and *La Révolution prolétarienne*, edited by Pierre Monatte, former CGTU leader, give now and then valuable information. In the end, nothing can replace a careful reading of Communist literature, in particular *L'Humanité*. When put alongside such papers as *Le Populaire*, *L'Oeuvre*, *La République*, and of course *Le Temps*, *L'Humanité* provides a good picture of Communist activities and goals. Among other Communist literature, the brochures are frequently the hardest to run down and are only infrequently of any real value. Those before 1936 are at times of good use, particularly when they report speeches at Central Committee meetings. From 1936 on, all significant speeches and reports were first published in their official—that is, edited—form in *L'Humanité*, then in brochures.

In my search for "inside" information, my major sources were memoirs, complemented where possible by interviews. Among the more reliable memoirs were those of Herriot, Reynaud, and, from the lesser lights, Pierre Cot, Jacques Keyser, and André Delmas. Interesting and generally reliable bits of information can be culled from the public testimony given by political leaders of the 1930's to a committee set up by the National Assembly after the war to look into the reasons for the collapse of France in 1940, published under the title *Les Evénements survenus en France de 1933 à 1945*. Renegade Communist leaders have unfortunately written very little concerning events which occurred during the period of the Popular Front. Albert Vassart wrote a short but extremely informative article after the war on his experiences as French Communist representative in the Comintern Executive Committee from 1934 to 1935. He also left very important information in the hands of M. Branko Lazitch, whose documents are now in the Hoover Institution at Stanford University. I was able to hold interviews with the following Frenchmen, all active in the Popular Front: Vincent Auriol, Henri Barbé, André Blumel, Marcel Capron, Henri Chambelland, P.-L. Darnar, André Ferrat, Jacques Kayser, Lucien Lamoureux, Giles Martinet, Daniel Mayer, Octave Rabaté, Oreste Rosenfield, and Mme. Cécile Vassart.

The bibliography that follows contains only selected primary and secondary sources of particular interest for the history of the French Communist party, the Popular Front, and the Comintern. It is not intended as a complete listing of everything about these subjects and does not include all the sources I have consulted.

I. Public Documents

Documents on German Foreign Policy, 1918–1945. Series C, 1933–1937. 4 vol. to date. Washington, D.C., 1957–1962.
——. Series D, 1937–1945. Vol. I: *From Neurath to Ribbentrop*. Vol. II: *Germany and Czechoslovakia*. Vol. III: *Germany and the Spanish Civil War*. Washington, D.C., 1949–1951.

Les Evénements survenus en France de 1933 à 1945: Témoignages et Documents. 9 vols. Paris, 1947.

France. Chambre des Députés. *La Commission d'Enquête chargée de rechercher les Causes et les Origines des Evénements du 6 Février 1934 et Jours suivants, ainsi que toutes les Responsabilités encourues*. Annexe au Procès-verbal de la séance du 17 mai 1934, Nos. 3383–87, 3391–93.

France. *Journal officiel, Débats parlementaires, Chambre des Députés*. Paris, 1932–1939.

France. Ministère des Affaires étrangères. Commission de Publication des Documents relatifs aux Origines de la Guerre 1939–1945. *Documents diplomatiques français, 1932–1939*. 2e Série (1936–1939). 3 vols. to date. Paris, 1963–1966.

Germany. Auswartiges Amt. Politische Abteilung V. Kommunismus in Frankreich. 2 vols. Serials 303 (June 1936–October 1937), 296 (November 1937–July 1939). Washington: National Archives, Microcopy T-120.

United States. *Foreign Relations of the United States, Diplomatic Papers: The Soviet Union 1933–39*. Washington, D.C., 1952.

II. Periodicals and Newspapers

Bol'shevik (Moscow). Theoretical journal of the All-Union Communist party (Bolshevik).

Cahiers du Bolshevisme (Paris). Theoretical journal of the French Communist party.

Correspondance internationale. Weekly informative publication in French of the Comintern.

La Dépêche de Toulouse. Leading Radical newspaper of southwestern France.

L'Emancipation de Saint Denis. Local newspaper put out by Doriot's Communist organization.

L'Enchaîné du Nord (Lille). Communist newspaper of the Nord Department.

L'Ere nouvelle (Paris). Right-wing Radical newspaper.

La Flèche de Paris. Newspaper published by Gaston Bergery's Common Front.

Front mondial. Monthly organ of the Committee of Struggle against Imperialistic War (Amsterdam-Pleyel). Title changed in 1935 to *Paix et Liberté.*

L'Humanité (Paris). Daily paper of the French Communist party.

International Press Correspondence. English-language edition of the Comintern's weekly journal.

L'Internationale communiste. Theoretical journal in French of the Comintern.

Izvestiia (Moscow). Official newspaper of the Soviet government.

Juin '36. Weekly newspaper of the radical wing of the Socialist party.

Kommunisticheskii Internatsional. Theoretical journal in Russian of the Comintern.

La Lumière (Paris). Liberal weekly newspaper.

Le Matin (Paris). Popular daily newspaper.

Le Midi socialiste (Toulouse). Regional Socialist newspaper for southwestern France.

Nuovo Avanti (Paris). Emigré Italian Socialist newspaper.

L'Oeuvre (Paris). Left-wing Radical newspaper.

Paix et Liberté. Monthly organ of Amsterdam-Pleyel. Title before 1935 was *Front Mondial.*

Le Peuple (Paris). Daily paper of the CGT.

Le Populaire de Paris. Socialist daily newspaper.

Pravda (Moscow). Newspaper of the All-Union Communist party (Bolshevik).

Que Faire? Monthly review of dissident left-wing Communists.

La République (Paris). Anti-Communist Radical newspaper.

La Révolution prolétarienne. Revolutionary syndicalist review.

Syndicats (Paris). Organ of the anti-Communist CGT leaders.

Le Temps (Paris). In Edouard Herriot's words, the "evening *Journal officiel.*"

L'Usine. Publication of French management.

La Verité (Paris). Trotskyite newspaper.

La Vie ouvrière (Paris). Organ of the Communist union leaders.

III. Partisan Pamphlets and Literature

Album des Parlementaires communistes. Paris, 1936.

Communist International. *Compte rendu sténographique du VI*ᵉ *Congrès de l'Internationale communiste.* Paris, 1928.

——. *Report of the Seventh World Congress of the Communist International.* London, 1936.

——. *Theses and Decisions: Thirteenth Plenum of the ECCI.* New York, 1934.

Les Communistes défendent les Paysans. Paris, 1935.

Déat, Marcel. *Le Front populaire au tournant.* Paris, 1937.

[Doriot, Jacques]. *Lettre ouverte à l'Internationale communiste.* Also referred to under title: *Les Communistes de Saint Denis et les Evénements du 6 au 12 Février;* also: *Pour l'Unité d'Action.* Paris, 1934.

Duclos, Jacques. *Corps à Corps avec le Fascisme.* Paris, 1934.

——. *La Défense des petits Propriétaires.* Paris, 1937.

——. *En avant pour le Front unique d'Action anti-fasciste.* Paris, 1934.

Duclos, Jacques. *L'Unité pour la Victoire.* Bourges, n.d.

Ferrat, André. *Lettre ouverte aux Membres du Parti communiste.* Paris, 1936.

Frachon, Benoît, and Monmousseau, Gaston. *Pour une CGT unique! Pour l'Action de Masse.* Paris, 1934.

La France du Front populaire et les Peuples coloniaux. Paris, 1938.

Frank, Pierre. *La Semaine du 6 au 12 Février. Pour l'Alliance ouvrière! Pour la IVe Internationale!* Paris, 1934.

Garmy, René. *Pourquoi j'ai été exclu du Parti communiste.* Paris, 1937.

Gitton, Marcel. *Les Elections cantonales de 1937: Les Leçons d'une Victoire.* Paris, 1937.

——. *La grande Famille communiste.* Paris, 1938.

——. *Le Parti communiste dans la Lutte anti-fasciste et l'Unité d'Action de la Classe ouvrière.* Paris, 1934.

Izard, Georges. *Où va le Communisme? L'Evolution du Parti communiste.* Paris, 1936.

Jouhaux, Léon. *La CGT et le Front populaire.* Paris, 1937.

Lozovsky, A. *Uroki sobytii vo Frantsii* [The Lessons of the Events in France]. Moscow, 1934.

Neuf Février 1934. Journée rouge. Paris, 1934.

Parti communiste. *Classe contre Classe: La Question française au IX Exécutif et au VI Congrès de l'Internationale communiste.* Paris, 1929.

——. *Compte rendu sténographique du VIIIe Congrès national de Villeurbanne.* Paris, 1936.

——. *Les Elections législatives de 1936: Instructions et Conseils aux Régions, Rayons et Cellules.* Paris, 1936.

——. *Elections municipales de 1935: Programme du Parti communiste suivi de Renseignements et Conseils techniques.* Paris, 1935.

——. *La France du Front populaire et sa Mission dans le Monde.* Paris, 1938.

——. Comité central. *Deux Ans d'Activité au Service du Peuple.* Paris, 1938.

——. *Une Année de Lutte pour le Pain, la Paix et la Liberté.* Paris, 1938.

Le Parti communiste français devant l'Internationale. Paris, 1931.

Parti ouvrier et paysan français. *Deuxième "lettre ouverte" aux Ouvriers communistes: Que veulent les Agents français de Staline?* Paris, n.d.

Parti socialiste, SFIO. *Compte rendu sténographique du XXXIe Congrès national.* Paris, 1934.

———. *Compte rendu sténographique du XXXIIe Congrès national.* Paris, 1935.

———. *Compte rendu sténographique du XXXIIIe Congrès national.* Paris, 1936.

———. CAP. *Les Communistes et Nous.* Paris, 1936.

Quatre Années de Luttes pour l'Unité. Paris, 1935.

Rassemblement du 14 Juillet 1935. Paris, 1936.

Ribard, André. *Le Chemin de la Liberté.* Paris, 1937.

Scherer, Marx. *Communistes et Catholiques.* Paris, 1936.

Thorez, Maurice. *Au Service du Peuple de France.* Paris, 1936.

———. *Un Bilan de Faillite. Six Mois de Gouvernement Laval.* Paris, 1935.

———. *Les Communistes et le Front populaire.* Paris, 1934.

———. *Dans la Voie de Lenine.* Paris, 1935.

———. *Le Front populaire en Marche.* Paris, 1934.

———. *La Lutte pour l'Issue révolutionnaire à la Crise.* Paris, 1934.

———. *Par l'Unité d'Action nous vaincrons le Fascisme!* Paris, 1934.

———. *Pour la Cause du Peuple.* Paris, n.d.

———. *Pour l'Unité de Lutte du Prolétariat.* Paris, 1933.

———. *L'Unité d'Action. Victoires et Perspectives.* Bourges, 1935.

———. *Sous le Drapeau rouge du Parti communiste.* Paris, 1934.

Le Triomphe du Front populaire. Paris, 1935.

IV. Memoirs

Barbé, Henri, and Célor, Pierre. "Le Groupe Barbé-Célor," *Est et Quest,* No. 176 (June 16–30, 1957), pp. 1–4; No. 177 (July 1–15, 1957), pp. 7–9.

Blum, Léon. *L'Oeuvre de Léon Blum (1940–45): Mémoires. La Prison et le Procès. A l'Echelle humaine.* Paris, 1955.

Cot, Pierre. *Le Procès de la République*. 2 vols. New York, 1944.

Coulondre, Robert. *De Staline à Hitler. Souvenirs de deux Ambassades*. Paris, 1950.

Delmas, André. *A Gauche de la Barricade*. Paris, 1950.

Dumoulin, Georges. *Carnets de Route. Quarante Années de Vie militante*. Lille, 1938.

Ex-Insider [pseud.]. "Comintern Reminiscences: Interview with an Ex-Insider," *Survey*, No. 32 (April–June, 1960), pp. 109–15.

———. "Moscow-Berlin 1933," *Survey*, No. 44–45 (October, 1962), pp. 153–64.

Ferrat, Jean. "Contribution à l'Histoire du Parti communiste français," *Preuves*, February, 1965, pp. 53–61.

———. "Le Parti communiste," *Esprit*, No. 80 (May, 1939), pp. 157–70.

Herriot, Edouard. *Jadis*. Vol. I: *D'une Guerre à l'Autre, 1914–36*. Paris, 1952.

Kayser, Jacques. "Le Parti radical-socialiste et le Rassemblement populaire, 1935–38," *Bulletin de la Société d'Histoire de la Troisième République*, No. 14 (April–July, 1955), pp. 271–93.

———. "Souvenirs d'un Militant (1934–39)," *Les Cahiers de la République*, No. 12 (March–April, 1958), pp. 69–82.

Krivitsky, Walter. *I Was Stalin's Agent*. London, 1939.

Lamoureux, Lucien. "Mémoires." Unpublished manuscript.

Lazareff, Pierre. *Dernière Edition*. Montreal, n.d.

[Lazitch, Branko (pseud.)]. "Informations fournies par Albert Vassart sur la Politique du PCF entre 1934 et 1938." Manuscript in Hoover Institution, Stanford University.

Lévy, Louis. *Vérités sur la France*. London, 1941.

Marty, André. *L'Affaire Marty*. Paris, 1955.

Paz, Maurice. "Echec de 1936," *La Nef*, Nos. 65–66 (June–July, 1950), pp. 100–16.

Paul-Boncour, Joseph. *Entre deux Guerres. Souvenirs sur la III*^e *République*. Vol. II: *Les Lendemains de la Victoire*. Paris, 1945.

Ravines, Eudicio. *The Yenan Way*. New York, 1951.

Reynaud, Paul. *Au Coeur de la Mêlée, 1930–45*. Paris, 1951.

———. *Mémoires*. 2 vols. Paris, 1960.

Thorez, Maurice. *Fils du Peuple*. Paris, 1960.

[Vassart, Albert]. "Compte rendu d'une Conférence d'Albert Vassart au Cercle Zimmerwald du 17 Janvier 1957," *La Révolution prolétarienne*, No. 414 (February, 1957), pp. 22–24.

——. "Le Rôle du Délégué du Comintern en France." Manuscript in Hoover Institution, Stanford University.

Ypsilon [pseud.]. *Stalintern*. Paris, 1948.

V. Secondary Sources

Allen, Luther A. "The French Left and Russia: Origins of the Popular Front," *World Affairs Quarterly*, XXX, No. 2 (July, 1959), 99–121.

Bécarud, Jean. "Esquisse d'une Géographie électorale du Parti communiste français entre les deux Guerres (1920–1939)." Unpublished doctoral dissertation. Faculté des Lettres de l'Université de Paris, 1952.

Beloff, Max. *The Foreign Policy of Soviet Russia*. 2 vols. London, 1947–49.

Belousova, Z. C. *Frantsuzskaia diplomatiia nakanune Miunkhena* [French Diplomacy on the Eve of Munich]. Moscow, 1964.

Bernard, Marc. *Les Journées ouvrières des 9 et 12 Février*. Paris, 1934.

Bodin, Louis, and Touchard, Jean. *Front populaire, 1936*. Paris, 1961.

Bonnefous, Edouard. *Histoire politique de la Troisième République*. Vol. V: *La République en Danger: Des Ligues au Front populaire (1930–1936)*. Vol. VI: *Vers la Guerre (1936–1938)*. Paris, 1962, 1965.

Bonnevay, Laurent. *Les Journées sanglantes de Février 1934*. Paris, 1935.

Borkenau, Franz. *European Communism*. New York, 1953.

——. *World Communism*. New York, 1939.

Cattell, David T. *Communism and the Spanish Civil War*. Berkeley, 1955.

——. *Soviet Diplomacy and the Spanish Civil War*. Berkeley, 1957.

Caute, David. *Communism and the French Intellectuals, 1914–1960*. London, 1964.

Ceyrat, Maurice [Tasca, Angelo]. *La Trahison permanente. Parti communiste et politique russe*. Paris, 1947.

Chastenet, Jacques. *Histoire de la Troisième République*. Vol. VI: *Déclin de la Troisième, 1931–1938*. Paris, 1962.

Collinet, Michel. *Esprit du Syndicalisme*. Paris, 1951.

Colton, Joel. *Léon Blum: Humanist in Politics*. New York, 1966.

"Le Communisme en France," *Bulletin de l'Association d'Etudes et d'Informations politiques internationales*, No. 126 (March 1–15, 1955), pp. 1–39.

"Les Conflits de Juin," *Etudes*, December 5, 1936, pp. 652–69.

Daniels, Robert V. *The Conscience of the Revolution: Communist Opposition in Soviet Russia*. Cambridge, 1960.

Danos, Jacques, and Gibelin, Marcel. *Juin '36*. Paris, 1952.

Drachkovitch, Milorad, and Lazitch, Branko. *The Comintern: Historical Highlights*. New York, 1966.

Dupeux, Georges. "L'Echec du premier Gouvernement Léon Blum," *Revue d'Histoire moderne et contemporaine*, X (January–March, 1963), 35–44.

——. *Le Front populaire et les Elections de 1936*. Paris, 1959.

Duroselle, Jean-Baptiste (ed.). *Les Relations germano-soviétiques de 1933 à 1939*. Paris, 1954.

Ehrmann, Henry W. *French Labor from Popular Front to Liberation*. New York, 1947.

Fauvet, Jacques. *Histoire du Parti communiste français*. Vol. I: *De la guerre à la guerre, 1917–1939*. Paris, 1964.

Ferlé, T. *Le Communisme en France. Organisation*. Paris, 1937.

Flechtheim, Ossip. *Die Kommunistische Partei Deutschlands in der Weimarer Republik*. Offenbach a.M., 1948.

Goguel-Nyegaard, François. *Géographie des Elections françaises de 1870 à 1951*. Paris, 1951.

——. *La Politique des Partis sous la Troisième République*. Paris, 1946.

Halévy, Daniel. *1938: Une Année d'Histoire*. Paris, 1938.

Histoire du Parti communiste français. 2 vols. Paris, 1960–62.

Joll, James (ed.). *The Decline of the Third Republic*. London, 1959.

Kennan, George. *Russia and the West under Lenin and Stalin.* Boston, 1961.

Kriegel, Annie. "Le Parti communiste français sous la Troisième République (1920–39): Evolution de ses Effectifs," *Revue française de Science politique,* February, 1966, pp. 5–35.

Larmour, Peter. *The French Radical Party in the 1930's.* Stanford, 1964.

Lefranc, Georges. *Histoire du Front populaire.* Paris, 1965.

——. *Juin '36.* Paris, 1966.

Leibzon, B., and Shirinia, K. *Povorot v Politike Kominterna* [The Change in the Policy of the Comintern]. Moscow, 1965.

Lederer, Ivo J. (ed.). *Russian Foreign Policy: Essays in Historical Perspective.* New Haven, 1962.

Ligou, Daniel. *Histoire du Socialisme en France, 1871–1961.* Paris, 1961.

McKenzie, Kermit E. *Comintern and World Revolution, 1928–1943.* New York, 1964.

Marcus, John T. *French Socialism in the Crisis Years, 1933–1936.* New York, 1958.

Maurice Thorez, Fils du Peuple. La Légende et la Réalité. Paris, 1953.

Micaud, Charles. *The French Right and Nazi Germany, 1933–1939.* New York, 1943.

Monnerot, Jules. *Sociologie du Communisme.* Paris, 1949.

Montreuil, Jean [Lefranc, Georges]. *Histoire du Mouvement ouvrier en France. Des Origines à nos Jours.* Paris, 1946.

Namier, L. B. *Europe in Decay. A Study in Disintegration, 1936–1940.* London, 1950.

Nicolaevsky, Boris. *Power and the Soviet Elite: "The Letter of an Old Bolshevik" and Other Essays.* New York, 1965.

Nollau, Gunther. *International Communism and World Revolution: History and Methods.* Trans. Victor Andersen. New York, 1961.

Paz, Maurice. *Le Six Février. Causes, Physionomie, Significations et Conséquences.* Paris, 1936.

Pickersgill, J. W. "The Front Populaire and the French Elections of 1936," *Political Science Quarterly,* LIV, No. 1 (March, 1939), 69–83.

Prost, Antoine. *La C.G.T. à l'Epoque du Front populaire.* Paris, 1964.

Prouteau, Henri. *Les Occupations d'Usines en Italie et en France (1920–1936).* Paris, 1938.

Renouvin, Pierre. *Les Crises du XX° Siècle.* Vol. II: *De 1929 à 1945.* Paris, 1958.

Rossi, A. [Tasca, Angelo]. *Les Communistes français pendant la Drôle de Guerre.* Paris, 1951.

——. *Physiologie du Parti communiste français.* Paris, 1948.

Schulz, Marcel. "Les Origines de la Crise ouvrière de 1936," *Le Musée social,* May, 1937, pp. 121–39, June, 1937, pp. 153–65, July, 1937, pp. 185–200.

Schwarz, Solomon. *Les Occupations d'Usines en France de Mai et Juin 1936.* Leiden, 1937.

Schapiro, Leonard. *The Communist Party of the Soviet Union.* New York, 1959.

Scott, William Evans. *Alliance against Hitler: The Origins of the Franco-Soviet Pact.* Durham, 1962.

"VII Kongress Kommunisticheskogo Internatsionala," *Voprosy Istorii KPSS,* August, 1965, pp. 48–62.

Seton-Watson, Hugh. *From Lenin to Khrushchev: The History of World Communism.* New York, 1962.

Le Six Février (après l'Enquête). Paris, 1934.

Soulié, Michel. *La Vie politique d'Edouard Herriot.* Paris, 1962.

Tabouis, Geneviève. *Vingt Ans de Suspense diplomatique.* Paris, 1958.

Thomas, Hugh. *The Spanish Civil War.* London, 1961.

Walter, Gérard. *Histoire du Parti communiste français.* Paris, 1948.

Werth, Alexander. *The Destiny of France.* London, 1937.

——. *France and Munich. Before and after the Surrender.* London, 1939.

——. *France in Ferment.* New York, 1934.

Wolfers, Arnold. *Britain and France between the Two Wars.* New York, 1940.

Index

Action française, 27-28
Amsterdam-Pleyel movement, 17-18, 39-41, 79; antifascist congress (1934), 54-55; *Rassemblement populaire*, origins of, 102; renamed Peace and Liberty, 105; Universal Rally for Peace (1936), 142-143
Aubaud, Raoul, 182-183

Barbé, Henri, 6 *n.*, 18
Barbusse, Henri, 17
Barthou, Louis, 51
Bergery, Gaston, 25, 46
Blum, Léon, 91, 124, 203, 244; *Camelots du Roi*, attack by, 129; on Clichy riots, 182; *Rassemblement national* coalition, 209, 211; on United Front, 64, 70
Blum governments: first (1936-1937), Communist party, relations with, 157, 172-175, 190-192, financial policy, 180, 184, 190, foreign policy, 159, 162, 169, formation of, 149, reforms, 156-157, resignation of, 192, sit-down strikes, 149-150, 153-154, 157; second (1938), financial policy, 215, 236, formation of, 211, resignation of, 215, Spanish policy, 212, and strikes, 215
Bonnet, Georges, 209, 216
Bouisson government, 96
Bourneton, Charles, 150
Brest riots, 108-109
Bukharin, Nikolai, 4, 9

Cachin, Marcel, 21, 59, 63, 150
Camelots du Roi, 27, 129
Célor, Pierre, 18
Chamberlain, Neville, 212, 222
Chautemps, Camille, and Communist party, 160, 202-204, 209
Chautemps governments: of 1937-1938, financial policy, 193, formation of, 193, resignation of, 204, Spanish policy, 200, and strikes, 201; transition government of 1938, 209-211
Chinese Communist party, *see* Communist party (China)
Churchill, Winston, 207
Class against class tactics, 3-4, 6; *see also* Communist party (France), class against class tactics, *and* Communist International, class against class tactics
Clichy riots, 181-183
Communist International: and Barbé-Célor group, 18; class against class tactics, 3-4; Communist participation in bourgeois governments, 141, 141 *n.;* and Communist party (France), 14-15, 107, 187-188, 233-235; defense of Soviet Union, 5; and Doriot, 47-48; Executive Committee Plenum (Thirteenth), 8-9; and fascism, 48-50, 241-242; and French foreign policy, 52, 107, 162-163, 225; and French labor unions, 98, 111; internal dissension, 7-9, 58-59, 82-83; International Brigades, 168, 186; and Munich, 225; organization, 5-6; and Pact for Unity of Action, 60-62; popular front tactics, 105-106, 177-178, 189-190, 193; and purges, 187-188; and Thorez, 6, 18, 47; united front tactics, 3, 52-53, 58, 60-62, 65-66, 80-85, 105-106; world congresses: sixth (1928), 2-3, seventh (1935), 56, 58, 82, 106-107
Communist party (China): class against class tactics, 4; united popular front, 105-106

261

DATE DUE

MAY 5 7			
MAR 31 '72			
FEB 26 '74 MAR 13 '74			
MAR 29 '88			
GAYLORD			PRINTED IN U.S.A.